Roots to Fruit

FAMILY STORIES WITH FAITH AS THE ROOT AND LOVE AS THE FRUIT

MARSHALL L. GRANT JR.

WESTBOW
PRESS
A DIVISION OF THOMAS NELSON

WestBow Press books may be ordered through booksellers or by contacting:

WestBow Press
A Division of Thomas Nelson
1663 Liberty Drive
Bloomington, IN 47403
www.westbowpress.com
1-(866) 928-1240

Because of the dynamic nature of the Internet, any web addresses or links contained in this book may have changed since publication and may no longer be valid. The views expressed in this work are solely those of the author and do not necessarily reflect the views of the publisher, and the publisher hereby disclaims any responsibility for them.

Any people depicted in stock imagery provided by Thinkstock are models, and such images are being used for illustrative purposes only.

Certain stock imagery © Thinkstock.

ISBN: 978-1-4497-5881-3 (sc)

Library of Congress Control Number: 2012912166

Printed in the United States of America

WestBow Press rev. date: 10/23/2012

FOREWORD

Though I speak with the tongues of men and of angels, but have not love, I have become sounding brass or a clanging cymbal. And though I have the gift of prophecy, and understand all mysteries and all knowledge, and though I have all faith, so that I could remove mountains, but have not love, I am nothing. And though I bestow all my goods to feed the poor, and though I give my body to be burned, but have not love, it profits me nothing.

Love suffers long and is kind; love does not envy; love does not parade itself, is not puffed up; does not behave rudely, does not seek its own, is not provoked, thinks no evil; does not rejoice in iniquity, but rejoices in the truth; bears all things, believes all things, hopes all things, endures all things.

Love never fails. But whether there are prophecies, they will fail; whether there are tongues, they will cease; whether there is knowledge, it will vanish away. For we know in part and we prophesy in part. But when that which is perfect has come, then that which is in part will be done away.

When I was a child, I spoke as a child, I understood as a child, I thought as a child; but when I became a man, I put away childish things. For now we see in a mirror, dimly, but then face to face. Now I know in part, but then I shall know just as I also am known.

And now abide faith, hope, love, these three; but the greatest of these is love. 1 Corinthians 13:1-13

Apostle Paul

PREFACE

Since I retired in 1991, I have often thought about writing some articles that could be shared with others. When I was working as a training officer for the State of Ohio, I did on a number of occasions write training programs which included case problems, in basket problems and game simulations. I did not take many writing courses in college and I have never considered myself a writer. But I have always maintained an interest in writing; however I never did anything about it before June 2009. On May 30, 2009, I attended a reunion of my Kappa Alpha Psi Fraternity Brothers at Ohio University in Athens, Ohio. Some of the brothers were swapping stories about their experiences when they were on campus back in the day and the suggestion was made that maybe each of us could submit a story or two that could be included in a publication. This publication could perhaps be sold to members of our national fraternity with the proceeds going to help our Ohio University chapter. Well I immediately wrote two short stories and submitted them to one of the reunion leaders. I believe that only one other fraternity brother has submitted a story and at this time, I do not know the status of this proposed publication. I hope that it will be eventually completed and published.

My nephew, Tony Grant, has done a lot of work on developing a family tree through the ancestry.com program. He has worked very hard to get the names, birthdates and other information from all our family members. I wrote this history because of his efforts. One of my third cousins, Warren Keith Leek, who is the son of Joanne Russell Ussery my Aunt Stella's grandchild, suggested that someone write a history on our family before it is too late. This along with my Kappa reunion inspired me to begin to write stories about my life experiences as it relates to being a member of my mother and father's family. I have many interesting members in my family and I would like to share my experiences about them with each other and anyone else interested in reading how faith in

Christ can produce the ability to love unconditionally. My life probably has not been any more interesting than a lot of other people but I have been inspired by God to write about it. As I think about the theme of my book, it could be that without Jesus Christ in my life, it would be helpless and hopeless. My story is not just about my family history but about the impact of Christ in my life.

These stories could not have been written without the help of my brother Robert Douglas Grant Sr. who is affectionately called Doug by family and friends. Not only has he provided me with material to write about, he has faithfully read and edited every piece that I have written. I told him that he has given life to every piece of my writings. It goes without saying, that I owe a tremendous debt to my wife, Delores A. Grant. She is the one who has, over the years, consistently informed me about my Lord and Savior, Jesus Christ. She did it not by constantly preaching to me but rather by letting her behavior speak for her. She has always encouraged me to seek the Lord for my salvation not only for the present but also for the future. I am also thankful to my sister, Alice Carole Grant, who is another source of material for my writings. Alice is a wonderful sister and like my brother, has been a blessing in my life. My brother's wife Addie Grant has also played an important part in my life. She is featured in one of my stories and has always made sure that I was treated with lots of goodies when visiting her and my brother.

I dedicate this book to my children, Charissa, Renita and Kathy and to my grandchildren Derrick, Kisha, Schena, Lavida and Kai. This book is also dedicated to my six nephews, Robert, Anthony, Timothy, David, Christopher and Kyle. I have written this book for them and their families and all the members of my family. I want to emphasize that Jesus Christ is the way, the truth and the life. I implore them and any one reading my book to put their faith in Christ and they will never regret it. He will give you a life so abundant that you will not understand how you could have ever lived without Him. He will help you to make good choices and decisions in living your life. And when your life on this earth is over, He has prepared a place for you and has promised to come and take you to be with Him. We will continue to pray for all of you and ourselves that we might follow our Lord and Savior, Jesus Christ's Commandments.

"As the Father loved me, I also have loved you; abide in My love. If you keep My commandments, you will abide in My love, just as I have kept My Father's commandments and abide in his love. John 15:9-10

TABLE OF CONTENTS

Chapter Three: High School

Chapter Four: College and the Marines

Chapter Five: Hello Civilian Life

Chapter Six: Return to College

Chapter Seven: After Graduation

Chapter Eight: Work Years

Chapter Nine: Spiritual Challenges

Chapter Ten: Spiritual Growth

Chapter Eleven: Spiritual Blessings

Chapter Twelve: More Family Stories

Chapter Thirteen: Special Stories

Chapter One:
FAMILY HISTORY

PROLOGUE

Over the past few years, I have collected a number of quotations from various known and unknown authors. One of my favorite quotations is the expression; "Faith is the root and love is the fruit." I decided to name this book: "Roots to Fruit," family stories with faith as the root and love as the fruit. After naming my book, I was reminded about the Pulitzer Prize winning novel titled "Roots" written by Alex Haley and published in 1976. In this book, Mr. Haley traced his family history from Africa to the present time. This book was an inspiration for all people seeking to learn about their ancestral history. This was a very difficult task for Mr. Haley but he was able to accomplish it through an exhaustive search of the census, slave records and extensive interviews with the keepers of oral history in Africa. This book was a huge success and was made into two television series. It dominated the television viewing for a significant period of time and was very instrumental in changing racial relations attitudes in America. I remember my son, who died when he was just seven years old, being able to read this book. The book, Roots, will always be special to me.

In my writings, I have focused on the life experiences of my family, the Grants and the Shobes. In doing so, I wanted to give the glory to God and relate how He has guided and directed me in making life changing choices and decisions. Alex Haley's Roots described a past time where the faith of our foreparents brought us to this point where we are now beginning to see the effect of their labors and sacrifices in the form of beautiful fruit such as equal rights and mutual respect between all races, religions and sexes. In my book, I have tried to emphasize the importance of Jesus Christ in my life. He is the one I look to for guidance and direction and He is giving me an abundant life here on earth with the promise to be with Him eternally after my life on earth is over.

My father was a better educated man than either my brother or me but he didn't have the opportunities that we both had. He was born in 1907 in a small southern Indiana town and for most of his life, had to face segregation laws, customs and attitudes. For example, as a young man starting married life in Columbus, Ohio, the only job he could get was that of a shoeshine boy even though he had a law degree from the Indiana School of Law. This law school became a part of Indiana University in 1944. Eventually my father was hired as a janitor at a local refrigeration parts factory and for most of his 30 year career, he was a machinist. He retired in 1972 as a machinist supervisor. He and my mother made sacrifices by putting their dreams aside and making it possible for my brother, sister and I to achieve our dreams. Because of the efforts of our parents and this includes all parents, black and white, we have succeeded to the point where our country recently elected Barack Obama as its first African American President of the United States of America. I don't believe that this happened by accident or by some kind of natural evolution or even by the efforts of many men, women and children. I believe this is all in God's plan and our accomplishments should glorify Him on this earth.

This struggle continues and, while we are on this earth, is never ending. We can only imagine what African American foreparents had to deal with. Can you imagine yourself being a slave and having another person control your every movement even to the point of what you thought about in your solitary moments? And even after being freed they tried to bring you back to as close to that condition of slavery as possible? Well this happened to African Americans in this country beginning in the seventeenth century and continuing until well past the middle of the twentieth century. But we are now free and we need to act as free people. We should make every effort to get the best education as possible. Not only should we vote but we should run for public office. A favorite saying of mine is: **"Be a lawmaker and not a lawbreaker."** Our struggles in this world are not against each other but against the forces of spiritual darkness and wickedness. Once we understand this, we can begin to reap the fruit of love and the other fruit of the spirit such as joy, peace, patience, kindness, goodness, faithfulness, gentleness, and self control. "Roots to Fruit" is indeed my family's story. Remember, without faith, as the root, there is no fruit.

You did not choose Me, but I chose you and appointed you that you should go and bear fruit, and that your fruit should remain, that whatever you ask the Father in My name He may give you. These things I command you, that you love one another. John 15:16-17

THE GRANTS

The recorded roots of the Grant family began in 1842 with the birth of David King in Kentucky. He was born a slave and united with Ellen, another slave, who was born in 1840 in Kentucky. They had three children, named Robert Grant born in 1862, Mary Grant born in 1865 and Clara Grant born in 1870. David probably had the King name because this was his owner's last name. I am guessing that he changed it to Grant after the Civil War in honor of General U.S. Grant. Anyway, his son, Robert (Bob) met and married my grandmother Lucy Mitchem, who was born August 13, 1867 in Indiana to Thomas Mitchem and Carrie Alexander. Bob Grant died in 1911 and Lucy Grant died in 1951. I had a great uncle named Hayes Mitchem, who was one of Lucy Grant's brothers. He lived in Columbus, Ohio and I believe he died in 1962. Therefore, we Grant Children in Columbus, Ohio were able to establish a good relationship with him and his wife Grace. In fact, our family lived with him while we were looking to buy our own home. Uncle Hayes and Aunt Grace along with my parents have long gone to be with the Lord.

In all, there were thirteen children born to Bob and Lucy Grant beginning in 1886 with the birth of Estella Grant. I had a chance to know her since she lived until 1964. At the time of her passing, I was a twenty seven year old man. Aunt Stella was a strong and talented woman who loved her family very much. I understood that she had been a school teacher and she was also an accomplished artist. In fact, she gave a couple of her paintings to my father and my sister still has them hanging in her house today. She was always looking out for her loved ones' best interests, which included me.

Aunt Stella was married to Fred Russell and together they had six children beginning with Corrie born in 1911. Then she had Thelma (1915), Fred Jr. (1916), Donald (1919), Bobby (1920) and Carolyn (1926). All of the children grew to maturity and all had children except for

Corrie and Donald. All are now deceased except for the youngest child, Carolyn, who is now in her eighties and still quite active. She has one son, Gerald, and many grandchildren and great grandchildren. When I was a young boy, my father and mother would take us on vacation to Indianapolis, Indiana to visit our relatives and we spent many a day over at Aunt Stella's house. She would let us have the run of the house and there were always a lot of cousins to play with. Sometimes, her son, Fred (Fritz) from Philadelphia was there with his wife, Mildred and their children Joanne and Norma Jean. Fritz was my first cousin but because of our age difference he was more like an uncle.

The family would sometimes meet at Aunt Stella's house for spaghetti dinners and other kinds of celebrations. Her second child, Thelma had five children with the first two being closer to me in age. Beverly Ann was born in 1936, about one year before me and Bobby Don was born in 1941, four years after me. Aunt Stella died in 1964. I remember Aunt Stella's funeral especially because of an accident that occurred in the funeral procession. A woman in, one of the cars, suffered a broken ankle with the bone coming out of the skin. I never forgot looking at that broken ankle. By the time Aunt Stella had died, she had lost her father, mother, one sister and four brothers, leaving only seven of Bob and Lucy Grant's children left.

The next child born to Bob and Lucy Grant was Robert Jr. born in 1888. He was an excellent swimmer but ironically died in 1904 while trying to swim the Ohio River between Indiana and Kentucky. He was only sixteen years old at the time of his passing. Upon hearing of his drowning, his mother was sorrowfully quoted as saying: "I told him to stay out of that river." Robert's drowning was probably the reason why my parents never encouraged us to learn how to swim. My brother did become a good swimmer by teaching himself. My father learned that he was swimming at the Maryland Park Swimming Pool and went there to confront him. Upon arriving there he saw my brother diving off the high board. My father just nodded his head and told my brother that he could continue swimming.

Born next in 1889 was Lillian, who lived only to 1896. The story goes that she was kicked in the head by a horse and as a result died from her injuries. Born fourth in 1891 was Guy L. Grant, the most famous of all the children. Uncle Guy is best known for being one of the ten founders of Kappa Alpha Psi Fraternity, which was founded at Indiana

University in 1911. This fraternity now has chapters at universities and colleges throughout the United States and alumni chapters throughout the world. Guy L Grant practiced dentistry in Indianapolis, Indiana for many years. His wife, Laura, was a podiatrist and passed away a few months before he did. He died in 1973 a few weeks before his baby brother and my father, Marshall L. Grant Sr. passed away at the young age of sixty six.

After Uncle Guy's birth, Aunt Carrie was born in 1894. I spent many hours at her house when my parents took me to Indianapolis, Indiana for vacation. She had one son from an earlier marriage, but she was now married to Tom Parker. Her son, Guy E. Russell was my first cousin but was twenty five years my senior. One day, when he and his family came to visit us in Columbus, Ohio, I introduced him to my friends as my uncle. I was trying to show him the respect that he deserved. He immediately corrected me and told my friends that he was my cousin. His response differed from that of my other cousin, Corrie who was born one year before Guy E. Before my introduction of him, I had introduced her as my cousin to some of my friends. She corrected me and said "I am his aunt." As you can see, this is why I referred to Guy E. as my uncle. His oldest child, Guy Evans, was only four years younger than me.

Uncle Tom and Aunt Carrie would drive from Indianapolis and visit us in Columbus in the nineteen forties. They drove a big black late thirties touring sedan. It was a beautiful automobile. Later, they replaced it with a black Chrysler sedan. They had a small but beautiful home with a garage to accommodate their automobile. They also had a swing on their front porch that everyone loved to sit in and swing. Across the street, there was a playground where we children had lots of fun. Uncle Tom's niece, Mildred Jean West lived with them and she was like a big sister to me when I visited them. I never forgot that as a child, she would always kiss me on the forehead as I was going to bed. It is funny how you never forget acts of kindness and love no matter how long you live.

Aunt Carrie was considered to be the matriarch of the Grant family. I believed that she functioned in this capacity even while my grandmother, Lucy Grant was alive. Aunt Carrie was a very strong person and demanded respect. The great Ohio State University football coach Woody Hayes reminded me of her. She was like the financier, E.F.

Hutton; when she talked everybody listened. Aunt Carrie died in 1975, a few years after the passing of Uncle Tom. And her only son, Guy E. Russell joined her in glory in 1996 at the age of 84. He had lived to be an older age than his mother.

The next child to be born to Bob and Lucy Grant was David or as we called him Uncle Dave. He was born in 1896 and lived until 1951. He lived all of his life with his mother and as far as I knew, he was never married. When I was a young boy, my grandmother Lucy was living with four of her children, Dave, Lawrence, Charlie and Bernice. I can still picture Uncle Dave sitting on the front porch of the family home reading the Sunday newspaper. He died in the fall of 1951 after the death of one of his younger brothers, Lawrence in March 1951 and his mother, Lucy Grant, in June 1951. Uncle Lawrence died of a heart attack, while watching a boxing match on television and his death was very much unexpected. Three months later, my grandmother died at age 83. My Uncle Dave came to Columbus to visit my father and our family. I am sure that he was grieving for the loss of his mother and brother

He stayed a few weeks and then returned home to Indianapolis. In August, 1951, we received word that he had been found dead on a city bus. It was reported that he had been running to catch the bus. These three deaths in a space of six months were a tremendous tragedy for our family. I remember that I had only seen my father cry once in my life and that was when Uncle Dave died. I did not see him cry for Uncle Lawrence and I did not see him cry for his mother. But with Uncle Dave's death, I guess the sorrow finally caught up with him.

Uncle Wilbur was born in 1897 and died in 1983. He was an attorney and served as a legislator in the Indiana House of Representatives in the nineteen forties. He and my father practiced law together before my father and my mother came to Columbus, Ohio in 1936. For many years, Uncle Wilbur served as a superior court judge for Marion County in Indianapolis, Indiana. In fact, he retired as a superior court judge. His wife, Lucille was a school teacher and died a few years after him. Even though my father had long ago moved to Columbus, Ohio, Uncle Wilbur kept my father's name on his letterhead which named the law practice as "Grant and Grant, Attorneys at Law." Uncle Lawrence was born in 1900 and lived until 1951. He had attended dental school but he never graduated. Why I don't know. The time that I knew him, he worked as a house painter. Like the entire family, he had a good sense of humor. It seems that he always had paint on his hands and clothes. If he saw you with a cup of coffee, glass of milk or pop, he would extend his paint covered finger and offer to stir your drink up for you. Needless to say, there were not any takers of his offers.

Uncle Elmer was born in 1902 and died in 1948. I never knew or saw him during the time we were both on this earth. He was in a mental institution in Indianapolis, Indiana and they tell me that he was a brilliant man who suffered a devastating mental illness. He was a dentist but I don't know if or how long he had ever practiced. His family would go and visit him but I was never given the opportunity to see him. Mildred Jean would go with Aunt Carrie to visit him and she describes him as not really connecting with them. Uncle Elmer died in 1948 and is buried in Indianapolis' Crown Hill Cemetery with many of the rest of his relatives. Uncle Charlie was born in 1903 and died in 1992. He did not marry until he was 48 years of age, which was after his mother had died. Before her death, he had lived with her, Dave, Lawrence and his sister, Bernice. His wife Julia was a beautician and she died a few years before he did. All of the Grant men were handsome guys but Uncle Charlie had those movie star looks. However, he never showed that we thought of him in that way.

Uncle Orville was born in 1905 and died in 1974. He had been married and had two children. He and his wife, Dorothy divorced and she died about 14 years before he did. His children are named Renee born in 1943 and Rita born in 1945. Although he went to college, I believe he worked in a foundry. He and his family would periodically come to Columbus and visit us. He had a nice car and a beautiful little house with a covered swing in the back yard. The next child born to Bob and Lucy Grant was my father; Marshall L. Grant Sr. He was a law school graduate and had practiced with my Uncle Wilbur in Indianapolis, Indiana before my birth. But he and my mother, Sara Jane, moved to Columbus, Ohio in order to have a better opportunity. However, once arriving in Columbus, the only work he could find initially was that of a shoeshine boy. He worked a number of years as a janitor and then was promoted as a machinist for a refrigeration parts factory. He began working during a time in America when segregation was practiced wide and deep. If you were black, there were few opportunities for you. My father retired as a machinist supervisor in 1972 and died in November

1973, a few weeks after, his older brother, Guy L. Grant. My mother lived 21 more years, passing in 1994.

The last child of Bob and Lucy Grant was Bernice Grant Coleman who was born in 1909 and died in 1984. She had previously been married but in 1951, she was living with her mother, who died that year in June. She was a petite woman and very pretty. I loved her sweet but assertive personality. She had been married to Rochelle Coleman but they were divorced at the time of her death in 1984. Rochelle had preceded her in death in that same year. They are all gone now with Uncle Charlie's passing in 1992 at age eighty eight.

Their descendents come from four of the children listed above: Estella's sons, Fred Jr. and Robert and daughters, Thelma and Carolyn; Carrie's one son, Guy E., Orville's daughter, Renee and Marshall Sr.'s two boys and one daughter, Marshall Jr., Robert and Alice Carole. Only Marshall Sr. had boys to carry on the Grant name and one of his sons Robert Sr. has five Grant boys. His other son Marshall Jr., which is me, had a son, Marshall III, but he did not live until maturity. I also have three adopted daughters named Charissa Ann, Renita Kay and Kathy Lynn. Charissa has one boy Derrick, and three girls Kisha, Schena and Lavida. Renita has one boy Kai. Robert's five sons are Robert Douglas Jr, Anthony Romero, Timothy Avery, David Todd and Christopher Tyrone. Timothy has a boy, Nicholas Avery and a girl, Marissa Nicole. David has a boy, Jon David and a girl, Julia Addie and Christopher has two boys, Joshua Ryan and Jacob Tyler. Marshall Sr.'s daughter Alice Carole has a son named Kyle Grant Gibson and a grandson named Grant Avery Gibson. He was given his first name of Grant to honor the entire Grant Family.

There are many other descendents of the Grant family including a large number of Russell's and Francis's, both of which are establishing their own family tree with its many branches. I would like to take the opportunity to mention some of those Grant descendents at this time. Aunt Stella's son Fred Jr. has two daughters, Joanne Russell Ussery and Norma Russell Pratt. Her Son Robert has four children: Sharon Maxey, Karen, Robert and Yvonne Russell. Her Daughter Thelma has five children: Beverly Ann Jenkins, Bobby Don Hamilton, Johnny, Tommy and Russell Wise. It should be noted that both Johnny and Tommy Wise have passed away. Her other daughter Carolyn has a son, Gerald Francis. Aunt Carrie's Son Guy E. has three children: Guy Evans

Russell, Gail Russell Coyle and Gwen Russell Green. He and his wife Doris' first child named Rosalind died when she was just five months of age having been born in 1940. Uncle Orville's daughter Renee Grant Eskridge has two children: Gerald and Barbara Eskridge. One of Renee's grandchildren through her son Gerald is Antonio Smith the all Big Ten defensive back for the 2007 Ohio State Buckeyes Championship Football Team. In addition to being a very good football player, he is an excellent student and an outstanding young man.

I had mentioned earlier that Guy L. Grant was one of the ten founders of Kappa Alpha Psi Fraternity. He was able to welcome five of his brothers into the fraternity. They were Wilbur, Lawrence, Elmer, Orville and Marshall. Another brother, Charlie, had pledged Kappa but he didn't want to play the part of a little brother and was never made a Kappa. My first cousin, Guy E. Russell was a Kappa and a Polemarach of the Indianapolis alumni chapter when he was in his early thirties. My own brother Robert Sr. is not a Kappa but he is a Thirty Second Degree Mason and Shriner. A few years ago, I was able to buy a gold coin depicting the likeness of Founder Guy L. Grant and I gave it to my brother. Although he is not a Kappa Brother, he was responsible for putting all of his five sons through college with four of them, Anthony, Timothy, David and Christopher, becoming Kappas. He also helped me, his big brother, who is also a Kappa, get through college. I figure that makes him an honorary Kappa in my book. But if any Kappas are reading this, don't show him any of our secrets. You have to cross the burning sands to be the real thing.

In addition, to four of my brother's sons being Kappas, my sister's son, Kyle, is also a Kappa. My brother also helped to contribute to Kyle's college educational expenses. There are also other Kappa Men in our family such as my second cousins, Guy Evans Russell, who is the son of my first cousin Guy E. Russell, the son of Aunt Carrie and Gerald Francis, who is the son of my first cousin Carolyn, the daughter of Aunt Stella. In October 2006, our family was presented a silver coin bearing the picture of our uncle Dr. Guy L. Grant, one of the ten Kappa Founders. Our family chose my cousin Guy Evans Russell to receive this coin for our family. He has been a great Kappa Man and follows in the tradition of his father Guy E. Russell and his great uncle Guy L. Grant.

I was just recently honored by the present and past Kappas of Epsilon Lambda chapter of Kappa Alpha Psi as being one of the two men most responsible for Kappa Alpha Psi Fraternity being on the Ohio University Campus in Athens, Ohio. The other man is Ronald Holman, who along with thirty five other brothers led in establishing the Epsilon Lambda chapter of Kappa Alpha Psi Fraternity at Ohio University in 1966. I remember that my grandmother, Lucy Grant was a believer in Jesus Christ and so were other members of the Grant Family. There was always one of her children who would make sure she was able to attend church every Sunday. She was a very outspoken woman and my brother remembers going with her to the grocery store one time when she got into a spirited discussion with the white grocer about children. He asked her what she would take for my brother. My grandmother replied by asking him what would he take for one of his children. He stated that his children were not for sale. My grandmother said that was not always the case because white people had sold some of their children. The grocer replied that they had not sold their children. My grandmother replied that they had sold the children which they had conceived with slaves. What could the grocer say; he knew that she was telling him the truth.

Every year at Christmas, she would send us a big box containing presents, candy and fruit. We always looked forward to receiving that box of goodies from her. She lived to be almost eighty four years old. I had experienced death in the family one year prior to her death when my older cousin on my mother's side, Dr. Walter Rhodes Shobe died. And again in March, two months before she died when her son, Lawrence died. So her death wasn't a complete shock for me. I am grateful that I had known her for almost fourteen years. It has been over fifty eight years ago since her death and I still miss and love her until this day. She was a wonderful God loving woman. Lucy and Bob Grant left a wonderful legacy for us to treasure and pass on to our children and their children. I pray that we can love one another and others as Christ has loved us. This is the only solution that we have in order to create a world where we can live in harmony and peace. Even though it seems impossible, we should never stop trying to work toward this goal of loving each other.

MARSHALL L. GRANT JR.

For this reason I bow my knees to the Father of our Lord Jesus Christ, from whom the whole family in heaven and earth is named, that He would grant you, according to the riches of His glory, to be strengthened with might through His spirit in the inner man, that Christ may dwell in your hearts through faith; that you, being rooted and grounded in love, may be able to comprehend with all the saints what is the width and length and depth and height—to know the love of Christ which passes knowledge; that you may be filled with all the fullness of God. Ephesians 3:14-19

THE SHOBES

Now I would like to tell you about my mother's side of the family, one of the African American Shobe families in Bowling Green, Kentucky. When I say one of the African American Shobe families in Bowling Green Kentucky, I mean that there were two African American Shobe families running parallel to each other in Bowling Green, Kentucky. They all gained their freedom from slavery after the thirteenth amendment was ratified. The name of Shobe came from white slave owners named Shobe. After the Civil War, the freed Shobes were given farm land in Bowling Green, Kentucky. One of the other Shobes' sons named Hayden married my mother's sister, Beulah Shobe. They had a number of children and we met one of them in this other Shobe family a few years ago when by mistake we attended a family reunion of the other African American Shobes. This cousin's name is Walter Gregory Shobe and he is my first cousin on my mother's side. Therefore he is directly related to both African American Shobe families in Bowling Green, Kentucky.

My mother also had a close friend by the name of Alice Shobe Holland who lived in Poindexter Village near us. She was related to the other Shobes. My mother and she would refer to each other as cousins but they were not related by blood. My Shobe family record goes back to 1824 with the birth of Benjamin Shobe and the birth of his wife Matilda in that same year. They had six children including my grandfather, Benjamin "Major" Shobe who was born in 1861. The other children born to Benjamin and Matilda were Wesley Shobe in 1855, Luther Shobe in 1857, Sally Shobe in 1859, Hobby Shobe in 1864 and Lizzie Shobe in 1872. In 1883, my grandfather Benjamin Shobe married Alice Cooke who was born in 1870 and died in 1931. Alice Cooke was the child of Sara Dunn and a white man named Will Cooke. My grandfather, Benjamin died before my grandmother Alice but I don't know the year of his death. They had thirteen children together including my mother Sara Jane Shobe born in 1907 and she died in 1994.

The first of Benjamin and Alice Shobes children was Aunt Ida born in 1883. She married Charles Brown and they had nine children. At least two that I know were older than my mother. This would be Nicholas and Alice Brown. Owen Brown was another one of her children that I became close to. He was very nice and considerate to my mother. In fact, he got a picture of her parents from one of his sisters and gave it to my mother. He said that she deserved the picture since she was the last surviving child of that family. Owen was a wonderful gift to me since I didn't really meet him until I was about fifty years old. He passed away of cancer about a year before my mother died. The last time that I saw him, he was very thin but in good spirits. Two of Ida's other children had sons who sang with the Counts, a singing group of the nineteen fifties. Their names are Chester Brown and Robert Wesley. In looking at a picture of Chester, he looks just like my mother. Two of their hit songs were "Darling Dear" and "My Dear My Darling."

Another one of Benjamin and Alice's children was named Oscar. I don't know when he was born but he died as a toddler in a fire accident. He died before my mother was born in 1907. The next child was Uncle Walter Lewis Shobe. He was born in Kentucky in 1886 and died there in 1956. I would see him when we were both visiting in Indianapolis, Indiana. He would always ask me where chocolate milk came from and I would always answer him that it came from brown cows. He would get a big kick out of my answer. He was married to Anna Rhodes and they had two children, Walter Rhodes Shobe M.D. and Judge Benjamin Shobe. Walter Rhodes was a physician and died very young in 1950 at age thirty two. His father took his death very hard and could not bear to attend his funeral. When Uncle Walter died in 1956, a broken heart over his son's death may have been a contributing factor. Uncle Walter's other son, Benjamin, became an attorney and because of segregation in Kentucky at the time, he had to attend law school in Michigan after his graduation from Kentucky State College now Kentucky State University.

Later on, as a civil rights attorney, he was instrumental along with The NAACP and Thurgood Marshall in overturning the segregation policies of the State of Kentucky. In 1976, Judge Shobe was appointed to the 15th Division of the Jefferson Circuit where he served until his retirement in 1992. For two of these years, Judge Shobe was the first African American chief judge of the Jefferson Circuit with its 16 divisions. Judge Benjamin Shobe is an honored resident of the State of Kentucky and is known as a prominent retired judge. Both Uncle Walter and Aunt Anna were educators in Kentucky. Aunt Anna was affectionately referred to as Sister Anna. In 2006, Judge Benjamin Shobe was chosen as the 42nd member of the Gallery of Great Black Kentuckians.

The next child was Uncle Ray who was born in 1888. I don't recall much about him but I know that he lived in Indianapolis, Indiana and he died in 1956. Another child was Uncle Everett who was born in 1890 and died in 1965. I was very close to him and his son Bernard. Uncle Everett married Aunt Mildred, who was born in 1898 and died in 1977. He started out as a janitor and invested his money well. He owned a restaurant named the Polly Parrot and this is where my mother worked and met my father. Uncle Everett also owned several houses and a small hotel which was located in what is now considered downtown Indianapolis, Indiana. My cousin Bernard died in 2000 at the age of sixty seven. He was survived by two children, Priscilla, LeAnn and his grandchildren with his one son, Bernie Shobe, dying one month before him.

Aunt Beulah was born in 1892 and died in 1952. She was married to Hayden Shobe, a member of the other African American Shobe Family. They had nine children including Walter Gregory Shobe who I previously mentioned. My Aunt Maude was born in 1895 and we would periodically go visit her in Louisville Kentucky. She had three children named Ida Mae Patterson, James Daniel White and Maude White Clay who we called Sis. James Daniel White also coached at Central High School in Louisville during the time Muhammad Ali attended. At the time of our visits, the children's fathers were dead and Aunt Maude was married to a man named Mr. Gus Gossum. He was very nice to us and I remember him always buying us ice cream. They are all now dead with the youngest Sis dying in 2008. Aunt Ada was born in 1897 and she married Jim Houchens. The record shows that they had nine children. I remember visiting them once when I was a child.

Uncle Owen was born in 1899 and died sometime in the nineteen forties when we lived in Poindexter Village. I remember my mother receiving the news and crying uncontrollably. In my mind, I can still see the pain that she was dealing with. Elizabeth Shobe was born in 1903 but she died as a teenager as a result of sickness. They called her Lizzie. The next child was Uncle Wood who was born in 1905 and died in 1984 at the age of seventy nine. I knew him very well. He was a life long bachelor and he worked for his brother, my Uncle Everett at his hotel. My mother, Sara Jane Shobe was born in 1907 and died in 1994 at the age of eighty seven. She married my father, Marshall L. Grant in 1936 and they had three children, Marshall Leland Jr., Robert Douglas and Alice Carole Grant.

Last but not least is my beautiful Aunt Hattie Belle who was born in 1912 and she died in 1987. She married Douglas Potter and they adopted their son Damon Potter around 1960. Whenever we visited Indianapolis, Indiana we would always stay at Uncle Doug and Aunt Hattie Belle's house. There was so much love for us in their home and we loved them dearly. In fact, my parents would let my brother, sister and I visit them during the summers when we were little. I would go by myself and my brother and sister would go together. The Shobes have many descendents and they are far too numerous to mention here. Unfortunately, I have first cousins that I don't remember ever meeting. Because my mother was the twelfth child born to Major Ben and Alice Shobe, a number of my cousins are closer to her in age than me. As previously mentioned, two of Aunt Ida's children, Nicholas and Alice were older than her.

I never had the opportunity to see my father's father or my mother's parents because they died before I was born. The only grandparent that I knew was my grandmother, Lucy Grant or as we called her Mama Grant. As a child, I knew and associated more with my Grant relatives than I did with my Shobe relatives. Aunts Hattie Belle and Maude along with Uncles Everett, Walter and Wood were the Shobes that I knew very well. The other Shobe aunts and uncles, I knew of but can't remember seeing often. I somewhat remember seeing Aunt Beulah, Aunt Ada and Uncle Ray but I can't remember where or when. Oscar and Lizzie died as children and the oldest, Aunt Ida, was born twenty four years before my mother. I don't remember ever seeing her and Uncle Owen. Still I was tremendously blessed with having such wonderful relatives on both sides of my family.

The Shobe family has many branches descended from Ben and Matilda Shobe with Judge Benjamin Shobe, the son of Walter and Anna

Shobe, being the patriarch for the Shobe family. Judge Shobe has ten Children: Carol, Benjamin Wills, Benita, Deanna, Charlene, Kirby, Anna Louise, Cherria, Deborah and Demetria. There are many more Shobe relatives that are too numerous to mention. But it is not always about blood relatives. In the end, it is about the relationships that we establish. My best relationships have been those established through Jesus Christ. These are the relationships that endure throughout good and bad times. Jesus summed up the Ten Commandments into Two when He said: *"You shall love the Lord your God with all your heart, with all your soul, and with all your mind. This is the first and great commandment. And the second is like it: You shall love your neighbor as yourself. On these two commandments hang all the Law and the Prophets."* **Matthew 22:37-40**

The love we should have for each other is described in First Corinthians Chapter Thirteen of the Holy Bible. This is greater than the family, friendly, or erotic love that we sometime have for each other. This love described in first Corinthians Chapter Thirteen is **"Agape"** love and is unconditional love. The Shobe cousin that I was closest to was Bernard Shobe, Uncle Everett's son. It is ironic that this is true since Bernard was adopted and not a blood Shobe. Whenever I think of the essence of being a Shobe, I always think of Bernard Shobe. I always knew that he loved me and through him I experienced unconditional love.

Another cousin I had through my mother's side of the family was Callie Scribner. She was a little older than my mother and lived in Los Angeles, California. She was an inspiration to my sister as she was a dancer and a bit movie actress. She had appeared in several movies including "Lydia Bailey." I don't know where she fits in our genealogical chart but I do know that she was a close family member and I would stay with her on weekends at her Los Angeles home in 1957-1959 when I was in the Marines at Camp Pendleton, California. I loved her very much but I don't remember ever telling her that while she was alive. I think about her often and what a beautiful human being she was. I last saw her in 1976 when I visited Los Angeles with my wife and children. She died a few years after that. My brother, sister and I have been trying to find a copy of the movie "Lydia Bailey" for many years but it appears to be out of print. We are so proud of Callie and her achievements.

The following stories I have written to tell you more about my family and how we were able to grow and become who we are today But these stories are not just about my family history but more about History. When I say History, I mean His Story, the story of Jesus Christ, my Lord and Savior and the impact that He has had on my life.

Now to Him who is able to do exceedingly abundantly above all that we ask or think, according to the power that works in us, to Him be glory in the church by Christ Jesus to all generations, for ever and ever. Amen. Ephesians 3:20-21

MY HERO

When I think of all of the great men in this world, I don't immediately think of Martin Luther King Jr., John F. Kennedy or Barack Obama. Although these men are certainly worthy to be thought of as great men, there have been other men and women who have done wonderful and marvelous things in their lives as well, perhaps on a smaller scale, but my thoughts don't immediately turn to them either. When I think of the man that I admire the most, I always think of my father, Marshall L. Grant Sr. This was a man who was the twelfth of thirteen children and grew up in a segregated America even though in his early years he went to an integrated school in New Albany, Indiana. He was the youngest son in a family of nine boys. He was very smart in school even though many times he said that his white teacher wouldn't call on him because of his color.

When he was a little boy, he was in a tornado and his leg was broken. As a result of this accident, this broken leg was a little shorter than the other leg. In fact, this injury and being about thirty five years old, married with three children kept him out of the army during World War Two. I can still remember him being happy about receiving the news that he would not have to go and be away from his family. He was a college trained lawyer but when I was just a toddler, he worked as a shoeshine boy downtown at a shoe repair and shoeshine stand. He could not find any work as a lawyer because of the wide and deep practice of segregation in this country at that time. This was around 1937 and 1938, shortly after he and my mother married in 1936 and moved to Columbus, Ohio before my birth in 1937.

In the 1930 census, He is listed along with his mother, and a few brothers as living together in the same household. At the time he was twenty two years of age and his employment was that of a lawyer. He practiced law with his brother, Wilbur, who subsequently became a state legislator and judge in Indianapolis, Indiana. When my father and my mother came to Ohio, he never resumed his law practice. He needed an immediate dependable job to take care of his family and he always put our security and safety above his own ambitions. When opportunities began to open up for African Americans, my mother would ask him to take a civil service test and try to get a government job. But he would not take the chance and once he had been hired by Ranco Refrigeration, he stayed for over thirty years until he retired in 1972. He started as a janitor and was finally given a job as a machinist. He retired as a supervisor machinist section chief. He accepted the position with the desire that there would be upward mobility for others of color.

I can't possibly at this time go into all the things that he did for my mother, brother, sister and me to give us the life that we had when he was living and the life that we have now. I was driving by his former place of work a number of years ago after he had died and I broke down and begin to cry. I thought of how he would come home after work tired with acid holes in his shirt from the chemicals he was working with in the plant. I thought about his level of education and how he could and should have done much better job wise. My heart welled up with gratitude for this hero of mine. I know my brother and sister share this feeling. The great Ohio State University Football Coach, Woody Hayes, had a saying that goes like this. **"You can't always pay back but you can pay forward."**

We children have tried to pattern our lives after his example and help our families in the best way that we can. I wish he could have lived longer so my brother, sister and I could have showered him with lots of monetary gifts and love for many years. We were able to do this for our mother. However, we did give him tremendous gifts of love and respect all of the days that we had him and we thank our Heavenly Father for giving him to us. He was truly our hero.

Behold what manner of love the Father has bestowed on us, that we should be called children of God! Therefore the world does not know us, because it did know Him. **Beloved, now we are children of God; and it has not yet been revealed what we shall be, but we know that when He is revealed, we shall be like Him, for we shall see Him as He is. And everyone who has this hope in Him purifies himself, just as He is pure, 1 John 3:1-3**

MY SHERO

As you have already guessed by now, my heroes are my mother and father. I have previously talked about my father and now is the time to tell you about my mother. Sara Jane Shobe Grant was probably born in 1907, the same year as my father but she always listed her birth date as being born in 1909. The 1910 census lists her birth date as being 1908. I just don't know for sure when she was born. She always kept that a secret. On my birth certificate, she is listed as two years younger than my father. I would look at her when she was going to a dance with my father and think how pretty she is. One of the main attributes that she had was a strong loyalty to her family members and children. We always knew that our mama was on our side. In the late 1960's, when my nephew, Robert Douglas Jr. was living with her and my sister in New York City, she had to take young Robert to the hospital. He was born with a chronic case of asthma and periodically had to go to the hospital emergency room for treatment. This particular time, the hospital refused to admit him when my mother thought that he should be admitted.

She refused to leave the hospital until they admitted him and she threatened if something happened to him while she was waiting in the emergency room, she would sue the hospital for everything she could. The hospital admissions staff changed their minds and admitted him. One evening, when I was a little boy, I was playing with a friend when my mother called me to come in for the night. I ignored her first two calls and finally she called me for the third time which I knew was my last warning. I told my playmates under my breath that the old witch is calling me and I would have to go. I don't know how she heard me but she did. She gave me a good whipping for that act of disrespect. Both of us laughed about that over the years as there was never a question about my love and respect for her. We children were well fed and cared for every day. She would daily bathe, dress us, polish our shoes and put us out on the backstoop to get some sun.

My mother loved all her children but her relationship with each one of us was different. My sister and I would sometimes try to talk back to her. While my brother was the one who never talked back, but still did what he wanted to do. If he got caught, he would take his punishment with a smile. One day, a few years after my father had died, the school board decided to take our property through eminent domain so that Columbus East High School could be expanded. My mother wanted to paint the property so she could get the best possible price for it. I had almost finished painting the ceiling of one of the rooms gray and my mother saw it and said she wanted it painted white. I said that it didn't make any difference what color it was, they were just going to tear the house down. My brother again asked my mother what color she wanted the ceiling painted. My mother said that she wanted it painted white and the walls a rose color.

She remarked that she had always loved that combination of colors. I continued to make my case that the school board was tearing down the house to expand Columbus East High School, therefore it did not make any difference what color the ceiling and walls were. Before I could finish my argument, I looked around and saw that my brother had already begun repainting the ceiling with the color of paint that my mother had requested. My brother then said that if she wanted it white and rose then that's how we'll paint it He knew that it didn't make any difference what color the ceiling and walls were painted but he would always agree with her. My brother recalls that one of his fondest memories as a youngster was smelling the sweet breeze of her breath as she gently kissed him when she placed his lunch money under his pillow as she was leaving for work.

When her baby sister died leaving her as the last of thirteen children, she talked about her sadness. Because of this, I tried to console her by saying that she still had us kids and grandchildren with her. This didn't cheer her up as she still talked about being sad. I kept trying to cheer her up when she finally told me that if I didn't shut up, she was going to give me a whipping. This was when I was in my fifties and my wife was present. I knew she wasn't really serious but I shut up anyway. My mother died in 1994 at the age of eighty seven. She lived a long and fruitful life and until the end she was the caregiver, protector and lover of her family. She outlived my father by twenty one years and we all made sure that she did not want for anything. We thank God for both of my parents. They were always loved, respected and honored by their children and grandchildren.

I thank my God upon every remembrance of you, always in every prayer of mine making request for you all with joy, for your fellowship in the gospel from the first day until now, being confident of this very thing, that He who has begun a good work in you will complete it until the day of Jesus Christ. Philippians 1:3-6

LITTLE PUG

My father and mother had three children: my brother, sister and me. I am the oldest and my brother is three years younger than me. My sister is two years younger than my brother. At times it was tough having a little brother especially the one I have. He was very adventuresome and liked to take risks. He was always climbing on buildings or doing other things that he shouldn't do. I would always get blamed for allowing him to do some of these things. When he was little, he could beat up everybody his age and stand up to guys my age. One boy after losing in a fight to my brother, and standing far enough away told him "I bet you can't whip Joe Louis." For those of you too young to know, Joe Louis was the former great heavyweight boxing champion. One time, I was talking to a friend and we saw someone my age chasing my brother down an alley. My friends said aren't you going to help your little brother. Before I had a chance to explain why my brother doesn't need help, roles were reversed and my brother had found a brick and was now chasing the older boy. Roy Houpe, the toughest guy in the neighborhood, nicknamed my brother Little Pug. Roy knew that he was Big Pug and he recognized the pugilistic talents of my brother.

My father loved boxing and one Christmas he gave us some boxing gloves. My father made me box my little brother on my knees, which enabled my brother to move around and punch me at will. As I said earlier, I never had to protect him from other boys, even those my age. My brother could beat everybody his age and would get a brick or stick to defend him against older boys. When we were little we would fight a lot after my father and mother had gone to work. Since I was older and bigger, he didn't have a chance of whipping me. But once the fight started, he wouldn't quit. I would put him out of the house and he would damage the French doors in the living room trying to get back in. He told me one time that he knew he could not beat me but he was going to fight me anyway. If you started a fight with him you probably

24

should have packed a lunch because he was not going to quit until you gave up. When I came home on leave from Marine Corps Boot Camp, I was in the best shape of my life. I was almost twenty years of age and my brother was almost seventeen. We started playfully wrestling like we always did and he picked me up and threw me across the bed. As I was landing, he said "So you been in the Marine Corps, so what."

My brother was probably in his twenties when he got into an argument, which may have been racially motivated, with a coworker. My brother is about five feet six inches and this co-worker was well over six feet tall. The co-worker suggested that they meet after work to settle their differences with a fight. Before the work day ended, this co-worker had a chance to talk to a guy who had attended school with my brother. This guy advised the co-worker that my brother was someone that he didn't want to mess with. The co-worker took this advice and saved himself a whipping and they later became friends on the job. As my brother matured, he learned that fighting was not the way to settle your problems. Years later, when my brother was in his mid fifties, I saw one of his childhood friends at a White Castle restaurant. We briefly exchanged hellos and then he asked me how my brother was doing. I responded that he was doing well. He then said: "Tell him when you see him again that I am not afraid of him anymore."

Over the years, I have seen my brother grow and develop as a follower of Christ Jesus. Not only is he reading and studying about God's word, he is also applying it in his life. He has served as the vice president and the president of his church board and is currently again serving as vice president and will serve as president when his vice presidential term is completed. My brother is teaching his grandchildren about the Bible including its values, the name of all the books and the names of the Major and Minor Prophets. He is also teaching them about the Presidents of the United States of America. My little brother has been and still is very special in my life. I was very proud of him as a young boy and prouder still of the man he has become. I don't need to tell you that my love for him is endless. Just as it is described in Isaiah 2:4, when he grew up, Little Pug beat his sword into a plowshare and turned his spear into a pruning hook. Little Pug grew up and became a Christian Soldier for Jesus Christ."

When I was a child, I spoke as a child, I understood as a child, I thought as a child; but when I became a man, I put away childish things. For now we see in a mirror, dimly, but then face to face. Now I know in part, but then I shall know just as I also am known. And now abide faith, hope, love, these three; but the greatest of these is love. 1 Corinthians 13:11-13

MISS BRONZE OHIO

As it was reported to me by my father, my mother decided to give birth to my sister in her hospital room without the doctor and nurse being present. The only other person in the room was my father, who heard my mother say" Marshall, the baby is coming." He immediately went over to my mother and pulled off the blanket covering. What he saw was this new born baby kicking and screaming. He then called the nurse for help. She was born on November 8, 1942 during World War Two and was named Alice after my mother's mother. My mother also gave her the middle name of Carole and she is usually called Alice Carole. She was born because my father did not have to go to the military service because he was over thirty five years of age, married with children and had a slight injury to his leg from a childhood accident. Therefore, he was able to stay home, provide us with excellent care and be able to father this little baby girl. I was five and my brother, Doug, was two years old when she was born. Although she discontinued the screaming, she has been kicking all of her life.

At an early age my mother provided for Alice to take dancing lessons. She started lessons under a local dance teacher, named Gwen Kagy, who had separate classes for whites and blacks. Gwen Kagy gave her a good beginning but eventually the group teaching under Miss Kagy was not challenging for my sister. In fact, my sister had become a disruption in class. My mother then decided to find another studio for her. She wanted to place her under Jorge Fasting, a well known teacher of ballet, but he would not accept her because of her color. He did, however refer her to Vicky Paige, who was just starting out as a ballet dancing teacher. Vicky also had to deal with the issue of white mothers not wanting their children in classes with black children so she decided to give Alice Carole private lessons. This was a blessing in disguise because my sister was always scheduled last and Vicky provided additional training at no extra cost. Alice Carole flourished under Vicky's teaching and developed a wonderful reputation as a ballet dancer. My sister always practiced more than she was required and my mother would have to stop her from practicing so much.

At one point in time, Vicky became ill for almost a year and Jorge Fasting agreed to teach my sister until Miss Paige recovered. When Vicky was ready to return to her teaching duties, Mr. Fasting wanted to remain my sister's teacher. My mother would not let her stay with him especially since he didn't accept her initially because of her color. He now recognized the talent my sister possessed and wanted to work with her. Alice Carole continued to be trained by Vicky Paige and began to win local talent contests. She dreamed of a show business career and would often daydream that she was performing with Nat King Cole and other nationally known performers. She continued practicing on the East High School gymnasium stage every day after my father came home from work. He would take her there and the janitor allowed her to practice on the school's big stage. This practice time was very important in turning her into the dancer she eventually became.

In the summer of 1959, my sister entered a local beauty contest to compete for the title of Miss Bronze Ohio. The competition consisted of evening gown, swimsuit and talent. My sister won the evening gown, talent and placed third in the swimsuit competition. She was crowned Miss Bronze Ohio and given an all expenses paid trip for two to Las Vegas, Nevada. Her dance teacher, Vicky Paige, accompanied my sister to Las Vegas as her chaperone. During this trip, my sister attended a performance by Pearl Bailey and was given the opportunity to meet with the star backstage. Alice Carole asked Miss Bailey for an audition but was informed she was unable to audition my sister at that time. Miss Bailey said that she would be performing in Cincinnati, Ohio later in the year and would be glad to look at her talent then. My sister auditioned for Pearl Bailey in her hotel hallway during the Ohio performance and based on that audition, Miss Bailey hired my sister to be a solo performer in her show.

The Miss Bronze Ohio Trophy turned out to be golden for my sister. But in later years, Alice Carole learned that receiving gold is good but accepting Jesus Christ as your Lord and Savior is the greatest gift that we could ever hope to receive.

Knowing that you were not redeemed with corruptible things, like silver or gold, from your aimless conduct received by tradition from your fathers, but with the precious blood of Christ, as of a lamb without blemish and without spot. 1 Peter 1:18-20

HATTIE BELLE AND DOUG

Along with my father, my Uncle Doug was one of my greatest heroes. He was a man that I admired and loved very much. Uncle Doug was married to my mother's baby sister, Hattie Belle. Doug and Hattie Belle would drive to Columbus and visit us almost yearly and when we went to Indianapolis, we would always stay with them. Uncle Doug always had a car but we didn't get one until 1949. My brother was named Robert Douglas Grant and given his middle name after Uncle Doug. He received his name Robert from my father's father, Robert Grant. My relationship with Uncle Doug began when I was born which was about twenty four years prior to him adopting his son, Damon. I was about five years old when Uncle Doug was drafted into the United States Navy. Since the armed forces were segregated, Uncle Doug probably served as a steward during World War Two. I don't know how long he was gone. But he came back to us safe and sound and we were so grateful.

After the war ended, Uncle Doug returned home to resume his life with Aunt Hattie Belle and his other family members and friends. This World War fought to protect freedom did not extend to the African-Americans war veterans coming home. They were still subject to the same racism that they had experienced prior to World War Two. Segregated schools, housing and jobs were the way of life in America. In the southern states there was total racism including periodic lynching of African-Americans. In 1948, President Truman desegregated the armed forces and in 1954, The United States Supreme Court desegregated the public schools. This marked the beginning of the Civil Rights Revolution in the United States with Martin Luther King Jr. as God's appointed leader to head this upcoming and lengthy battle. I had just graduated from high school in 1954 and had no idea of what was about to happen in the future. During the next ten years, I would be struggling to mature, serve in the Marine Corps, go to college and work odd low paying jobs to help finance my education.

Uncle Doug returned to a job as a lot boy for Monarch Buick in Indianapolis, Indiana after his World War Two military service. Many young men today would not take a job like this because they would consider it beneath them. They would rather hang out and do anything but get a menial job. But Uncle Doug was what a real man is all about. He worked hard to take care of his wife and eventually the son that he adopted. Uncle Doug and Aunt Hattie Belle purchased a lovely home, bought new cars, wore quality clothes and really lived a good life. They always had plenty of food to serve us when we would visit them. In looking back, some of the best times in my young life were spent with them. When he finally retired, he was the supervisor in the printing section of a government agency. I remember, as a young child, going to stay with him and Aunt Hattie Belle in the summer at their apartment in Lockfield Gardens. My brother and sister also visited them in the summer when they were young children.

They would keep us for extended periods of time but they never had all three of us at the same time as they usually kept me one time and then my brother and sister another time. One time my mother came to get me and I said that I wanted to stay with Aunt Hattie Belle and Uncle Doug. My mother started to cry and said "My baby doesn't love me any more." Well of course that wasn't true but I sure did love my Aunt Hattie Belle and Uncle Doug. In 1961, they adopted a beautiful baby boy and named him Damon after a close friend and neighbor. They loved Damon very much and I am so happy that they got their chance to be parents on a fulltime basis. Damon is living in Indianapolis, Indiana and has children of his own.

In 1980, Aunt Hattie Belle became ill with Alzheimer's disease and eventually, Uncle Doug was unable to care for her because he was struggling with bladder cancer. He brought her to Columbus to stay with and be looked after by her sister, my mother. I am sure that was the hardest thing he ever had to do. Uncle Doug loved Aunt Hattie Belle very much and always showed it throughout their married life. He died a couple years later and she died a few years after him. I often thought that I probably would not be able to bear their eventual passing someday. But the Lord is good and worthy to be praised. Not only did

He prepare me for their passing, He has prepared me for my parents, son and my other loved ones passing including my own.

Jesus said to her, *"I am the resurrection and the life. He who believes in Me, though he may die, he shall live. And whoever lives and believes in Me, shall never die. Do you believe this? She said to Him,* **"Yes Lord,"** **I believe that you are the Christ, the Son of God, who is to come into the world," John 11:25-27**

EVERETT AND BERNARD

U ncle Everett was a very important and beloved member of my Shobe family. He was born in 1890 and lived until 1965. He was one of my mother's older brothers. My mother had six brothers and six sisters and she was next to the youngest sister, Hattie Belle. Aunt Hattie Belle and my mother looked up to Uncle Everett. They were careful not to drink or smoke in front of him. If they were doing any of these activities, they would immediately get up and leave the room when they saw or heard him coming. In addition to being well respected by his family members, he was an honest and Christian man.

He was also a good businessman. He worked as a janitor in a shoe store but he had purchased property in his city of residence, Indianapolis, Indiana. He owned a small hotel near downtown Indianapolis and had several rental properties in addition to his own beautiful residence. He also owned a restaurant called the Polly Parrot. My mother worked in his restaurant and this is where she met my father. All of this, he accomplished while continuing to work as a janitor in a shoe store. He eventually retired from his janitor job and devoted his fulltime attention toward his businesses and investments. I can remember that he had air conditioning in his house at a time when almost nobody had their house air conditioned. Every few years, he would buy himself a new Cadillac automobile.

But before owning a Cadillac, he and his son Bernard would drive to visit us in Columbus, Ohio in a Plymouth sedan. During their visit we would get a chance to play with Bernard, who was like an older brother. We would go to the zoo and ride on the amusement rides. Whenever Bernard came to visit, he would like to put a little muscle on me. This was how I treated my little brother at times but unlike me, my brother would fight me back. One time when I was visiting Bernard, he took me to three double feature movies. When I left the last movie, I had a headache from seeing all those movies.

When Bernard was a teenager, Uncle Everett bought him a yellow 1946 Ford convertible. This was a beautiful car and I wished that I could have had a car like it when I was a teenager. Bernard also had a motorcycle as a young man and later on, he became a motorcycle traffic officer for funerals. Whenever I think about Bernard, I am reminded of the Andy Hardy movies starring Mickey Rooney. Andy Hardy was the privileged son of a judge, and he also had his own car. Almost all of the African American teenagers that I knew during the 1940s and 1950s did not have their own cars or motorcycles.

I remember that Uncle Everett loaned my father some money for a down payment on our house. He also gave my mother a present of beautiful silverware. When I was returning to the Marine Corps after being on leave, my mother asked Uncle Everett to give me money to help pay for my way back. Of course he did so as he was a very generous man. Bernard married very young at age seventeen and had three children and a wife to support. He needed a lot of help from his father, who was right there to help raise those children. Uncle Everett provided for them in a way that they wanted for nothing. He even left his grandchildren his real estate property.

Uncle Everett died suddenly and surprisingly in 1965 at the age of seventy five. My cousin, Bernard, moved to Colorado and I did not see him for many years. But he did move back to Indianapolis and married a woman named Willa. I had the opportunity to visit him and Willa on many occasions and was treated very hospitable by them both. They also came to Columbus to see us several times. Bernard lived for thirty five more years after Uncle Everett's death and died in 2000 at the age of sixty seven. I will always remember Bernard for his unconditional love and Uncle Everett as someone who shared his material possessions with his relatives.

But if anyone does not provide for his own, and especially for those of his household, he has denied the faith and is worse than an unbeliever. 1 Timothy 5:8

HAYES AND GRACE

There was only one great uncle that I had the opportunity to know and that was my Uncle Hayes Mitchem. Uncle Hayes was my grandmother Lucy Grant's brother and he and his wife Aunt Grace lived here in Columbus, Ohio. He, like my grandmother, was originally from New Albany, Indiana but eventually found his way to Columbus. Aunt Grace had been a school teacher but she was older and blind when I first met her. Uncle Hayes had been a state employee for the State of Ohio but I don't know what type of work he did. I believe that it was some kind of white collar job. I know that he was a Prince Hall Shriner and I remember seeing the sword that was part of his ceremonial uniform. He and Aunt Grace lived on Rich Street in Columbus in one half of a double that they owned. It had a living room, dining room, kitchen, three bedrooms and one bathroom. I am very familiar with this house because my family and I lived there for three months in 1950.

We had been living in Poindexter Village but we were evicted three days before Christmas in 1949. My father had bought a rooming house and had not informed the housing authority. They found out and gave us three days to find other housing. Our family including Uncle Hayes and Aunt Grace went to Indianapolis, Indiana to visit our other relatives. Upon our return we moved in with Uncle Hayes and Aunt Grace for the next three months. At that time, they were raising a girl named Sharon Jackson and for three months we were all one big happy family. Sharon and I attended the same school, Franklin Junior High School and she was a half grade ahead of me. We didn't pal around at school and the only time I saw her was at home. After three months, my father bought us a home on Long Street in Columbus and I didn't see Sharon much after that except for holidays such as Thanksgivings, Christmas, Easter and July the Fourth. My mother and father always included them in all of our holiday celebrations.

When living with Uncle Hayes and Aunt Grace, they always treated us very nice. Uncle Hayes was especially easy going and was very kind to us. Aunt Grace was more of a disciplinarian and she would make attempts at times to punish us for our misdeeds. She didn't want us to speak bad language or talk back and she would try to wash out our mouths with soap if she heard any bad words. Since she was blind, she wasn't always successful in catching us so she could administer this punishment. In looking back, she never punished us if we didn't deserve it. Both Sharon and I attended Columbus East High School in Columbus, Ohio and even though Sharon was a half grade ahead of me, we both graduated in June of 1954. During my time at East High School, I had earned extra credits which I used toward my graduation. My only memories of Sharon at East High School were those of her in the marching band where she played the clarinet. After we graduated, I never saw her again until Uncle Hayes died in the early 1960's. After he died, Aunt Grace went to live in a nursing home and she subsequently passed a number of years later. My memories of them were and continue to be an important part of my life.

In May of 2004, Sharon contacted me to tell me that she and her husband were planning to attend the fiftieth reunion of our 1954 graduation class. Unfortunately, I was not able to see her since I didn't attend the reunion and we couldn't make arrangements to meet with each other. For some reason, I was not close to my fellow high school students having only attended one reunion in 1974. I have been closer to my college friends and have tried to keep in contact with them periodically and attend reunions when I can. I realized that since my young son died in 1978, I haven't wanted to look back but instead look ahead. These stories about my family are my first attempt to look back in time and try to remember the past. I thank God for allowing me to be able to do this at this time. In looking back, I think about the gift of Uncle Hayes and Aunt Grace in my life and I thank God for them and all the rest of my family and friends that played such an important part in my wonderful life. I remember them with love. **But there is another who we are to always remember in our heart with thanksgiving and that is our Lord and Savior, Jesus Christ.**

For I received from the Lord that which I also delivered to you; that the Lord Jesus, on the same night in which He was betrayed took bread; and when He had given thanks, He broke it and said, *"Take eat; this is my body which is broken for you; do this in remembrance of me."* In the same manner He also took the cup after supper, saying, *"This cup is the new covenant in my blood. This do, as often as you drink it, in remembrance of me."* For as often as you eat this bread and drink this cup, you proclaim the Lord's death till he comes. 1 Corinthians 11:23-26

Chapter Two:
EARLY YEARS

POINDEXTER VILLAGE

My parents and I moved to Poindexter Village when I was almost three years old. It was one of the first public housing projects in the United States. My brother was born at home in the village shortly after we moved there. My sister was born two years and five months after my brother. But she was born in a hospital. We always laughed that my brother was born on the kitchen table. I guess this was not true. Before Poindexter Village was built, this area consisted of a slum called the Blackberry Patch. In looking back, Poindexter Village was a wonderful place to live and grow up. My earliest recollections of living in Poindexter Village were in the spring when workers would come around and put our screen doors on. This would tell us that school was just about over and summer vacation would soon begin.

I can still remember the milkman from Moore and Ross coming down the alley with his horse drawn wagon bringing us the milk in bottles. In those days, milk, bread and ice were delivered to our apartment. There were no supermarkets but there were small grocery stores where we could buy food. Anderson Gibson would bring us ice for our icebox which we used for refrigeration before electric refrigerators. I can still remember him letting his seven or eight year old son, Vernon drive the truck down the alley while he delivered the ice. John Henderson owned the neighborhood grocery and Carl Brown sold produce at the East Market. Today we have places like McDonalds and Wendy's that sell hamburgers but the best hamburger that I have ever tasted came from Stephens Pharmacy operated by Doc Stephens.

Another pharmacy in the area was Tyler Pharmacy owned by Waldo Tyler Sr., who we referred to as Dr. Tyler. In addition to the business people important in our community there was William Colwell, who was the third manager of Poindexter Village. Mr. Colwell didn't want children playing football or baseball on the lawn and encouraged us to go to the playground. We would still continue to play on the lawn so he took my football one day and I never got it back. When he took my football, I didn't like him very much. Years later, when I had grown up, I would tease him about this and ask him where was my football? One of these children, who played on the lawn, grew up and like Mr. Colwell, became a manager of Poindexter Village. His name is Bernard Cherry and he is the little brother of my friend Sam Cherry, who was also called Little June.

Other places we played baseball was in the small alley between the apartment buildings. When I look at that alley today, it is hard to believe that we had enough space to play a baseball game. In fact, there were many times that some of us would knock the baseball through someone's window. The windows were made into multiple panes so you only had to replace a small window pane. We also played baseball on our street called Metro Place and its parking lot. When we were small, no one had a car so the street and the parking lot were always empty. We could always play on the playgrounds of Poindexter Center and Beatty Park Recreational Center. I especially remember Mrs. Frances Murray and Mrs. Flora Foster who were both wonderful women with a profound influence in my life. Mrs. Murray would baby sit us for my mom and was like a family member.

Sometimes when she baked pies, she would put them on her window sill to cool. We neighborhood children would grab one every now and then. Mrs. Foster was my Cub Scout Mother and she had twin sons my age named Newton and John. They were among my closest friends that included Sam Cherry, Bobby Martin, Jackie Lee, Cecil Smith, Paul and Billy Shearer. We loved and admired Doug Comer, a Poindexter Village resident, who was our recreation leader at Beatty Park Center located next to the Poindexter Village. There are so many more people that I could name at this time. We grew up, playing baseball, football, basketball, and fighting each other. I lived there until I was twelve years of age when my parents bought our home. I then had a new neighborhood and met new friends. But I never forgot all the valuable lessons learned and friendships given to me in Poindexter Village so long ago and far away.

Brethren, 1 do not count myself to have apprehended; but one thing I do, forgetting those things which are behind and reaching forward to those things which are ahead, I press toward the goal for the prize of the upward call of God in Christ Jesus. Philippians 3:13-14

POINDEXTER VILLAGE CAST

I have written previously about my experiences growing up in Poindexter Village but my brother, Doug Grant, has asked me to write about some or many of the children that we grew up with. I am trying to tell him that I am not the Census Bureau. But he won't listen. He thinks that he is still Little Pug and the straw that stirs the drink. As my mind rolls back in time, I think of Roy Houpe, who gave my brother the name of Little Pug. Roy was one of the toughest guys that I have ever known and on the other hand he could be quiet and gentle, if not provoked. Fortunately for me, I never provoked him. I always considered him one of my good friends. Lawrence Estice lived across from Roy in the village and he was among the guys who played football and baseball together as kids. Also in that section of Poindexter Village lived James and Robert Griffin, and Charles "Chuck" Comer, former Columbus, Ohio East High School and Western Michigan running back. Chuck's father was Doug Comer, whom I have talked about previously as our beloved recreational leader. I also remember Marcelyn Keyes, who is today a member and secretary at my brother's church, St. Philip Lutheran in Columbus, Ohio. I wasn't that close of a friend with the girls but I need to include them as they are an important part of my childhood friends.

In our section, there is Evelyn, Barbara and Marilyn Kendrick, who according to my mother hit me in the head with a rock. I really don't remember this from my own memory. My mother told me that I would pick on some of the other kids. Marilyn took exception to me picking on her. I saw her a few years ago at the ninetieth birthday party for Mrs. Foster, our beloved Cub Scout leader, and she reminded me about hitting me with the rock. There was another time when I got hit in the head with a rock. Some kids started calling me tomato head because of the bloody head wound. I always thought that Johnny Thompson had thrown the rock but a few years ago, Sam Cherry confessed that he had done it. He waited until I was a senior citizen to tell me. Another family in our section was the Hughes' family which included the twins and their brothers, Mary, Marilyn, Richard and George. Pauline Fulton and her daughter Susan were also our close neighbors and friends. Next door to us lived Anna, Wendell and Jenny Lee Brown. Another friend of mine is Birtho Arnold, who I just saw recently and is doing very well. I can't forget James, Hugh and David Black and Jimmy, Dickie and Bruce Rogers. Jimmy was a well known and talented professional drummer.

In 1947, the twins, Newton and John Foster, moved out of the village and Paul, Billy and Nikki Shearer left also. I can still remember Billy standing on the running board of the family Nash Rambler Automobile as they drove away with him broadly smiling. I have previously mentioned Bobby Martin, Jackie Lee, Sam and Bernard Cherry and Cecil Smith in other writings. I also need to include Jimmy, Johnny and Patsy Thompson, Jackie Lee's sister and brother, Maxine and Donald Lee, Lucille Cherry and Gaynell Smith. Lucille is the big sister of Sam and Bernard Cherry and Gaynell, who passed many years ago, was the sister of Cecil Smith. In other buildings, lived Bernard Blackwell, Calvin Ward, Shellie and Grady Doughty, Howard and Roger Tidwell along with Jean, Richard, Charlene and Marilyn Robinson and Wilford, Hubert and Ann Tuney. Last to be mentioned but certainly not the least is Sue and Aminah Brenda Lynn Robinson, the great African American artist and writer, who has done a wonderful job in telling the world about Poindexter Village through her paintings, quilts, sculpture and writings.

Some of the young married adults living in the village were Earl S. Sherard Jr. who had been a Tuskegee Airman during World War Two and had been shot down in combat. At the time I knew him, he was going to medical school at The Ohio State University. He graduated and became a renowned neurologist. Another young married adult was John Holland who was attending The Ohio State University Dental College. After he graduated, he moved his family to Toledo, Ohio where he set up his dental practice. There is also Reverend Jack and Helen Watkins, Carol Watkins' parents, who celebrated their sixty eight wedding anniversary in October 2009. There are so many more of my childhood friends that it is impossible to list them all here at this time. When I think of the past, I could choose to be sad but instead I am glad. The Lord is so good that He has given me another day and I am grateful for that. My father, Marshall L. Grant Sr., had a saying about time that he frequently quoted and I have kept it unto me all these years. **"Time by minutes slips away. First the hour, then the day. Small the daily loss appears. Yet soon it amounts to years."** Another one of his favorite sayings was: **"Don't worry about it."**

Be anxious for nothing, but in everything by prayer and supplication, with thanksgiving, let your requests be made known to God; and the peace of God, which surpasses all understanding, will guard your hearts and minds through Christ Jesus. Philippians 4:6-7

INDIANAPOLIS

It seems like only yesterday, that we were getting into the taxi cab and going to Union Station to catch a train for Indianapolis Indiana to visit our relatives. As we heard the sound of the station announcer saying: "All aboard for Indianapolis, Chicago and all points west," we grew more excited since we were finally ready to board the train. As the train made its way out of Columbus, Ohio, we opened our basket of chicken and other food our mother had made for us. We would also purchase cheese and other sandwiches along with milk or soda pop to drink. The trip only took about two and one half hours but it seemed much longer than that at the time. We were not used to going on long trips like this but rather on short bus trips in our neighborhood and city. Riding on the train to Indianapolis was indeed very special.

Once we arrived, Uncle Doug was there to pick us up at the train station. Even though we would mostly visit with my father's relatives while in Indianapolis, we would always stay with my mother's sister, Aunt Hattie Belle and her husband, Uncle Doug. Aunt Hattie Belle would have plenty of food prepared for us and a lovely home for us to stay in. During our visit, we would visit my grandmother, Lucy Grant, and her household which included Uncles Lawrence, Dave, Charlie and Aunt Bernice. These relatives were on my father's side of the family. One time during one of our visits, Aunt Bernice took me to get a haircut. She didn't ask my parents for permission. She just did it and that's the way it was.

We would also get together at Aunt Stella's house and the family would eat, play cards and games. I remember this as being so much fun. We also would have a chance to see all of our younger relatives including Beverly Ann, Bobby Don, Guy Evans, Gale, Renee and Rita. A couple of nights, I would stay at Aunt Carrie and Uncle Tom's house, which was a few streets over from Aunt Hattie Belle and Uncle Doug's house. Aunt Carrie's house was small but a wonderful place to stay. It had a beautiful swing on the front porch that we spent plenty of time swinging back and forth. There was a small playground across the street where we would play on the swings, teeter totter and sliding board. At bedtime I remember Mildred Jean, who was Uncle Tom's niece, kissing me goodnight. I was born into a loving and caring family on both sides and I thank God for this blessing.

Of course, we would always spend time with Uncle Everett and his son, Bernard. Bernard would take us to movies, shopping and sporting events. I would go to Uncle Everett's hotel and this would give me a chance to see my Uncle Wood, who was the youngest Shobe male in the Shobe Family. Uncle Wood was a life long bachelor who never married but had plenty of girlfriends. My mother would visit her other relatives living in Indianapolis such as Alice Wesley, Nicholas Brown and Geneva Henry. Sometimes we were fortunate in visiting Indianapolis at the same time that Uncle Walter and Aunt Anna were visiting from Louisville, Kentucky. Both Uncle Walter and Aunt Anna were educators in the State of Kentucky. When I was little boy, Uncle Walter would always ask me where does chocolate milk comes from. And I would always answer him that it comes from brown cows. He always thought that my answer was very funny but I thought brown cows did give us chocolate milk

We would mostly go to Indianapolis around my grandmother's birthday on August 13th which was one day after my birthday. We would celebrate her birthday at Uncle Guy's five acre estate where we had a picnic and played games. The big event of the day was when he would give us a tractor ride. This was so much fun as we would show by clapping our hands and laughing as we rode. Generally all of my father's relatives attended this birthday party, which continued every year long after my grandmother's passing. When the vacation ended, we would again board the train for Columbus, Ohio. The ride going home was never as exciting as the ride going to Indianapolis. But once the taxi pulled up to our apartment in Poindexter Village, we were happy to be home. Every time we visited our relatives in Indianapolis, we would return home with a greater love for each other. Even though all of the older relatives of my childhood have now passed away, I still hold a fondness for Indianapolis, Indiana and all of its wonderful memories in my heart.

"A new commandment I give to you, that you love one another; as I have loved you, that you also love one another. By this all will know that you are My disciples, if you have love for one another." **John 13:34-35**

BOXING

My father was a big fan of boxing when I was a little boy. Before television, he would listen to boxing matches involving Joe Louis, Sugar Ray Robinson and others. In fact, he was such a big fan that he had Santa Claus bring us boxing gloves one Christmas day. This was probably the worse gift that I have ever received. I would often have to box my brother, who was three years younger than me. Well you are probably thinking what is so hard about boxing someone who is that much younger than you. Nothing, except that I had to box him on my knees while he could run around me and hit me at will. And Little Pug, my brother, enjoyed beating on me very much.

My father would also have boxing matches out in the center of the yard between the rows of apartments in Poindexter Village. There was a big light there and he would hold the boxing matches under the light. Can you imagine how it felt to get beat on with your own boxing gloves by the other boys in the neighborhood? Looking back, I understand that my father was trying to teach me to defend myself. He had observed other boys picking on me. There were occasions when a childhood playmate would chase me home. I would run from him and just barely get into my house. One day this boy began to chase me home and my father locked the door and would not let me come in. My brother remembers this incident because he was home at the time. My brother said that he was coming to unlock the door when my father commented that he didn't think anyone was knocking. So my father simply pulled the shade down on the windows and would not let me come in. I found out something important that day. I could beat that boy and he never chased me home again. I also found that if you fight back people won't pick on you. The lessons learned that day served me for the rest of my life and especially when I was in the Marine Corps.

One day when I was in boot camp, I was told by some of my fellow recruits to come to the head which is the Marines' name for the bathroom. They were going to punish me for some offense that I had allegedly committed. Back then, the Drill Instructors' hands were tied in giving out punishment to recruits because of an accidental drowning of a number of recruits a few years earlier. So the Drill Instructors used recruits to administer punishment to their fellow recruits. Sometime a recruit would show up with a black eye or busted lip and when asked by the Drill instructor what had happened. They would answer by saying: "Sir I tripped over a locker box sir. The Drill Instructor would really know what had happened. But this was his way of letting everyone know that punishment was being dealt out. Well back to me and my order to go to the head for punishment. I went to the head but I took a bayonet with me. I told those who had called me there that I was not going down without a fight. Evidently they believed me and they left me alone. I never had any trouble with anyone else again. So the lessons that I had previously learned from my father paid off when I was in the Marines.

But back to boxing and my father. When television came along, he watched the matches on his black and white television set. Remember the Pabst Blue Ribbon and Gillette Razor sponsors of the weekly televised fights. My father would watch the fights every week with his bottle of beer and bag of potato chips. He would sit in front of the television set and throw a punch for every punch that the fighters were throwing. This activity ended in 1951 after the death of one of his older brothers, Lawrence, from a heart attack while watching a fight. Lawrence was only fifty one years old and the excitement of watching this fight probably heavily contributed to his death. After his brother's death, I can't remember my father having the same interest in boxing ever again.

I also remember an experience like an excited heartbeat, when I was watching the Hagler-Hearns fight on April 15, 1985. As I watched the fight my heart started beating faster. I remembered what had happened to my Uncle Lawrence and I stopped watching the fight for a while until my heart beat decreased. Boxing and other sports are wonderful to watch but it is not life and death unless you make it out to be that important. We are born with the natural tendency to fight against each other; but God wants us to fight our battles with spiritual power through His Son, Jesus Christ.

For we do not wrestle against flesh and blood, but against principalities, against powers, against the rulers of the darkness of this age, against spiritual hosts of wickedness in the heavenly places. Ephesians 6:12

FLORA MAE

I have known Mrs. Flora Mae Foster since we moved to Poindexter Village in 1940. Our families moved into the newly built Poindexter Village, one of the first public housing projects in the nation, a few months before my third birthday. She had twin boys who became some of my closest playmates and lifelong friends. I remember that the twins, named Newton and John would fight each other however, if anyone else tried to fight one of them, they would join together to protect each other. These boys were very strong, athletic and intelligent individuals. Their family moved out of Poindexter Village in 1947 when they were ten years old and from then on we went to different schools. Both of them were good high school athletes and excellent students. They eventually graduated from The Ohio State University with engineering degrees and both served as second lieutenants in the United States Army.

Mrs. Foster was very special in my life because she was my Cub Scout Mother. As children, we were very involved in scouting activities. She would have our meetings at the Poindexter Village Recreational Center. Sometime we would have father and son banquets. She would also take us on field trips to places of interests in Columbus, Ohio and to see movies such as "The Song of the South". One of the places I remember her taking us was Lockbourne Air Force base, now known as Rickenbacker, where Colonel Benjamin O. Davis Jr., was the base commander of the 447th Composite Group also known as the Tuskegee Airmen. Colonel Davis was the most famous of all of the Tuskegee Airmen, who were an all African American outfit. Colonel Davis, before he died, was elevated to Four Star General in the United States Air Force. I can still remember sitting in an airplane and later on eating ribs for lunch during that visit to Lockbourne Air Force Base which has been over sixty years ago.

Another place that Mrs. Foster took us was to the Ohio Penitentiary located on Spring Street in Columbus, Ohio. I remember seeing the prisoners marching in their striped prison outfits. We looked at the cells they slept in and we saw some of the places where they worked. We then went to the room where they executed the prisoners on death row. I actually sat in the electric chair. We could also look at all of the pictures of those who had been executed. This was a place that I definitely did not want to come back to when I grew up. This visit may have been instrumental in keeping me on the straight and narrow path of doing lawful things during my growing years. The old Ohio Penitentiary has long been torn down and a new penitentiary was built in Lucasville, Ohio in Southern Ohio.

Mrs. Foster was also very active in her church, Asbury United Methodist in Columbus, Ohio. She was a member there for many years. This church was on my paper route when I was a teenager carrying newspapers for the Columbus Dispatch. The church had been mostly composed of white people but changed when the neighborhood changed from white to black. During her membership, the old church building was torn down and a new church was built to replace it. They built a room in the church and named it in her honor. When she died, her funeral was held in that church. My sister in law's mother, Edith McCall was also a member of that church and her funeral was held there also. She died a couple of years before Mrs. Foster.

There were other mothers who served as Cub Scout Mothers when I was growing up in Poindexter Village. I remember Edna Griffin, Isabel Shearer and my mother Sara Grant, who replaced Mrs. Foster when she moved out of the village. They have all passed away with Mrs. Griffin just recently dying at the age of ninety eight. Mrs. Foster touched a lot of young children's lives and gave them wonderful experiences that guided them in the right direction as they developed into adults. She reigned until she was ninety four as the matriarch over a large family including her surviving son, nieces, nephews, cousins and grandchildren. Her husband, Newton, had died some years ago and shortly before her death, her son, John died. John was a civil engineer and had owned his own engineering company. The other twin, Newton, a retired mechanical engineer, is now the patriarch of this great family.

Mrs. Foster was a wonderful example of motherhood and a practicing Christian and I believe that we will meet again some day with our Lord and Savior, Jesus Christ. I give thanks to the Lord for sharing her with us on this good earth.

Now there stood by the cross of Jesus His mother, and His mother's sister, Mary the wife of Clopas, and Mary Magdalene. When Jesus therefore saw His mother, and the disciple whom He loved standing by, He said to His mother, *"Woman behold your son!"* Then He said to the disciple, *"Behold your mother!"* And from that hour that disciple took her to his own home. *John 19:25-27*

EAST LONG STREET

After living in Poindexter Village for almost ten years, in early 1950, we moved to 1507 East Long Street. Even though we were only about two miles away from our previous apartment in Poindexter Village, it was almost like being in another city. We had new geography to discover and navigate and we had new friends to meet and learn about. But we did have one advantage in becoming accustomed to our new environment. Our Poindexter Village friends, Paul and Billy Shearer had moved two years earlier to our new neighborhood. In fact, they lived one street over on Menlo Place, which was north of Long Street and ran parallel to Long Street. Their house was on the south side of Menlo Place and our house was on the south side of Long Street. We would visit each other quite often. When we both lived in Poindexter Village, we lived across the alley from each other. We had cans hooked to a long string and used them as a makeshift telephone. We would also cook food and share it when our parents were not at home.

After we moved on Long Street near them, our relationship resumed and I believe became better. That was probably because we were all older. We didn't hang out together because both Paul and Billy were older than me and in different grades at school. But we were still close with each other. I can still remember their father becoming ill and dying in 1953. He was only forty four years of age when he died. He was a very intelligent man and a leader in his community and I don't just mean the black community. I remember him as being a strong democrat and a fighter for equal rights. His children were raised to become somebody and they have become very accomplished. His oldest son, Paul Jr. was a member of the Best Dam Band in the Land in 1951 when he was about sixteen years of age. If you don't know what band I am talking about. It is the Ohio State University Marching Band. I was so very proud of him.

Even though Paul Jr. was about three years older than me, He turned out to be one if not the very best friend that I had. His friendship to me was invaluable during my young adult years before I had graduated from Ohio University. In fact, he was the only one of my childhood buddies to come to my college graduation in August 1964. I love all of my childhood friends but I have a special love and affectation for Paul Jr. His brother Billy was my good friend also. He wrote me wonderful letters after my parents and son's death that gave me hope and inspiration to carry on. Billy and my father had a special relationship because after Billy's father died he came to my father for guidance and advice. After Billy had joined the Marine Corps, my father started calling him captain. My father knew that Billy had high goals and this was my father's way of encouraging him. Upon his discharge from the Marines, Billy joined the reserves and worked his way up to lt. colonel. However, before he became a lt. colonel, he made captain.

He very proudly came over to tell my father that he was a real captain now. I haven't mentioned their sister Nikki, since she was younger than me. She grew up and became an accomplished writer. Also their mother Isabel was a beautiful woman who had a lively and spirited personality. She was also a very intelligent woman and it was hard to believe when she passed away as she always seemed so full of life. It was after I moved on East Long Street when I met Herbie Foster and Luther Guynes. They both became very good friends of mine and understandably we spent a lot of time together. I would play sandlot basketball with Luther; and Herbie introduced me to lifting weights. Some other friends I met after moving to East Long Street were John Robinson, Harold Cundiff and the Long Brothers, Albert, David (Doogie) and Wylie. We spent a lot of time playing basketball at Saint Cyprian Catholic Church on Hawthorne Avenue next to Poindexter Village where I lived as child. As I grew older, I also attended dances on Saturday nights at Saint Cyprian Catholic Church.

When I was a newspaper carrier for the Columbus Dispatch, I carried papers to the house of William Cy Butler, the outstanding basketball coach of Champion Junior High School and his lovely wife Dr. Julia Butler. Their children, Courtney and Bill, were younger than me but Courtney was a contemporary of my sister, Alice Carole. I also met another boy younger than me named Norval McAllister who was the son of one of my customers. I haven't seen Norval in over fifty five years, but I still remember him fondly. In 1976, our house on Long Street was torn down to make way for improvements to Columbus East High School. Even though my mother was now living in a beautiful new home, she broke down and cried upon hearing the news of our family home being destroyed.

He heals the brokenhearted and binds up their wounds. He counts the number of the stars; He calls them all by name. Great is our Lord, and mighty in power; His understanding is infinite. Psalm 147:3-5

My New Hood

The house my father had bought for us was located at 1507-1509 East Long Street. It was a spacious duplex, which we lived in the lower half. One of the first things we did upon moving in was to sand and refinish the floors. Then my father divided the upper half into two apartments. When we first moved in, I remember there was a booth in the kitchen where we could sit and eat. The booth did not last too long and it was taken out and replaced with a table and chairs. I can remember watching wrestling on television and my father cooking steaks for us on Saturday night. Gorgeous George, Don Eagle and Antonino Rocca were some of the wrestlers that we enjoyed watching. This house had a big beautiful front porch where we could sit and watch the traffic go by. In the back yard my father built an outdoor fish pond where we had a few goldfish. There was one in particular that we named Little Shorty. I don't remember what happened to Little Shorty and the rest of the fish. I imagine a cat went fishing and ate them all. We also had a three car garage that we never used to park our car. My father built a basketball rim on the garage and all of us including my father would play basketball in the alley where the garage was located.

Eventually my father, brother and I had to tear the garage down because it needed too many repairs. We never did replace it. Across the street was a vacant lot where shortly after we moved there, St. Philip Lutheran Church was built. This is the same church where my brother and his wife, Addie attend today and where he has served as the church president. Next to the church on the northeast corner of Long and Taylor avenue was a building that included a Kroger Store, a delicatessen and a barber shop. This Kroger Store was different from any Kroger Store you see today. It was not a market or a supermarket. The first supermarket in Central Ohio was built by Big Bear in the nineteen fifties. This Kroger Store was small and you had to ask a clerk for what you wanted to buy. For example, if you wanted to buy a box of cereal, the clerk would take a long handle grabber and get the cereal off a high shelf. All the merchandise for sale was behind the counter and you needed a clerk to get it for you. This building today houses the Willis Beauty Supply Company's store for Hair N Stuff which is owned by my childhood friend, James Willis and his brother Sherman.

On the northwest corner of Taylor and Long was another building containing three or four businesses. I remember one of them being Barney's Market and the other being a bakery shop. I finally became old enough to work for Barneys and drive his delivery truck like the older guys that I had looked up to. Of course I was a frequent customer of the bakery shop. I loved the donuts and brownies they baked. I would buy some baked goods and a quart of milk and have a party. I remember going out for the football team with its two a day practices. In between the practices, I would get a loaf of freshly baked bread and a jar of jelly to eat. No wonder, I didn't make the football team. This building was torn down and a building for Tyler's Pharmacy was built. After Tyler's Pharmacy went out of business Willis Beauty Supply bought the building. This was before they moved across to the building next to St. Philip Lutheran Church.

Today, Ohio State University Hospital East occupies the northwest and southwest corners of Long and Taylor. The hospital acquired the northwest property from Willis Beauty Supply in exchange for the property on the northeast corner. On the southwest corner was a large apartment building containing the Tyler's Pharmacy which later moved across the street. On the southeast corner was a gasoline station. This was eventually torn down and replaced with a house. Behind our house on East Long Street was Eastwood Avenue where there were houses and a large building housing the Eastwood Storage Company. My brother would climb to the roof of this building for the challenge. This was done of course, without my parent's knowledge. All the property between Long Street, Eastwood, Taylor and Parkwood Avenues was torn down to make way for the expansion of Columbus East High School. This included our beautiful home on Long Street which was replaced with another newer beautiful home in the City of Whitehall, suburb of Columbus, Ohio where my sister, Alice Carole, owns and lives today. When I think about the creation of this earth, sun, moon, stars and universes, I become breathless in thinking about how awesome my Creator is. But yet He sent His Son to pay for my sins.

Who has measured the waters in the hollow of His hand, measured heaven with a span and calculated the dust of the earth in a measure? Weighed the mountains in scales and the hills in a balance? Isaiah 40:12

LONG STREET CAST

A long with reuniting with Paul, Billy and Nikki Shearer, we met new friends such as Luther C. Guynes, Albert, David (Doogie) and Wylie Long. Luther became a close friend of mine. He lived on Hawthorne Avenue, which was three streets over from my street. We had attended Franklin Junior High School and also went to Columbus East High School together. Luther was a good dresser and enjoyed delicious soul food cooking prepared by his grandmother and mother. He lived with his uncle and his aunt who he considered as his mother and father. In fact, years later, after the death of his grandmother and uncle, he came and took his aged mother back to California with him so he could watch over her. Herbie Foster is another close friend I met when we moved on Long Street. We not only became pals but also study buddies. We would study our Spanish homework together and visit each others homes.

In 1954, Paul and Billy Shearer joined the Marine Corps and went to boot camp at Paris Island, North Carolina. Luther Guynes followed them about a year later when he joined the Marines. One time when he was home on leave, he went with me as I looked for a job. I got an interview and to my surprise he also got an interview knowing that he could not accept a job. When asked by the interviewer what type of job was he looking for? He said that he wanted to be vice president of the company. I thought this was so funny that he would say this. I had never thought of him as someone who would aspire to such a high position. He was eventually discharged from the Marines but after an interval he decided to re-enlist. This was during the time that he had married and gone to California to live. After that, I lost track of him until he showed up in Columbus to get married again.

This was in 1968 after the assassinations of Martin Luther King Jr. and Bobby Kennedy. He asked me to be his best man. I learned that he was now a college graduate and doing very well. I understand that he became a vice president of a community college in California after receiving his Doctor of Philosophy. The last time that I saw him was when he came to get his mother and take her back to live with him. I am very proud of Luther and his accomplishments. We need more of our children to dream like he did and then to work toward achieving that dream. In 1957, I also joined the Marines as a result of following in the footsteps of Paul Shearer, Billy Shearer and Luther Guynes but I was sent to the Marine Corps Recruit Depot in San Diego, California. Unlike those guys, I was a Hollywood Marine. I also finished college after I was discharged from the Marines and eventually found my dream job as a training officer for the State of Ohio Rehabilitation Services Commission.

The Long Brothers were friends of my brother and I. Albert Long was a tremendous high school football player. He just seemed to grow overnight from the first time that I saw him. He first went to Ohio State and than transferred to Nebraska. His brother, David was called Doogie after his middle name of Douglas. I remember Doogie as being strong with a tough personality. Their little brother Wylie became a good friend of my brother. They were close when they were in school and remained friends until Wylie's recent death. Doogie had died some years before. Some of our other friends were Harold Cundiff, Richard and Donald Spurlock, and Gastor Taylor, who was Luther Guynes' stepbrother. Richard Spurlock also died just before Wylie in 2009. I also met and became friends with a guy younger than me, named Norval Mc Allister, when I delivered the newspaper to his house. I can't forget John, Gene and Ernestine Robinson, who lived next door to us on Long Street. They moved here from the State of Texas. I started Franklin Junior High School about sixteen months before moving on Long Street and one of the friends I met when I started going there was a boy named James Willis. We became good friends and ran away from home together after graduating from high school. But that is another story that I will talk about later. I seldom get the chance to talk to these friends of mine who are still alive but I will always cherish their friendship.

Therefore, as the elect of God, holy and beloved, put on tender mercies, kindness, humility, meekness, longsuffering; bearing with one another, and forgiving one another, if anyone has a complaint against another; even as Christ forgave you, so you also must

do. But above all these things put on love, which is the bond of perfection. And let the peace of God rule in your hearts, to which also you were called in one body; and be thankful. Let the word of Christ dwell in you richly in all wisdom, teaching and admonishing one another in psalms and hymns and spiritual songs, singing with grace in your hearts to the Lord. And whatever you do in word or deed, do all in the name of the Lord Jesus, giving thanks to God the Father through Him. Colossians 3:12-17

Chapter Three:
HIGH SCHOOL

ORANGE AND BLACK

H ooly kanook kanack kanack. Hooly kanook kanack kanack. Get
off the track. Get off the track. Get out of the way of the Orange
and Black. I probably heard this cheer at an East High School basketball
game while I was still in Franklin Junior High School. This was in
early 1951 and Columbus East High School was just about to win the
State of Ohio Class AA Basketball Tournament. Prior to this time,
no big city high school basketball team had ever won. This includes
Cleveland, Toledo and Cincinnati. The 1951 East High Tigers made
basketball history by defeating Hamilton Public for the championship.
This was a great team of guys that came mostly from Champion Junior
High School, an all black school in the inner city. There were also guys
on the team from Franklin Junior High School, which was integrated.
East High started out predominately white but gradually turned mostly
black as housing patterns changed and blacks were allowed to move into
previously white areas. However in 1951, East High School was still
mostly white. My family was one of those that moved from an all black
public housing project into an integrated neighborhood. However over
the years, that neighborhood turned into an almost black housing area
but is now showing signs of reintegrating.

I remember a little white boy, named Dickie Luzader, who became
my brother's friend. He told my brother that they both spit white spit
and they both bled red blood. This was his attempt to say they were
equal. All this happened before the 1954 Brown vs. Board of Topeka
School Board Decision. Basketball was becoming more popular in the
inner cities of this nation. Bigger city schools were getting the talent to
challenge the more rural communities that had been producing those
outstanding white basketball players like the great Jerry Lucas and
John Havlicek, who won a national championship at The Ohio State
University in 1960. African American players like Bill Russell, K.C.
Jones and Oscar Robertson were also gracing the national scene. More

black players were being recruited to play basketball at major colleges and universities. But let's get back to the 1951 East High Tigers. What a great team that was. The starting five were Romeo Watkins, *guard*, Bernie Granger, *guard*, Dick Linson, *forward*, Bill Truss, *forward* and Rollie Harris, *center* who just recently passed away and Fred Andrews, the most colorful player of them all, who described himself as the best sixth man in the state. And I believe that he was.

There were also great subs on that team including Richard Kendall, Bill Sowards, Ray Burton, Ike Clegg, Fred Modena, Bill Kramer and Norman Ingram. They were coached by the young and talented twenty eight year old Bucky Walters. But again four of the five starters were black even though the majority of students at East High School were white. It should be mentioned that there was only one African American coach in the junior high school system in Columbus at this time. His name was William Cy Butler who provided Bucky Walters with all of these great black players and a lot of valuable advice. Mr. Butler was unable to coach at a senior high school because of his color and he retired as the coach of Champion Junior High School. Columbus East went on to win again in 1963, 1968, 1969 and 1979. My favorite East team was in 1955 that lost to Cincinnati Hughes in the semifinals of the state championship. That team was led by one of the greatest players to ever come out of Central Ohio by the name of Frank Wade, *guard*. He was nicknamed Mr. Ice because of his winning game shots in the last seconds. The other starting four players on that team were; Nate Harris, *forward* and brother of Rollie Harris, Reuben Young, *forward*, Jack Steptoe, *guard* and Joe Roberts, *center*.

There have been many other schools in Columbus and Central Ohio to win the state championship including triple winner, Linden McKinley, one time winners, South and Walnut Ridge, whose coach was Jack Moore, the assistant coach to 1951 East's coach, Bucky Walters. Other Columbus and Central Ohio winners are Westerville North, Brookhaven and Northland High Schools with these latter two schools being coached by African Americans. In 1966, Texas Western, played all black players and won the NCAA basketball tournament against an all white basketball team from Kentucky coached by Adolph Rupp. This victory by Texas Western helped to start the wave of black players being recruited to play basketball for majority colleges and universities. Columbus East High School and hundreds of other inner city schools produced black players, who were pioneers in advancing this cause, like Joe Roberts and Mel Nowell, both of whom were starters on the 1960 Ohio State NCAA Basketball Champions.

Do you not know that those who run in a race all run, but one receives the prize? Run in such a way that you may obtain it. And everyone who competes for the prize is temperate in all things. Now they do it to obtain a perishable crown, but we for an imperishable crown. 1 Corinthians 9:24-25

STATION 62

Station 62 was where I first learned about the world of work. This was my first job outside of doing chores for my parents for an allowance. You see I followed in the footsteps of the older guys in my neighborhood and became a paper boy for the Columbus Dispatch. In those days the Dispatch was delivered in the hours after school and not early in the morning like today. The only time we had to deliver papers in the morning was on Sunday morning. We would carry our papers on our backs, in a wagon or we used a bicycle to transport them. In the summer it was hot inside the paper station as there was no air conditioning. The heat probably didn't affect us as much since we were so young. But in the winter, we had one of those old fashioned potbelly stoves to keep us warm while we folded our newspapers and packed them in our paper bag. Many times we would huddle over that stove to get warm and prepare for the cold weather outside.

Once our bags were packed, we would take our newspapers to our route. My route was located in a neighborhood near my home. One of my customers was an artist named Emerson Burkhart, who was a well known and talented painter. When I went to his house to collect my money, I would be able to see many of the paintings that he had completed. In fact, it seems that he had paintings in every room of the house. I didn't see all of his rooms but the ones I saw were filled with paintings. At the time, I didn't know just how famous he was going to become. Billy Shearer, my friend and fellow paper boy posed for him in a painting depicting a young teenager praying. I always wondered what happened to that painting. By the way, Billy Shearer was the only paperboy that I knew who transported his newspapers once in a taxi cab. I guess that particular Sunday morning he was pressed for time and wanted to be sure he delivered his papers on time in spite of the extra transportation expense.

One of the paperboys, Sherman Green, had a route where he took most of his papers into one big apartment building. A lot of us would have loved to have had that route. Sherman grew up and became a school principal. Part of being a paperboy was to be able to play baseball in a league for paperboys sponsored by the newspaper. I was a starting pitcher and I think that I was pretty good. I know that we won more games than we lost. One of the saddest days that I remember as a paperboy was when our station manger died of a heart attack. I can't remember his full name but we called him Chaz, which I believe was short for Charles. I can still see him lying in that casket not believing that he was gone. A guy named Bud took his place and although it was never the same, we all took a liking to Bud.

My friend Adger Cowans, who motivated me to attend Ohio University, was my family's paperboy. Adger went on to graduate from Ohio University and he became a renowned photographer in New York, City. My brother also carried papers at the same station that I did and some of his memories of being a paper boy are as follows: He was able to recognize the existence and value of the capitalist enterprise system. He learned how to interact and respect different people from all walks of life. He further learned that the public demands a high performance level but generously rewards efficient and polite customer service. Fats Waller has a song with lyrics dealing with this very issue. The lyrics are: "Find out what they like and how they like it and let them have it just that way."

Having a paper route was also a means for getting other jobs from customers such as cutting grass in the summer and shoveling snow off of driveways and sidewalks in the winter. I worked for one of my customers in addition to carrying his paper; I would clean his floors and fill his coal bin for his furnace. My brother further reports that our little sister assisted him on his paper route. She became good at folding his newspapers so they could be thrown on to the customers' porches. He paid her a few dollars and on collection day, which was Friday, they stopped at Tyler's Drug Store and enjoyed a coca cola and cashew nuts. My brother says that this experience was so valuable that he would have paid the newspaper company to train his sons if it was necessary. But that wasn't necessary, since his sons became paper boys and the older boys passed their routes on to the younger ones. Our father would often tell us that those who work eat and those who don't work do not eat. Work is also spiritual and a gift from God.

For even when we were with you, we commanded you this: If anyone will not work, neither shall he eat. 2 Thessalonians 3:10

WEASEL AND SCAMP

My father had a unique talent in picking out nicknames for his and other children in the neighborhood. He along with the rest of my family and friends would call me Junebug. I don't know the origin of that nickname but I would like to believe that some thought it was because I was as cute as a little Junebug. When he wanted to make a point with me, he would then call me Junior. I don't remember him ever calling me Marshall or Marshall Jr. There was a friend of mine named Billy Shearer who was always striving to be the very best he could be and did grow up to be a very successful man. After Billy graduated from high school, he joined the Unites States Marine Corps and came home from Boot Camp as a private. My father immediately began to address him by the rank of captain. My father was letting Billy know in a joking way that he could do better than private. After Billy was discharged from the Marines, he joined the Ohio National Guard. A number of years later, when he actually achieved the rank of captain, he proudly came to see my father and gave him the good news.

Billy continued his service in the National Guard and obtained his highest rank of lt. colonel. By this time, my father had passed away but I know that he would have been very proud of him. Billy has often talked about how my father became a substitute for his wonderful father who had passed away the same year he graduated from high school. Another friend of mine named Herbert Foster was given the name of Philbrick after the character in the 1953 television series; "I Led Three Lives." This series starred Richard Carlson and was loosely based on the life of Herbert Philbrick who infiltrated the Communist Party on behalf of the F.B.I. in the nineteen Forties. After my father started calling Herbie "Philbrick," the name stuck and I still think of Herbie Foster today as Philbrick. My middle daughter, Renita was nine years old when I adopted her and my father gave her the name of Neetsie Noodle. She already had the nickname of Neet but he added the Noodle. He has been deceased for thirty six years but her mother, my wife, still calls her Noodle.

My father also had special names for my brother and sister. I remember that he would call my brother "Weasel" and my sister "Scamp." In looking back, I wonder why he chose to call my brother Weasel since that name is not the most flattering of names. My brother describes his youthful qualities as having the ability to redirect and occasionally mislead, to be evasive and talk with a smooth and persuasive tongue. These qualities gave him the ability to do many of the things he wanted as a child. My brother would sneak out of the house by exiting through a window instead of a door. When he returned, he would sometimes knock on the window so I would let him back in. One night, He stayed out late and my mother and father were waiting up for him. My father finally became tired of waiting and went to bed. But my mother continued to wait up. Finally my brother put his key, which he would grease with Vaseline so it wouldn't make noise, in the lock while carrying his shoes in his hands. He was always considerate in that he didn't want to wake anybody up when he came in late. I wonder why? My mother met him at the front door and bounced his head against one side of the hall to the other side. Unfortunately, for my brother, we had a long hall. But one of his most positive character traits was that he always took his whipping like a man.

My brother always smiled at his nickname. He realized that our father, trained as an attorney, was able to see in him a natural ability to play his cards close to the vest while displaying a poker face. The nickname Weasel provided the motivation to always use his talent and negotiation skills in a positive manner. Not surprisingly he received the least disciplinary action from our parents and we often called him the Golden Boy. Now Scamp was just the opposite of Weasel. One time when my father was going to give her a spanking, she ran and he couldn't catch her. She was an expert at disappearing under a bed. From that time on, he would call her his little Scamp. My sister says that my father never gave her a spanking again. He left her spanking up to my mother who didn't try to chase her. My mother would tell her that she had better not run. One day, I was picking on my sister and she kicked me in the groin. I immediately fell to the floor and she began to cry out "I'm sorry. I'm sorry" As I was lying on the floor, I said that I was going to kill her when I got up. That was one time she got the best of me. Today both my brother and sister are grandparents but I still think of them sometimes as Weasel and Scamp. My parents loved all of us very much and better yet they always showed it. I give thanks to God for choosing them to raise us. We were very much loved.

And above all things have fervent love for one another, for love will cover a multitude of sins. 1 Peter 4:8

MAGIC BOXES

Growing up in the nineteen forties I would listen to the radio for my daily entertainment. There were such wonderful shows like Gang Busters, The Lone Ranger, The Shadow, The Fat Man, Lux Radio Theater, Fibber McGee and Molly and Amos and Andy. You had to use your imagination when listening to these shows because there weren't any pictures to go along with the sound. The only time we had pictures with sound was when we went to the movies. At the movies, we would watch cowboy movies starring Gene Autry, Roy Rogers, Johnny Mack Brown and Hopalong Cassidy. Of course the Tarzan movies were a favorite of ours. I believe admission was about twenty five cents and a bag of popcorn was ten or fifteen cents. In those days, You always saw two movies for the price of admission. One time when I was visiting my cousin, Bernard Shobe in Indianapolis, Indiana, he took me to three double feature movies. At the end of watching all of those movies, I had big headache. I have never tried to watch that many movies in one day again.

The radio, however, was my primary source of commercial entertainment. I would listen to Ohio State Football Games with my mother on Saturday autumn afternoons and to the championship boxing matches with my father. There was also the music of Bing Crosby, Frank Sinatra, Fats Waller and Nat King Cole to enjoy on the radio. Who can ever forget some of the great comedians like Jack Benny and Bob Hope who kept us constantly laughing throughout hard times like the after affects of the depression, segregation and during World War Two? When I was a little boy, radios were big pieces of furniture that stood on the floor. Gradually over the years, they became smaller and smaller until today, they can fit in your hand. Some of our greatest music was written and recorded before television came upon the scene such as "Long Ago and Far Away," a popular World War Two song and Ain't Misbehavin, which was written and sung by one of my favorite entertainers of all time, Fats Waller. In this song, Fats sings about no one to talk with but him and his radio.

This song and Fats Waller was before the commercial use of television. Fats Waller died in 1943 while traveling on a train. In 1948, I saw my first television that a door to door salesman was trying to sell. The screen was so small that you had to watch it through a magnifying glass. I remember begging my father to buy it but he said no way. One of our close friends and neighbor, Pauline Fulton, bought a television set and our family would go to her apartment and watch The Toast of the Town Television Show hosted by Ed Sullivan. We were still living in Poindexter Village, at that time, which was in 1949. We moved out of the village in December of 1949 and finally got our own television set in 1950 after we moved to Long Street. It was a Philco brand and we would watch wrestling matches every Saturday night while eating steaks my father bought for our enjoyment. We also watched "Your Show of Shows" starring Sid Caesar and Imogene Coca. Back in those days you hardly ever saw a person of color on television. During the rare time that one would come on, whoever was watching would holler out; "Come quick, there is a colored person on television."

Another show that I remember but only lasted about a year was Broadway Open House hosted by Jerry Lester and featuring a blonde female performer named Dagmar who has been described as the original dumb blond. This show preceded Steve Allen's Tonight Show about three years. Steve Allen of course was before Jack Parr, Johnnie Carson, Jay Leno and Conan O'Brien on the Tonight Show. Television has been somewhat maligned over the years as being referred to as the Boob Tube. Like anything positive, it also had a negative aspect. Children would spend more time watching television than they did doing their homework. The television also promoted sedentary activity over being outside and participating in physical activity such as baseball, football and basketball. Like anything we have and enjoy, too much of it can be detrimental to our well being. I would spend countless number of hours watching television when I could have been doing something more productive like reading, studying or exercising.

Today, television is so much a part of our society that it is impossible to imagine life without it. The only threat to it has been the development of computers and the internet. But this technology is so interwoven together that your television screen can be used as your computer screen.

The video cassette recorder (VCR) and now the digital versatile disc (DVD) have been part of the television revolution in my lifetime. I thank God for His blessing of these magic boxes.

Enter into His gates with thanksgiving, and into His courts with praise. Be thankful to Him, and bless His name. Psalm 100:4

DYNAFLOW

We were still living in Poindexter Village in 1949. My father had just bought a new 1949 blue Buick Super Sedan. This was his first car as far as I knew. In Poindexter Village there was a parking lot for cars, but there weren't many cars to occupy the parking spaces. People primarily used the public transit system to get around since everywhere you had to go could be reached on a bus line. We would play baseball in the empty parking lot. You can imagine how my father's new car looked in a parking lot with very few other cars. It stuck out like a sore thumb, especially if it wasn't your new car. The first thought many people probably had is how did he buy this car? People living in Poindexter Village were not supposed to be making enough money to buy a new car. My father like all the other fathers living in the village did not make a lot of money even though many had good educations. People living in the village at that time were almost all African Americans except for Mrs. Ward, wife of Calvin Ward who was a well known gospel singer. The Ward family, one of the many great families living in Poindexter Village, consisted of a black father and a white mother. Mr. Ward along with Mrs. Ward had four children including, Sergeant Calvin Ward, a retired Columbus, Ohio police officer. Their other children in that family were Owen, George and Alice Ward.

At that time there were people living in the village with college degrees working as janitors, garage attendants, and delivery boys and cleaning maids. The civil rights revolution was not to start until the mid nineteen fifties; so segregation was everywhere including the workforce. So when this big new car suddenly appeared in the parking lot, everybody seemed surprised. The big question was:" Where did my father get the money?" One rumor I found out years later was that he had hit the numbers. I don't know where this rumor came from, maybe he put it out. But his children all knew a secret that we could not tell anyone. The secret was that my father had bought a rooming house some years earlier and was making money from the rent he collected. Well, the public housing authority found out about his extra income and took action to evict us from Poindexter Village three days before Christmas in 1949. We stored our furniture at our rooming house and then drove to Indianapolis, Indiana for the holidays.

We then moved in with my great Uncle and Aunt, Hayes and Grace Mitchim for about three or four months until my father bought us a beautiful and spacious duplex located at 1507-1509 East Long Street in Columbus, Ohio. We lived in the bottom half and rented out the top half, which helped pay the mortgage. After moving on Long Street, I had a lot of good times riding in and driving that 1949 blue Buick Sedan. My parents let me get my license when I was fifteen years old because they wanted me to drive them to and from work. Therefore I had the use of the car during school hours. After I took my father to work, I would pick up my girlfriend and her sister and bring them to Columbus East High School which I also attended. Even though the school was located behind my house, I would be late quite frequently. In the evening, I felt free to take the car without asking permission since I had my own set of keys.

In fact, the first time that I drove the car was shortly after my father bought it and we were still living in Poindexter Village. I was only twelve years of age and I drove the car around the block with my friend Sam Cherry as my first passenger. Unfortunately, Mrs. Estella Tyler saw me and told my parents. I remember getting a spanking for that incident. After we moved on East Long Street, I distinctly remember the second time that I took the car. I drove it west on Eastwood Avenue and then turned north on Winner Avenue to cross East Long Street. Because of my driving inexperience, I got out of the car at Winner and Long Streets and looked to see if any cars were coming down Long Street. When I saw that Long Street was clear of cars, I proceeded to drive across it. I would also take the car while my parents were sleeping and then drive it between Midnight and 5:00 a.m. making sure to get home before my parents woke up. In looking back, I don't know where I got the nerve to do all of that.

I drove this car so much that my friends referred to it as my car. This car lasted until 1957 when my father replaced it with another new Buick Sedan. I was in the Marine Corps when he got his new car, a 1957 Buick Sedan. Sixty years have passed since my father bought that

1949 blue Buick Super Sedan with its descriptive **Dynaflow Automatic Transmission**. My father was a loving, giving and sharing man. He shared that car and his love with me throughout my high school and college years and until he died. I am always thankful to God for giving him to me as my father.

Command those who are rich in this present age not to be haughty, nor to trust in uncertain riches but in the living God, who gives us richly all things to enjoy. Let them do good, that they be rich in good works, ready to give, willing to share, storing up for themselves a good foundation for the time to come, that they may lay hold on eternal life. 1 Timothy 6:17-19

JUNEBUG, JUNEBUG

My family and friends have called me Junebug for as long as I can remember. I believe it started when my mother said isn't he as cute as a little Junebug. Most of my childhood friends have always called me Junebug. Although my closest childhood friend, Sam Cherry, always called me by my given name of Marshall. I don't know why this is so, maybe it is because his nickname is Little June and he wanted to keep the name of June to himself. The Foster twins always called me Bug and sometimes Billy Shearer would call me this also. But just about everybody would call me Junebug including my parents, brother and sister. I have always accepted this name and I am still called by it today by my wife and other family members. My brother modified the name of Junebug a few years ago and starting calling me Junniebuggie.

When my son was born, we named him Marshall Leland Grant lll. The day he was born, I hadn't selected a name for him. I did not plan on naming him Marshall but I had no other name in mind. I called my father, Marshall Sr. to inform him that my son was born and he asked me what I was going to name him. I replied that I did not know. He then surprised me by saying: "Why don't you name him Marshall." I immediately said yes I would. My father and my son have both passed away but fulfilling my father's request of naming my son after him is one of the greatest memories I have. My father was called Marshall and my son was called Little Marshall. Of course I was referred to as Marshall in college, on my job, in the Marines and at church. But you can always tell my childhood friends, because they always call me Junebug.

My father had a 1949 Buick Super Sedan that he let me drive him and my mother to and from work. This meant that I had the car during school hours. I didn't need the car to drive to school since I lived right behind the school. Even though I had the use of a car, I was late a lot. I would wait for the first bell to ring before I took off for school. One day I was in the tardy line where students coming late had to report to the teacher assigned to check in the tardy students. There was a boy ahead of me who was a high school star football player by the name of Jim Marshall. After playing for Woody Hayes and the Ohio State Buckeyes, Jim Marshall played a few years for the Cleveland Browns and eventually played for the Minnesota Vikings for many years. In addition to being a high school friend of mine, Jim Marshall also became my Kappa Alpha Psi fraternity brother during his college years at The Ohio State University. The teacher asked Jim Marshall his name and Jim responded "Marshall." The teacher then said are you Marshall Grant? Unfortunately, at that time, I was more famous than Jim Marshall as a frequent participant in the high school tardy line.

My Father liked my name of Junebug so much that he would say it twice. Since I drove the car everyday to take my parents to and from work, I would take the car in the evening without asking for permission. For some reason, my father would let me do this. Even though it was his car, it seemed more like mine. On occasion, he would let me know that he was still in control of the car. I can remember getting ready to go out the back door to take the car when I would hear his booming voice from the front of the house saying: **"Junebug, Junebug, don't take that car."** I would pretend I didn't hear and go on about my way. During the time between my high school graduation and beginning college, I would meet a friend named, Millard Upshaw, at his house around eleven p.m. and we would go to Children's Hospital and pick up our girlfriends.

Every night I would just take the car without asking. My father never said stop taking the car. One night I drove to my friend's house and went inside to wait while he got dressed. When I came outside to get in the car, it was gone. I immediately thought the car was stolen. I called my father and told him the car had been stolen. He replied by saying: "Oh really." I knew then that he had come and got the car. This was his way of letting me know that the car belonged to him and not me. Of course the next night, I took the car again without asking and he permitted this by not saying anything.

After my graduation from high school at age sixteen, I ran away to Atlantic City, New Jersey with two other friends. My father eventually found out where I was and he came and got me. When I think of him, he reminds me of the father in the story of the Prodigal Son found in the Gospel of Luke chapter 15:11-32, where the father forgives and welcomes back his son. My father was a wonderful daddy to my brother, sister and me. Yes, we children all called him daddy. He helped all of us in different ways. Sometimes when I am thinking about my father I can still hear him say: **"Junebug, Junebug, don't take that car."**

"And he arose and came to his father. But when he was still a great way off, his father saw him and had compassion, and ran and fell on his neck and kissed him. "And the son said to him, "Father, I have sinned against heaven and in your sight, and am no longer worthy to be called your son." But the father said to his servants, "Brings out the best robe and put it on him, and put a ring on his hand and sandals on his feet. And bring the fatted calf here and kill it, and let us eat and be merry. For this my son was dead and is alive again; he was lost and is found." And they began to be merry. **Luke 15:20-24**

SEPARATE BUT EQUAL

The United States has long been described as the greatest country in the world and I have never disagreed with that description. But in 1937, I was born into a land where its stated values didn't coincide with its practices. Because of the evils of slavery and segregation, the United States has always been tarnished by its sins practiced against its own citizens. My two grandfathers, Benjamin Shobe and Robert Grant were born in Kentucky prior to the beginning of the Civil War in the United States. They were children when the war started but they were both born into slavery. After the Civil War, the former slaves now had to contend with this terrible practice of Jim Crow laws enacted after the war ended and continued until President Lyndon Johnson strongly called on Congress to enact the Civil Rights Act in 1964 and the Voting Rights Act in 1965. Public schools, transportation accommodations and the U.S. Military were all segregated when I was born. There was a famous or should I say infamous Supreme Court decision that established the Separate but Equal doctrine in the South for over fifty years and practiced somewhat in the North also. That Supreme Court decision was titled Plessy versus Ferguson and named after Homer Adolph Plessy a Louisiana resident who was only 1/8th black. Plessy had an African American great grandmother but his entire family had passed for white. However, the State of Louisiana considered him black.

Louisiana had recently passed a Separate Car Act that required blacks be separated from whites while traveling in Railroad cars in the state. Homer Plessy decided to challenge this newly created law by purchasing a railway ticket and sitting in the Whites' only car. He then informed the conductor that he was 1/8th Black and refused to move to the Colored car. Well he was arrested and taken off of the railroad car. This case went to court and the judge who decided against Plessy was named John Ferguson and this is how we got the name Plessy versus Ferguson. In an eight to one decision against Plessy, the United

States Supreme Court upheld the lower court decision. In a decision written by Justice Henry Brown, The Supreme Court established the Separate but Equal doctrine which said that requiring blacks to ride in separate but equal cars did not violate the fourteenth amendment of the U.S. Constitution. The United States Supreme Court further said that the fourteenth amendment established legal equality but not social or political equality between the races. In his lone dissent, Justice Harlan stated that the Constitution is color blind and neither knows nor tolerates classes among citizens.

This Supreme court decision stood for many years until it was overturned in 1954 with The Brown versus the Topeka Board of Education decision. With this court decision, the modern Civil Rights Revolution was started highlighted by the Montgomery Bus Boycott in Montgomery, Alabama in 1956 and inspired by Rosa Parks and led by Dr. Martin Luther King Jr. During all this time, it was legal to discriminate against African Americans. We were denied equal employment opportunity and segregated in the armed forces until 1948 when President Truman issued an executive order prohibiting this terrible practice. We also had to attend separate schools, and travel separately on buses and trains especially in the South. The Doctrine of Separate but Equal was never true. We were separate but never equal. But even if there had been a true attempt to have us separate and equal, it would have been impossible because as the Supreme Court stated in the 1954 decision; Separate but Equal is inherently unequal. Once the Supreme Court ruled that school children could not be segregated because of their color, then the fight was on to bring down all forms of segregation laws.

Today, I live in a different country than I did when I was a child. In traveling in the South, I don't have to sit in the back of a bus and drink from a colored only fountain. I can go to a restaurant without fear of not being served because of my color. I can marry any woman who wants me in the United States even if she is of a different color. I can attend college and not have to send in my picture with my application so the college can place me in a dormitory room with someone of my own race. I can use the restroom and not worry about whether or not the restroom is designated for Whites only. I can run for the office of President of the United States and know that there has been someone of color who has occupied that high office. My children, grandchildren and great grandchildren now know that they can achieve their dreams by finding out what to do and then working as hard as they can to be successful. God will answer their prayers if they ask Him in faith. And most importantly, there is something else, we can never be separated from and that is the love of God.

Yet in all these things we are more than conquerors through Him who loved us. For I am persuaded that neither death nor life, nor angels nor principalities nor powers, nor things present nor things to come, nor height nor depth, nor any other created thing, shall be able to separate us from the love of God which is in Christ Jesus Our Lord. Romans 8:37-39

ATLANTIC CITY

It was the summer of 1954 and I had just graduated from Columbus East High School at the age of sixteen. In two months, I would have turned seventeen years of age. But at the time of graduation, I was feeling like a grown man. I probably was as tall as I was going to get and I thought that I was as smart as I was going to get. Well my parents didn't believe that I was a grown man yet and they still made me come home before midnight. In fact, they treated me the same way that they had before I had graduated. I had a close friend, James Willis, who just graduated with me and his parents were treating him the same way even though he was ten months older than me. We both began thinking about what it would be like to be on our own. The more we thought about it the more we started thinking about running away. We had no idea of where we could go but finally I thought about Atlantic City, New Jersey. I was there on vacation, with my family, a couple of years earlier and it sounded like a good place to go again.

The problem was that I had no money to travel there and no funds to rent a place to stay upon arrival. My friend had some money because he had a part time job. But the question was where could I get some money? We came up with the idea to use some money from the club that we both belonged to. In our mind, this was just a loan that we would pay back. But in reality, this was what the law called embezzlement. I had always thought of myself as being an honest and truthful person but somehow I didn't see taking the money without asking as stealing from my club members. As I later learned in life, Jesus Christ would guide and direct my footsteps on the right path if I accepted Him as my Lord and Savior. I learned that if we love him, we will follow His commandments and love our neighbor as we love our self. But at this time I was not following Christ or using good common sense. All I knew was that I wanted to be treated as an adult and to achieve this goal, I did one of the most childish things that I could do, which was to steal money and run away from home.

We developed a plan and then we began to work our plan. We took the club's money and proceeded to wash and pack the clothes that we were going to take. Another one of our fellow graduates, Joe Woods, decided to go along with us to Atlantic City. Joe was a little older than us and more on his own. He wasn't really running away since he was going to be living on his own anyway. We were all going to wear white caps and white shoes as our traveling outfit. The day that we left, I remember my sister trying to get in to the family laundry room in order to see what we were doing. We would not let her in and later she would talk about that incident to my parents. That evening we left on a Greyhound Bus to Atlantic City, New Jersey arriving the next day in the morning. The first thing that we did was to find a place to stay and we were able to rent a room from a woman whose name I don't remember. James still remembers our address as 350 Ocean Terrace. I imagine that house is probably torn down now. We then started to look for a job. Some people were trying to sell us a job for five or ten dollars. I don't remember if we fell for this con and actually paid money to buy a job.

I finally found work as a dishwasher at a restaurant called the Kitty Kat and James got work as an elevator operator in a hotel. I can't remember where Joe found work. We were in Atlantic City for about one month when I finally called my parents to let them know where I was. They came immediately to take me back home with them. I acted like I didn't want to go back but I really was glad that they came to get me. My brother told me that if I had wanted a job washing dishes, I could have found one in Columbus.

My father made me repay the money that I took from the club. I didn't realize it at the time, but later as I matured, I deeply regretted running away. I am so sorry for the anguish that I put my parents through. I understand that my mother would spend hours crying for me and she also lost some weight. If one of my children had run away, I would have been very concerned about where they were and what they were doing. In my parents' eyes, I was lost. But they found me and took me back home and helped me go to college. Today I am retired from a job that I loved doing very much. I was also lost spiritually but it took Jesus to find me and save me from myself. **Jesus Saves.**

"What do you think? If a man has a hundred sheep, and one of them goes astray, does he not leave the ninety-nine and go to the mountains to seek the one that is straying? And if he should find it, assuredly, I say to you, he rejoices more over that sheep than over the ninety-nine that did not go astray. Even so it is not the will of your Father who is in heaven that one of these little ones should perish. **Matthew 18:12-14**

Chapter Four:
COLLEGE AND THE MARINES

OHIO UNIVERSITY

OHIO UNIVERSITY CAST

ONLY ALPHAS

KAPPA KONCLAVES

VIRTUOUS WOMEN

MUSICAL MAGIC

THE ORLANDOS

SEMPER FIDELIS

OHIO UNIVERSITY

It was in the fall of 1955, that I entered Ohio University in Athens, Ohio as a freshman. I had first heard of the university through my childhood friend and schoolmate Adger W. Cowans. He had begun the study of photography the previous year and talked very favorably about the university. When I sent in my application, I was asked to submit my picture. At the time, I wondered why they needed it. Maybe they just wanted to know as much as possible about me. Upon my arrival, I was assigned a room with two other black roommates named Aljah Butcher and James Moore. I subsequently found out that all the other black students roomed together.

Other than this overt act of racism, there weren't many more restrictions on the black students that I could see except for joining white fraternities. There was only one black fraternity on the campus and the university frowned on granting fraternity privileges to another one. Its reasoning was that all the blacks should support the one black fraternity now in existence. Another restriction was that we couldn't get our hair cut in the city of Athens because there were no licensed black barbers. A few years later, Don Hilt, a big mean looking Ohio University Basketball Player would go to a white barber shop and demand a haircut. When the barber said that he did not know how to cut a black man's hair, Don responded, "Well it's about time you learned." Don received his haircut that day. Before then, black male students had to go to Parkesburg, West Virginia to get a haircut. I suppose the females had the same or worse problem.

Both of my roommates were from Ohio with Aljah being from Cleveland and James coming out of Sandusky. I took an instant liking to both of them. Aljah was a member of Alpha Phi Alpha Fraternity, the only black fraternity on campus and later on, James became a member also. One of my uncles, Guy L. Grant, was a founder of Kappa Alpha Psi Fraternity, one of the other two big black fraternities in the country

93

but not on the Ohio University campus. The other being Omega Psi Phi. Not only was my uncle a Kappa founder, but four of his brothers, including my father were also Kappa Men. Also my cousin, Guy E. Russell, became a Kappa man; therefore I had no interest in becoming a member of Alpha Phi Alpha Fraternity. I must admit that I admired and respected both Aljah and James and probably would have joined them as Alpha Men if my heart had not already belonged to Kappa Alpha Psi. But I along with some other young black men started an interest group for Kappa Alpha Psi Fraternity on the campus.

As Ohio University students, we could watch feature length movie films at the auditorium for twenty five cents admission. After the movie, we would sometimes be served watermelon and other types of snacks. I remember being ashamed to eat any watermelon in public because of the negative stereotype of it being associated with black people. I am ashamed to say that was how I thought then. Thank God for those who helped me and others change that way of thinking. During this time black students for the most part tried to go along and get along with the powers in charge. Because I was not doing well in college, I decided to join the United States Marine Corps in 1957. I stayed in the Marines for two years and upon my honorable separation as a Lance Corporal, I returned to the university to work on my degree.

After returning from the Marines, I noticed a difference in the attitudes of the African American students on the Ohio University Campus. There was less of a go along and get along attitude. There were more African American students on the campus; therefore more diversity among the black students. While I was away there had been efforts to get Kappa Alpha Psi on campus as a fraternity. While not successful in establishing a fraternity, Ron Holman and others were able to get the Kappas accepted as a social club named Kappa Psi Phi. In 1966, after I had graduated, Kappa Alpha Psi received its charter and became a full fledged fraternity on the Ohio University Campus. Eventually the other big African American fraternity, Omega Psi Phi received fraternity status to join Alpha Phi Alpha and Kappa Alpha Psi on the Ohio University Campus. After undergoing many trials and tribulations, I finally graduated from Ohio University in August 1964.

I have returned to the campus for a black alumni reunion in 1991 and a Kappa Alpha Psi reunion in 2009. I have also returned to the campus for my two nephews' graduation ceremonies in the late nineteen eighties and mid nineteen nineties … I will always have wonderful thoughts when I think about Ohio University and my days spent there.

Finally, brethren, whatever things are true, whatever things are noble, whatever things are just, whatever things are pure, whatever things are lovely, whatever things are of good report, if there is any virtue and if there is anything praiseworthy—meditate on these things. Philippians 4:8

OHIO UNIVERSITY CAST

Aljah Butcher and James Moore were previously mentioned as my first two roommates at Ohio University. They were my roommates in Johnson Hall which was located on the East Green Campus. I have also talked about Don Hilt's haircut and Ron Holman efforts in establishing Kappa Alpha Psi on the Ohio University Campus. There were so many more friends mostly Kappas that I can tell you about. My closest friend on the campus was my fraternity brother, Leon Chapman. I met him after I returned from the Marines. We became good friends and usually talked every day by telephone when we could not see each other. Leon was a member of the university's tennis team and also a good athlete in other sports. We would play each other one on one in basketball and I could never beat him. After he beat me, he would give me his usual victory smile.

He graduated a couple of years before me and was gracious to send me a few dollars my last semester before I graduated to help me with my financial needs. I tried to pay him back by taking him out to dinner a couple of times many years later. But that kind of debt, you can never pay back, you just have to pay forward as Ohio State Football Coach Woody Hayes would say. Some months ago, Leon and his lovely wife Shirley invited Delores and I to Cleveland, Ohio to attend a Cavaliers basketball game. We stayed at their beautiful home and enjoyed their wonderful hospitality. It was a pleasure to see him again at the 2009 reunion of the Epsilon Lambda chapter of Kappa Alpha Psi at Ohio University. Some of my other Kappa Brothers are Cyril Weathers, Michael Preston, Cliff Coursey, Henry Scott, Frank Wise, Les Bowman, Gerald Smith, Freddy Moore, Austin Brown, George Hall, Martin Tyler and Arthur Hopkins.

We were more than guys who belonged to a fraternity. We were all good friends. Just belonging to the Kappas helped me to focus and desire to return to college. Cyril Weathers was a fun loving guy that I cannot imagine not ever knowing. He told wonderful stories and always kept you laughing. Michael Preston was from Lancaster, Ohio and became a social worker in Columbus, Ohio. Henry Scott was our Kappa president at one time and after graduation moved to California. Frank Wise was interested in becoming a military man. He was very active in ROTC while in college. I don't know if he ever joined the military. Les Bowman and Gerald Smith moved to Detroit, Michigan and Les became a hospital administrator. Gerald received his PhD. and became the executive director of a large social work agency. Unfortunately, Gerald died recently and he is missed very much. Freddy Moore became a chemical engineer and he has also passed away.

I just recently saw Austin Brown and Martin Tyler at our fraternity reunion and they have done very well. Austin and his lovely wife, Phyllis took some wonderful pictures of the reunion and shared them with everybody. Martin is a renowned dentist practicing in Canada and has achieved the rank of captain in the Navy Reserve. Cliff Coursey was an Athens, Ohio native but has since moved to Oregon. When in Columbus, he would always visit me. I last saw George Hall in 1991 at a reunion for Black Students. George became a school principal. Arthur Hopkins was close to my heart. He had moved to Detroit, Michigan but would always call me when he made a trip to Columbus to visit relatives. Arthur died a number of years ago and that was much too early. He was a very intelligent and gentle man. Another close Kappa friend of mine was Bert King who always came by to see me when he was in Columbus. Bert graduated with me in 1964 and went on to receive his Masters Degree from Harvard University. He also passed away a number of years ago and left me with wonderful memories of him.

There were so many others including Donna Moore, LaWanna McKinley and Barbara Ellis who were great examples for the women students on campus. Another good Ohio University friend of mine is Rita Osborne who wrote to me while I was in the Marine Corps. We still talk to each other periodically. There was also a basketball player on campus named Stacy Bunton, who at the time was the tallest person that I had ever seen. However, his playing ability did not match his height, but on his wedding night, he played a game in which he tipped in the basketball with one second left to win the game for Ohio University. I will never forget the crowd leaving the stands and hoisting Stacy up on their shoulders as a hero. Stacy subsequently became divorced and has since passed away. But that night of triumph for him will stay in my mind forever.

Beloved, if God so loved us, we also ought to love one another. No one has seen God at any time. If we love one another, God abides in us, and His love has been perfected in us. 1 John 4:11-12

ONLY ALPHAS

On the Ohio University campus in 1956, there were approximately sixty black students and there was only one black fraternity which was named Alpha Phi Alpha. This fraternity was the source of any dances and parties for the black students; and these events were usually held in a small rented hall owned by the Knights of Columbus. Black students could attend dances held by the university but that was it for us. There were many other fraternities on campus but they only had white members and did not socialize with black students. There was no overt segregation on campus but there was the covert practice of segregation. The university placed black students together in dormitory rooms and this practice continued for many years. Until this day, I have no memories of any white friends from my Ohio University days. The Alphas filled the void in our lives for personal intimate parties unless they were having a closed party. If this was the case, then only Alphas, their dates and invited friends could attend. Both of my roommates were affiliated with Alpha Phi Alpha Fraternity, Aljah Butcher being an Alpha and James Moore being a pledge.

There was another place on campus where blacks along with other students could go dance and socialize and that was at the John C. Baker Center. A couple of times a year, the university would sponsor dances that all the students could attend. During the spring of 1956, I invited a girl friend of mine from Columbus, Ohio. I had dated her once or twice before at home in Columbus. She was a very attractive and popular girl. In my youth, I considered it quite an accomplishment to get her to come to Athens. During this particular weekend, The Alphas were having a party. I thought that I would take my friend and see if we could get in the party. As we tried to enter, the guy at the door told me that I could not come in but he would let my friend come in. I declined this invitation but he again asked my friend if she wanted to come in. She looked to me for approval and I reluctantly said ok but I really didn't want her to go in without me. But to my surprise she said she wanted to go in. She went in for a little while and than came back out again. I am sure that the Alphas knew that I was interested in becoming a member of Kappa Alpha Psi Fraternity so that was probably why they would not let me come into their party.

I learned some valuable lessons that weekend. One lesson was that we needed another black fraternity on campus and another was I learned how it felt to be excluded. As a result of this and other incidents, some other young men and I decided to start our own fraternity interest group and we decided to try and establish a chapter of Kappa Alpha Psi Fraternity on our campus. This effort began in 1955 when I first arrived on the Ohio University campus and ended when the chapter was established in 1966. I had graduated by then but was invited back for the celebration. Since that time two of my nephews Tim and Chris Grant have graduated from Ohio University and both became members of Kappa Alpha Psi through the chapter that I help to found. Just recently I attended a reunion of my Ohio University Kappa Brothers in May 2009 at Athens, Ohio and I was honored as being one of two brothers most responsible for founding the Epsilon Lambda Chapter of Kappa Alpha Psi at Ohio University. The other man who I really consider to be the brother most responsible was Ronald Holman who led in the actual work of founding our fraternity on campus.

This was not a one or two man effort but the combined effort of many young men wanting to become Kappas. I won't try to name all of them but first there is Henry Scott, our president, and other members such as Alvin Adams, Austin Brown, Leon Chapman, George Hall, and Robert Harrison. Leroy Massey, Ralph White and Ronald Holman were the first members of Kappa Alpha Psi Fraternity on the Ohio University campus as they had joined the fraternity on other university's campuses. Our chapter of Epsilon Lambda of Kappa Alpha Psi Fraternity has been in existence since 1966. Kappa Alpha Psi is not a Christian fraternity but rather a social fraternity. But its principles are consistent with Jesus' commandment to love one another. As a member of Kappa Alpha Psi Fraternity and as a citizen of the United States of America, I am free to choose and practice what ever religion I want to. Thanks be to Christ for choosing me.

Blessed be the God and Father of our Lord Jesus Christ, who has blessed us with every spiritual blessing in the heavenly places in Christ, just as He chose us in Him before the foundation of the world, that we should be holy and without blame before Him in love, having predestined us to adoption as sons by Jesus Christ to Himself, according to the good pleasure of His will, to the praise of the glory of His grace, by which He made us accepted in the Beloved. Ephesians 1:3-6

KAPPA KONCLAVES

While at Ohio University, I helped to start a social club named Kappa Psi Phi. Our goal was to affiliate ourselves with the national fraternity of Kappa Alpha Psi which had chapters at many colleges and universities throughout the United States and some foreign countries. We would periodically meet to conduct fraternity business but many times we would just get together in a dormitory room to enjoy each others' company. During these informal meetings, we would tell stories about what was going on at the campus, which almost always encompassed talking about the girls. We would talk loudly and laugh with gusto. We would try to out do each other in the stories we were telling.

One particular night however, everyone decided to meet in my room which was in a private house, a mile or more walk from the campus. We started our conversation with everyone trying to top each other with their stories. We had the usual laughter and loud talking and this behavior probably went on for two or more hours. Finally, when everybody became tired and went home, I went to bed and immediately fell asleep. The next morning, I saw Mr. Warner who was the landlord. He started our conversation, as he always did, asking how I was doing and how school was going. Then all of a sudden, he blurts our "Who won the game last night?" I responded that Ohio University didn't play a game last night. He said, "I am not talking about Ohio University playing a game. I am talking about that game you had in your room last night."

When looking back, I always think of Mr. Warner as being a very considerate person. He could have told everyone to get out and go home. He could have given me a good talking to about the loud noises in my room last night. However, he chose not to do that. He did let me know that my behavior was unacceptable and I never had another meeting in my room again; however, when we had our business meetings, we would have them in a university meeting room. During one of our Kappa business meetings, we were having an unusually strong discussion. It seemed as if almost all the brothers had something to say. I can't remember what the issue was but no one could get a word in without another brother cutting them off. This spirited discussion went on for some time with no resolution. In this group of brothers was Phil Williams, who hardly ever had anything to say. I remember him as being polite and quiet during meetings. In fact, in the past meetings there were efforts to include him in the discussions, but usually he was quiet and would only participate by listening.

During this meeting, as usual, Phil wasn't saying anything. As the discussion continued with everyone still trying to talk, Phil suddenly raised his hand. Immediately everyone saw that Phil had raised his hand and several brothers began to say that Phil wants to say something. Other brothers chimed in and said: "Let Brother Williams talk". "Let's hear what he has to say." Everybody stopped talking and looked at Phil. Now for the first time in a long while, the room was quiet and Phil finally began to talk. What he then said, to everyone's surprise, was "May I be excused to go to the bathroom." The room then burst into laughter as Phil left to go to the bathroom. I have remembered this incident and Phil over the years. I remember his quiet and gentle spirit. I didn't know him very well but as I have gotten older and hopefully wiser, I appreciate more and more his humbleness and gentleness. I can't remember the issue we were discussing but I can never forget Phil Williams.

It has been over forty five years since I attended classes on the campus of Ohio University but just recently I was reunited with some of my Kappa Brothers at the Ohio University Inn on May 30, 2009. We were a little older, wiser and some of us heavier but we still had the love and respect for each other that we had over forty five years ago. It was good seeing all of those guys and reminiscing about old times and swapping Kappa stories. A history of our fraternity chapter at Ohio University was presented to all the brothers present at the reunion. **God is so good.**

The Lord is gracious and full of compassion, slow to anger and great in mercy. The Lord is good to all, And His tender mercies are over all His works. All Your works shall praise You, O Lord, And

Your saints shall bless You. They shall speak of the glory of Your kingdom, And talk of Your power, to make known to the sons of men His mighty acts, And the glorious majesty of His kingdom. Your kingdom is an everlasting kingdom, And Your dominion endures throughout all generations. Psalm 145:8-13

VIRTUOUS WOMEN

When I was a student at Ohio University, I can remember telling my friends that when I married I wanted it to be to a woman of substance. I had no idea of what a woman of substance was but I believed that I would recognize one when I saw her. In looking back, I now know that the Bible describes a woman of substance or a virtuous woman in the 31st chapter of Proverbs. But when I was a student at Ohio University, I unfortunately was not reading the Bible. There have been many virtuous women listed and described in the Holy Bible such as Sarah, wife of Abraham (Hebrews 11:11); Ruth, daughter in law of Naomi (Ruth); Esther, who like Ruth has a book in the Bible written about her (Esther); Deborah, who rendered judgment for and encouraged submission to God (Judges 4:4-10); Mary and Martha, sisters who exemplified the qualities of grace and works (Luke 10:38-42). and The Virgin Mary, the mother of Jesus Christ (Luke 1:26-38).

Over the past 50 years, I have sometimes thought of Barbara Ellis, who was one of my fellow students at Ohio University in the 1950's. I remember her as a woman of substance. We were not close friends. I just knew her in a casual sort of way. If you were to see her walking on campus, she would probably blend in with the other girls as far as appearance. But there was something that set her apart from the other girls and people in general. In looking back, I ask myself, what were those qualities that she had that made me remember her over the years? She had character, which included wisdom, humility and compassion. She had a beautiful spirit about her. You might say she had some if not all of the Fruit of the Spirit described in the fifth chapter of Galatians. In a way I admired her very much. I remember hearing about her marrying Les Carney, who was the 200 meters silver medal winner of the 1960 Olympics in Rome Italy.

Although I didn't know Les except for the fact that he was an Olympic champion, which is a wonderful achievement. But I knew that he had been very fortunate in marrying Barbara Ellis. Recently, I thought about Barbara but I could not remember her maiden name. I remembered Barbara Carney but that was all. I am at the age when I forget names while I still remember the person. My wife reminds me that this information that I have temporarily forgotten is in my file. And I will be able to retrieve it at some point in the future if I am patient. Just the other day, I was reading the Ohio University Alumni Magazine and saw that Barbara Ellis Carney had passed away. Even though I have not seen her for over fifty years and we were never close friends, I still had my feeling of sadness for her husband and children. I will always remember those brief days we spent at Ohio University and will keep her, Les and the children in my heart.

Another woman of substance I met on the Ohio University campus was LaWanna McKinley White. I met her after I completed my enlistment in the Marines and returned to the university campus. She was a leader among some of the African American women at the university. She tried to encourage the women to respect themselves and demand respect from the guys they were dating. Some of the guys resented her efforts in influencing the women and talked negatively about her. She didn't care what they said because she kept doing what she knew to be the right thing. I just saw her on May 30, 2009, after forty five years, at the Ohio University Epsilon Lambda chapter reunion of Kappa Alpha Psi Fraternity and she seems the same as when I last saw her. Her outer and inner beauty is still there for all to see. For me seeing her again was like time stood still.

Last but not least is my dear friend of over fifty three years, Rita Osborne Lewis. I met Rita in the fall of 1956 at Ohio University. I can't remember why or how but we became good friends. I think Rita was a good friend to all of those she knew. She has the ability to make you think that you are the only one. When I joined the Marines, Rita wrote me letters consistently. My sister, Alice was the only other person to write me letters like Rita did. After I was discharged from the Marines and returned to college, Rita would give me her dinner at the cafeteria. She wanted to stay trim and I lacked the money to buy all the food I needed so we helped each other out. In 1991, I learned that the black alumni were planning a reunion for that July. I wasn't going to attend until Rita called me and said "You are coming aren't you?" I hadn't talked to her for twenty six years but I immediately answered her "Yes." Periodically, we still talk on the telephone although I have not seen her for a number of years. Rita has been and always will be a wonderful friend.

There are many other virtuous women that I could write about and I have mentioned them in other writings. My favorite of course is my virtuous and beautiful wife, Delores who I will talk about later in a separate writing.

Who can find a virtuous wife? For her worth is far above rubies. The heart of her husband safely trusts her; so he will have no lack of gain. She does him good and not evil all the days of her life. Proverbs 31:10-12

Musical Magic

M y love for the piano began when I heard one of my college friends, Delmont Hopkins, play for me in 1956 at Ohio University. Delmont was the older brother of my future fraternity brother, Art Hopkins, who I met in 1960. We were both awaiting our rides to take us home for the Thanksgiving Holidays and the dormitory was mostly empty of students. I never knew Delmont could play the piano and this was an unexpected treat. As I listened to him, I fell in love with the beauty and magic of the piano. As I am beginning to write this piece on music, I am listening to a CD of Beegie Adair on my computer. If you have not heard of Beegie, she is a wonderful light jazz pianist who lives and works out of Nashville, Tennessee. I particularly like her because we are the same age and graduated from high school in the same year. I have written many of my stories while listening to her brilliant playing of so many of my favorite songs written by some of the great songwriters of the twentieth century. I just recently discovered her beautiful talent when I saw an advertisement about her on television. I have bought over ten CDs by her since I first became aware of her.

Not only do I love the piano, I love all the musical instruments that go into making musical magic. I can remember as a little child enjoying the music of Fats Waller. One of my favorite songs when I was about five or six was: "I gonna sit right down and write myself a letter." Since then I have collected and listened to almost all of his music. He has so many great songs that it would be impossible to mention them all at this time. My favorite female singer is Dinah Washington who made a number of great recordings and some with another favorite of mine, Brooke Benton. I am also a big fan of Billie Holiday, Ella Fitzgerald and Louis Armstrong. My favorite male singer is of course, the chairman of the board, Frank Sinatra. Following a close second is the incomparable Nat King Cole, who I believe has the sweetest voice ever. I have also become a huge fan of Rod Stewart, who sings the romantic songs that

Beegie plays. I like most of the music written in the 1920s through the 1940s.

I am also a big fan of Rock and Roll or as it was also called Rhythm and Blues. My teenage years consisted of listening and dancing to all of the famous groups such as the Platters and their hit "Earth Angel"; Clyde McPhatter and the Drifters singing "Money Honey;" and Lloyd Price singing "Lawdy Miss Clawdy." There were many other Rock and Roll groups too numerous to mention. One of my favorite groups of that era was the Counts who had a couple of hits: "Darling Dear and My Dear My Darling." These guys were favorites of mine especially after I learned that two of the four members were my second cousins on my mother's side named Robert Wesley and Chester Brown. Also during this time, my brother, Doug and three of his friends, George Davis, George Gibbs and Ronald Harris formed a doo wop group called the Orlandos. They would sing at different events with other competing singing groups. One time I saw them perform at the Veteran's Memorial Building in Columbus, Ohio and they were wonderful. The building had an overflow crowd and they along with the other groups brought down the house singing the popular hits of the day. I also love country music with the great stories told in their songs. Loretta Lynn and Patsy Cline are my favorites.

The music that has made the greatest impact on my life is gospel music and worship songs. After my son died in 1978, I started listening to gospel music. One of my favorite Christian artists is Andre Crouch and the Disciples. Andre uses a lot of scripture in his music and this was probably my first experience in listening to the Word of God. My wife knew about him much earlier than I did and the same night I went to see George Foreman fight Joe Frazier, she was going to an Andre Crouch concert. At the time, there was no way that I would select Andre Crouch over a Foreman vs. Frazier fight. A little over two years after my son's death, my wife and I opened a Christian book store and we stocked a lot of gospel music. I had an opportunity to listen to much of this music and I believe that this gospel music was instrumental in leading me to Jesus Christ as my Lord and Savior.

About thirteen years ago, I decided to take piano lessons as an adult but unfortunately my talent lies somewhere else. I then decided to take the money that I was spending and pay for my three year old grandson's piano lessons. Kai has been taking piano lessons ever since and he is now fifteen years old. He says that he wants to major in piano when he goes to college and then make music his profession. I am encouraging him to become whatever he wants but I am glad that he will have choices in life. The most important music in my life at the present time is worship music that gives praise to God. I am thankful that God has provided music to entertain and minister to us while we are here on earth.

Let the word of Christ dwell in you richly in all wisdom, teaching and admonishing one another in psalms and hymns and spiritual songs, singing with grace in your hearts to the Lord. And whatever you do in word or deed, do all in the name of the Lord Jesus, giving thanks to God the Father through Him. Colossians 3:16-17

THE ORLANDOS

B ack in the middle 1950's, while I was attending Ohio University, my brother, Doug, became a member of a local doo wop singing group named the Orlandos. I was three years older than my brother so I didn't associate with him and his friends. But I do remember expressing an interest in joining his group but they turned me down for some reason. Maybe they thought that I wasn't good enough to sing with them. I look on it as their loss. Who knows I might have been the missing piece that would have made them famous. I remember that they had these gold outfits with Bermuda shorts including gold shoes. They were a distinct singing group and they could really sing. They had many good singers and especially their lead singer, Ronald Harris had a voice like Frankie Lymon, the lead singer of the Teenagers who died in 1968 at the age of twenty six due to a drug and alcohol problem. One of Frankie Lymon's greatest hits was "Why do fools fall in love?" And Ronald was wonderful in singing the lead on this song with the other guys.

The Orlandos were founded by their bass singer, George Davis who had a beautiful and far ranging bass voice. George was a family friend that I knew through my brother. I remember that I bought a car from him for fifty dollars after I got out of the Marine Corps in 1959 but I forgot to pay him the money. In 1975, I put together a Poindexter Village Reunion and upon seeing George, he told me that I had never paid him for the car he sold me. At first I was taken back by this reminder but then I quickly realized that I had indeed not paid him. I gave him his fifty dollars but laughingly told him that I was not giving him any interest. He agreed and gladly took my money. George Davis in my opinion was a hero. As an army paratrooper, he served with honor and courage in the Vietnam War. One of his legs was amputated as a result of injuries received in combat and some years later he died.

Ronald Harris was another family friend who lived next door to us on Long Street. He and his older brother John came to our house on a regular basis. We loved those guys and considered them to be like family members. Ronald loved a good meal and had a tendency to put on weight. He accepted Jesus Christ as his Lord and Savior and was not shy in telling you about it. He became an assistant pastor at a church here in Columbus, but he eventually moved to Chicago, Illinois and pastored a church there. When my son died in 1978 at the age of seven, two months shy of his eighth birthday; it was Ronald who ministered to me. It is ironic how things turn out in life. A kid that I grew up with was now placed by God to console me in one of the worst times that I could imagine in my life. I will never forget the words of comfort that he gave me and I will never forget him. Ronald Harris died a few years ago and joined his brother John, sister and parents in glory.

The other member of the Orlandos that I remember well is George Gibbs or as he was also called George Richardson. George had a beautiful falsetto voice and has served as the historian of the group. He remembers for the most part what happened back in those days concerning the group and has written e-mails to my brother reminding him of when they got started and what they had accomplished. George is now living in Dayton, Ohio and periodically keeps in contact with my brother. My brother credits George with promoting what the Orlandos called the presentation concept, which is: outstanding appearance, composure, and conduct both on and off the stage. George Gibbs is one of the two remaining original members still living. George became a Methodist minister and served as the pastor of several churches including one here in Columbus, Ohio. Other young men joining the Orlandos as vacancies occurred were: Robert Wallace, lead and first tenor, Steve Martin, lead and first tenor, Robert Clark, first tenor, Keith White, first tenor, Leroy Foster, baritone and James Eskridge, bass.

The other original member of the group living is my brother Doug Grant. George Gibbs relates that he and the other group members would be fearful about performing but not my brother Doug. George says that Doug was not fearful of the devil himself. This is how I remember my brother because as a little boy, he was not fearful of anything. George goes on to say that Doug had a habit of doing wild stunts without notice. Doug would pretend to pass out so that one of the other guys would be there to catch him. By doing this Doug would get the crowd involved into giving the group a standing ovation. This would take some of the fear out of performing. George Gibbs talks about the group members going to church to obtain spiritual answers to their questions about the group succeeding. Occasionally they would receive criticism from the church elders and deacons for singing the devil's music. But as George says they were strong young black men who kept on moving ahead. **And move ahead they did.** Doug also has served his church, St. Philip Evangelical Lutheran as the president of their board.

Have you not known? Have you not heard? The everlasting God, the Lord, the Creator of The ends of the earth, neither faints nor is weary. His understanding is unsearchable. He gives power to the weak, and to those who have no might He increases strength. Even the youths shall faint and be weary, and the young men shall utterly fall, but those who wait on the Lord shall renew their strength; they shall mount up with wings like eagles, they shall run and not be weary, they shall walk and not faint. Isaiah 40:28-31

SEMPER FIDELIS

It was February nineteen hundred and fifty seven, and I had just joined the United States Marine Corps. I can remember taking my first plane ride from Cincinnati, Ohio to Chicago, Illinois. And then I boarded another plane to San Diego, California. This was in the days before jet passenger planes. That was the only time I ever flew on propeller driven airplanes except when I returned home after being discharged from the Marines. Upon arrival at the airport in San Diego, the other recruits and I were met by Marine Corps' Drill Instructors. They were shouting at us telling us to get in a formation and spit the gum out of our mouths. We were then loaded into buses and transported to the Marine Corps Recruit Depot. Upon arriving at the Recruit Depot, we had our heads shaved and were told to get rid of any personal items including food and medicine.

The next day we were awakened at five a.m. and the first thing the other recruits and I did was go to the bathroom. This was the pattern we followed during my entire sixteen weeks of training. After the early morning drills, we went to breakfast for a big meal. The rest of the day consisted of physical and mental training but mostly physical. Our only breaks after breakfast were lunch, dinner, periodic smoking breaks and nightly showers. We were constantly doing exercises and had to run everywhere we went. The discipline was intense and we had to call everyone above the rank of recruit, including privates, by the name of sir. In between the hours of five a.m. and 10:00 p.m. when we went to bed, it was pure physical and mental hell. At least that is what I thought at the time. However, looking back, it was one of the most important and productive times of my life. When I graduated from Marine Corps Boot Camp, I was in the best shape of my life and then I was assigned to a Marine Corps Infantry company.

This is when the real fun began. I was assigned a B.A.R. which is the short name for a Browning Automatic Rifle. This was primarily my weapon, but others would carry it from time to time if we were on hikes or long walks. This weapon was heavier than the M1 rifles that most of the infantrymen carried. One time, our regiment went on a one hundred mile hike and when we returned no one could walk. Everybody was given liberty but no one took advantage of the offer. Everyone just took a shower and went to bed. Another time, I went with my regiment to a place called Pickle Meadows that was used to provide us with cold weather training. Until I went to Pickle Meadows, I never realized how cold it could get. We used snowshoes to walk in the snow because it was so deep. The snow would come up to our waist making it almost impossible to walk without snowshoes. One day, my hands became so cold that I could barely stand it even with gloves on. My corporal, who was a white southerner, came over to me and had me, put my hands under his armpits.

My hands became warmer and I never forgot this act of kindness, especially since I thought he might be prejudiced against me because I was an African American. I learned that I was prejudging him before I knew all the facts. In my experience, the Marine Corps was a truly integrated outfit. I enlisted only nine years after the armed services were integrated but I saw or heard no instances of segregation. In fact, we were all treated equally, like dogs. One of my reasons for joining the Marines was to hopefully get into better shape. When I joined the Marine Corps I was probably in the worst shape of any recruit reporting for duty. There were two obstacle courses we had to successfully complete to become Marines. The beginning course was very difficult for me. Out of seventy six recruits running the course, I was the seventy fifth to finish it. In looking over at the advanced course, I never thought that I would be able to complete it. When the time came for me to complete the advanced course, I had no problem at all.

The Marine Corps' motto is **Semper Fidelis** which means always faithful. The Marine Corps was faithful to me in that it took an overweight boy and made him into a trim and fit man. I ended my enlistment in the Marine Corps as a main gate sentry at a naval prison in San Diego, California. This happened over fifty years ago. I may not now look the part but I am still and always will be a United States Marine.

MARSHALL L. GRANT JR.

Let a man so consider us, as servants of Christ and stewards of the mysteries of God. Moreover it is required in stewards that one be found faithful. 1 Corinthians 4:1-2

Chapter Five:
HELLO CIVILIAN LIFE

D ALLEY

HIS PLANS

ROBERT GRANT

PEARL'S GIFT

LITTLE BLACK SWAN

ALICE CAROLE AND MISS PEARL

TRAINS AND PLANES

PAY FORWARD

D ALLEY

As a young man, I knew that my little brother was a good worker. He started with a paper route and worked his way up to a management position with AT&T previously known as Western Electric. He started with Western Electric at the age of eighteen. He had also been hired at the United States Post Office and for two weeks worked both jobs in order to decide which one he wanted to keep permanently. He would work the day shift at Western Electric and than go to the second shift at the post office. Well as I have indicated, he decided to go with Western Electric. I think that he would have been successful wherever he went to work. He started out as a newspaper boy for the Columbus Dispatch Newspaper in Columbus, Ohio. This was where he learned about the world of work. He recalls earning about $45.00 dollars a week and the Christmas holidays really bought extra money for him.

My brother describes his paper route as being a gold mine in terms of performing additional customer service such as cutting grass in the summer and shoveling snow off driveways and sidewalks in the winter. He was also able to obtain other jobs from his customers such as cleaning, painting rooms and washing their automobiles. One of his greatest achievements as a paper boy was the many prizes and trips that he won through his newspaper and magazine sales. He won baseballs, basketballs and gloves as a result of his sales record. He also won trips to Washington D.C., the Rose Bowl in Pasadena, California and to see the Cleveland Browns play football. He even won trips to see the Liberty Bell in Philadelphia, Pennsylvania and the Statue of Liberty in the State of New York. I had the opportunity to work for my brother after I had been discharged from the Marines. I was now twenty one years old and my brother had got me a job parking cars at the parking lot where he was an attendant.

I learned a lot working for him. Although he didn't make a big salary, he knew how to supplement his income just like he had done when he was a paper boy. One day the lot was full of cars but people were still coming to park their cars. I asked my brother where are we going to park these additional cars since the A, B and C lots were full. He told me to park them in the D lot. I told him that we did not have a D lot. He said of course we have a D lot. I asked him where the D lot was. He said the D lot was in **D Alley**. This was his parking lot and he kept the funds earned by parking cars in the alley. We would also ask the parking lot customers if they wanted their cars washed. If they said yes, than I would drive their car to a car wash and get them washed. We would charge the customer more than it cost to wash the cars and this was our profit. Sometimes, we just washed the cars on our site using the water from the bank next door. My brother would do favors for the bank manager and he didn't mind my brother using their water.

When my brother started to work for Western Electric, he was fully prepared to compete with all the other workers. My father advised him to do the jobs that other workers didn't want so he would always be needed more. If there was a meeting, my brother would volunteer to take the minutes. This was a job that nobody else wanted and my brother was relied upon to do this job. He also was in control of what was recorded and quickly picked up the nickname Scribe. He became active in union politics and finally was elected to the executive board of the local union. In doing so, he became the first African American to be elected to this local board. He decided that with his excellent work record, he deserved to be promoted to supervision. Well he found out that there was resistance to his promotion. It could have been because of his color or it could have been because of his union activity but they would not promote him.

At the time, I was working for the Columbus Urban League in the employment section and it was my job to help our clients obtain employment. We had an excellent relationship with Western Electric through my boss, Irvin Lowery. Irvin knew the plant manager, John O'Neil of Western Electric personally and they also played golf together. When Irvin became aware of my brother's problem, he quickly went to Mr. O'Neil and got my brother into their management training program. The rest is history as my brother retired as a supervisor in 1996 after having served in many management positions. Just as he had helped me so many times in the past, I was able to help him when it counted. He always tells me that I have been a great brother; but the truth is he has been a brother's keeper to me.

Let brotherly love continue. Do not forget to entertain strangers, for by so doing some have unwittingly entertained angels. Remember the prisoners as if chained with them—those who are mistreated—since you yourselves are in the body also. Hebrews 13:1-3

HIS PLANS

When I was in high school and even when I first went to Ohio University I didn't have any idea of what I wanted to be. I started out in pre med without taking anything in high school that would have prepared me for this field. I remember my first test in chemistry, which I received an A. Then my second test came which required more math than I knew. Guess what, I received an F. It all went downhill after that. After a year and a half, my grades were not sufficient to allow me to continue and I enlisted in the Marine Corps. I served honorably for two years and was discharged as a Lance Corporal. I then decided to return to the university but I had to decide what I wanted to major in. I had a good friend who had also attended Ohio University but had graduated while I was in the service. In fact, he was my influence for going to this university. His name is Adger W. Cowans who had been a boyhood friend and had also been our family paper boy. He is still to this day a wonderful and talented photographer and personal friend.

Well I decided that I wanted to be a photographer also. I began to read about and look at some photographs taken by some of the great photographers of that era including Ansel Adams, Gordan Parks, Margaret Bourke-White, Alfred Eisenstaedt and Yousef Karsh. I had not begun my college courses again so I had time to do some pre study in photography before returning to the university. I bought a camera, some photography books and began studying photographic techniques. I was reading about shutter speed, use of a light meter, hyperfocal distance and other photographic topics. One day there was an accident in front of my house involving a little boy being hit and knocked under a car. Fortunately he wasn't hurt and I took his picture while he was still under the car. My picture was published in the local African American newspaper and should be in a 1959 summer issue of the Columbus Sentinel Newspaper in Columbus, Ohio. That is one of the few pictures

I remember taking. I remember feeling guilty at the time because I didn't try to help the boy, I just took his picture.

Unlike me, Adger Cowans was always taking pictures. Years later when he came to town for his mother's funeral, he brought his camera to the funeral and the cemetery. He used it to document what was going on in his life that particular time and moment. One of Adger's heroes was the great Life Magazine Photographer Gordon Parks. Adger met and worked with Gordon and remained close to him until his death a few years ago when Gordon was in his nineties. In fact, there was a picture taken of Gordon Parks, his son and two daughters for Jet Magazine shortly before his death. Adger is included in that picture and looks so much like Gordon that he could be mistaken for his son. Adger admired Gordon's work very much and I am sure that Gordon was very proud of Adger. I know that I am.

As I was preparing to return to Ohio University, most of my time spent in studying photography was in reading books and magazines on the subject. I guess I liked the thought of being a photographer rather than actually taking pictures. My father took an interest in my desire to major in photography and began to ask me questions. I guess I didn't provide him with adequate answers so he began to question my intent and desire to be a photographer. When pressed, I answered him somewhat defensively that I did indeed want to be a phographer. He then asked me a question that I really had no answer for. He said "you say that you want to be a photographer but I never see you taking any pictures." I had to ask myself that same question. I didn't have a good answer and it was probably then that I decided to choose another major. I chose to major in political science because I had an interest in politics and this major didn't require many prerequisite courses.

I eventually graduated with a BA in Political Science and had a great career that I loved in staff training and development where at times I did use a camera in the performance of my duties. **God had His plans for me.**

For I know the thoughts that I think toward you, says the Lord, thoughts of peace and not of evil, to give you a future and a hope. Then you will call upon Me and go and pray to Me, and I will listen to you. And you will seek Me and find Me, when you search for Me with all your heart. Jeremiah 29:11-13

ROBERT GRANT

My nephew, Robert Douglas Grant Jr. was born on May 10, 1959 at The Ohio State University Hospital in Columbus, Ohio. His mother, Claudia Grant, completed her God given mission and delivered a wonderful baby boy. When this was done, she went on to glory to be with our Lord and Savior, Jesus Christ. She had cardiac arrest following the delivery and despite extraordinary medical attention, she could not be revived. My brother was in the room and witnessed the heroic measures taken by hospital personnel. Although in shock, he recalls the presence of God and the awareness that Claudia wouldn't want her untimely death to overshadow the joy of the baby's birth. She would know that he would be raised in a nurturing atmosphere of family love. When Claudia was pregnant with Robert, she did tell my brother and sister that she had a very detailed dream of her baby growing up, being on television, in movies and yes, even on the stage. My brother, Robert Douglas Sr. brought the baby from the hospital and moved from his apartment to the family home to live with his parents, my sister and me.

My mother was working for the federal government at that time but resigned her position to take care of the baby. All of us pitched in to help care for little Robert who became the focus of our attention. He was a smart little fella and began talking at an early age. When we were pushing him in his stroller, he would speak to people by saying; "Hi how are you doing?" The startled strangers would respond by answering; "Fine, how are you?" Little Robert would answer by saying; "Pretty good how about yourself?" He probably got his method of greeting from my father, his grandfather, Marshall L. Grant Sr. The same year that Robert Jr. was born, my sister won the Miss Bronze Ohio Contest and this started her show business career. Around 1961, my mother, my sister and little Robert moved to New York, New York so my sister could continue her career in the Big Apple which is the nickname for

New York City. My brother missed his son but he knew that my mother had to be with my sister in New York. And she also had to continue to care for Robert.

When Robert was a toddler, he was diagnosed with Asthma and had to be hospitalized several times. During one of these hospitalizations, little Robert's condition was so serious that he fell into a coma. His father, Robert Sr. (Doug) flew up to New York and I took a train. My father, Marshall Sr. drove up later in the week. Little Robert was probably around three years of age when this particular hospitalization occurred. During his hospital stays, some of the hospital staff would attempt to address him by the name of Bobby but little Robert would tell them emphatically that his name was Robert not Bobby. In 1963, my brother married the former Addie McCall. Doug had known Addie as the little sister of Jean McCall who was married to one of Doug's best friends, Jimmy Bettis. Doug and Addie were married in April of 1963 in a small ceremony at her house. My father and I attended with me serving as best man. Doug and Addie moved into the upstairs of our family duplex and stayed there for ten years until they built their beautiful home off of Sunbury Road in McDaniel Estates.

Once they had settled in, little Robert returned home to live with his father and new mother. In January of 1964, Doug and Addie had a baby boy they named Anthony Romero Grant and then in November of that same year, they had another son, they named Timothy Avery Grant. So now little Robert had two little brothers he could protect and play with. One day, they were all thinking about playing Superman and jumping out of the upstairs window. But before this plan could be carried out, it was found out and guess who got the spanking. Yes, it was Robert because he was the oldest and should have known better. This was how it was when I was little. I was always getting the blame for what my brother did. When he would climb on the roof of our apartment building, my father would blame me for letting him do it. Now my brother was doing the same with little Robert. Little Robert attended Eastwood Avenue Elementary School through the second grade before he left on a summer vacation to visit my sister and mother who were still in New York City. Before going on this vacation, Robert would sing the hit song," Sitting On the Dock of the Bay," made famous by the late great Otis Redding. Robert would sing this song for us all the time and especially when we had company. We were beginning to see signs of his talent at an early age because of his ability to communicate and memorize what he had read. We had no idea that he would one day accomplish the things that he did. But during this summer vacation, Robert Grant turned into actor and singer, Douglas Grant. But again, we have to remember the dream that his mother, Claudia had about him. That one day he would be in movies, on television and the stage. **I believe the Lord speaks to us in dreams.**

But while he thought about these things, behold an angel of the Lord appeared to him in a dream, saying, "Joseph, son of David, do not be afraid to take to you Mary your wife, for that which is conceived in her is of the Holy Spirit. And she will bring forth a son and you shall call His name Jesus, for He will save His people from their sins." Matthew 1:20-21

PEARL'S GIFT

After being discharged from the United States Marine Corps in January of 1959, I subsequently found a job as a laborer at a paper company and was planning on returning to college in the fall. My sister, Alice Carole, who is five years younger than me had grown up and was now a senior at Columbus East High School. She had been taking ballet dance lessons since she was about five years old and had become a very good dancer. We saw an article in the local African American newspaper about a beauty pageant for young teenage girls. The pageant was named Miss Bronze Ohio and the winner would receive an all expense paid trip for two to Las Vegas, Nevada. I encouraged my sister to enter the contest since I knew that she had outstanding talent and was very pretty. Well she won the title of Miss Bronze Ohio with the prize of a two week vacation for two. As a result of this contest and trip, my sister met the incomparable Pearl Bailey and was eventually selected to appear as a solo performer in the Pearl Bailey Revue.

My sister initially appeared with Pearl Bailey in Las Vegas at the Flamingo Hotel. My mother, Sara Jane Grant went with her as her chaperone. Las Vegas at that time was still segregated and finding housing was a problem for African Americans including those performing in some of the finest hotels on the Las Vegas Strip. Even Pearl Bailey could not stay in the hotel but the Flamingo Hotel owners built a special house for her on the hotel property. That behavior seems strange today about forty five years after the civil rights act of 1965 but that's the way it was back in 1959. In trying to find housing for her and my sister, my mother was told that if she passed for a Hispanic, then she would have an easier time of finding a place to stay. My mother who was light skin with straight hair refused to be other than what she was, a proud black woman. They finally found a place to stay without pretending to be Hispanic.

My sister Alice Carole performed with Pearl Bailey in Las Vegas for sixteen weeks and my mother was relieved as chaperone by my sister's dance teacher, Vicky Paige, halfway through the Las Vegas engagement. Vicky met her future husband Joe while in Las Vegas with my sister. They married shortly after meeting in 1960 and remained together until he died about ten years ago. Vicky Paige passed on about two years ago and is buried in Green Lawn Cemetery in Columbus, Ohio beside her husband Joe. Alice went on to perform with Miss Bailey in the Midwest including Chicago, Illinois. During this time, My Aunt Hattie Belle served as her chaperone. While my mother was with my sister in Las Vegas, My Aunt Hattie Belle cared for Little Robert in Indianapolis, Indiana.

The show made a West Coast appearance beginning in San Francisco, California and going on to Vancouver, Edmonton and Calgary in Canada. The show than performed in Seattle, Washington and Portland, Oregon with me as the West Coast chaperone. My sister, her other chaperones and I had a wonderful opportunity to travel and meet some very interesting people. Miss Bailey was very kind to me and always called me big brother. Her husband, the great drummer, Louis Bellson was her orchestra leader and they had a great life of working together.

My sister went on to perform on her own as a solo act but she returned to work for Miss Bailey when Pearl took over from Carol Channing as the star in "Hello Dolly" on Broadway. My sister went on to perform many times before assuming responsibility for her young nephew's career in show business. His name is Robert Douglas Grant Jr. and he is my brother Doug's oldest son. With my sister's help, he has appeared in movies, television and on Broadway. They both finally left show business and obtained their undergraduate and Masters Degrees and their certificates in teaching. My sister is now a retired teacher who teaches part time and my nephew is currently married to his talented wife Eileen Smith Grant. They are both artists and he is a public school art teacher in New York, New York; and God continues to shower His blessings on all of them. Pearl Bailey indeed gave my family a precious gift in selecting Alice Carole to perform in the Pearl Bailey Revue and Hello Dolly on Broadway. Another gift given to Alice Carole by Pearl Bailey was a beautiful pearl ring which my sister still wears today.

Again, the kingdom of heaven is like a merchant seeking beautiful pearls, who, when he had found one pearl of great price, went and sold all that he had and bought it. Matthew 13:45-46

THE LITTLE BLACK SWAN

M̲y Sister, Alice Carole Grant, had just auditioned for Pearl Bailey in October 1959 when Pearl had performed in Cincinnati, Ohio. It was now November 1959 and a reporter from the theater editor's desk at the Columbus Journal had come out to give her an interview. The following is a reprint of that story by Norman Nadal as it appeared in the newspaper on November 11, 1959.

She flies through the Air with the Greatest of Ease

"There were only three of us in the almost-bare, strictly functional dance studio. Vicky Paige who operates her own dance school at 1666 W. First Ave. in Grandview was putting a record on the phonograph turntable. Alice Carole Grant, her 16-year pupil, stood in that gracefully relaxed but ready position that ballet dancers assume in the moment before they perform. Seated on a bench by the wall, I watched, and speculated. The kid (Alice Carole) might be really good, of course, you never could be sure. Regularly, dance (or music or drama) teachers call the theater editor's desk to report on a new talent. You couldn't blame them for being enthusiastic about their best performer. But you still had to watch or listen to decide if the youngster rated a story. Vicky had said on the phone that Alice Carole was accelerating her senior year at East High School so that she could graduate in January, and go professional.

She auditioned for Pearl Bailey in Cincinnati a couple of weeks ago, and the noted singer had been impressed. It was at her urging that Alice Carole aimed for a January graduation, so that she can turn professional and join Miss Bailey's night club and theater act. Only a few minutes earlier, I'd had my first look at Alice Carole, when she arrived at the studio with her mother, Mrs. Marshall Grant, Sr., 1507 E. Long St. In flat shoes, school clothes and with books under her arm, the child just didn't look like the popular concept of a ballerina. For one reason, ballerinas traditionally are tall, thin, and willowy, with an ethereal look about them. This youngster standing four feet, nine-and-a-half inches tall, was 105 pounds of solid muscular energy. She looked purposeful rather than ethereal. And she didn't look even her 16 years.

Somehow, I just couldn't see her in "Swan Lake." But there she stood, in her little costume, erect, attentive and ready as the introduction to the Fourth Act of Tchaikovsky's "Swan Lake" filled the room. And with a step, a leap and a turn, she was off.

During the next several minutes, the sterile-looking studio, evaporated into the stage of the Met Opera. It took a little imagining picturing the orchestra, conductor and stage; because Alice Carole's dancing seemed so entirely appropriately for such a setting. It was all speed, precision, grace, lightness and light. Not only were her traditional ballet steps and figures exact, but they were eloquent and integral parts of the whole ballet concept she was recreating. The music and the dancing ended. I found myself breathless from the exhilaration of watching such a performance. Little Miss Grant soberly related how she had won the Miss Bronze of Ohio competition at Valley Dale on Aug. 2, in which the three categories were talent, bathing suit and formal dress. Then with Miss Paige, her teacher, as chaperone, she had taken the prize trip to California, visiting San Francisco, Los Angeles and Las Vegas. It was at Las Vegas that she and Vicky met Miss Bailey, but didn't have the chance to audition. So when Pearl played Cincinnati recently, Alice Carole danced for her here.

The singer then asked her about joining the show after graduation and negotiations are now in progress. Alice Carole's family includes her parents and two brothers—Marshall Jr., 22 and Robert, 18. She has been Miss Paige's pupil for six years. The picture-taking, interview and audition over, she changed back into school clothes and marched purposefully out of the studio, just as she had marched in. Only this time, I could look at her healthy little figure and imagine her doing "Swan lake." *Written by Norman Nadel, 11/11/1959*

This Article was written over fifty years ago and I could not have said it any better if I had tried to put it in my own words. Alice Carole's dancing was like a light that burned bright and gave joy to all who had the opportunity to look at her.

Then Jesus cried out and said, *"He who believes in Me, believes not in Me, but in Him who sent Me. And he who sees Me sees Him who sent Me. I have come as a light into the world, that whoever believes in Me should not abide in darkness."* John 12:44-46

ALICE CAROLE AND MISS PEARL

Just before her opening night at the beautiful Flamingo Hotel in Las Vegas, Nevada, Alice Carole Grant had received a novelty elongated telegram from her Columbus friends and members of the Columbus Sentinel Newspaper which sponsored the Miss Bronze Ohio Contest. Alice answered as follows: "I received the wonderful telegram and I thank the members of the staff very much, for I realize this could not be possible if it were not for my winning the Miss Bronze title. Tonight was a very wonderful night. Everything seems to go my way. Everyone acts as if they enjoyed my dancing. Miss Bailey seems very pleased with me. She has put my name in the lobby and on all the programs. It is the thrill of a lifetime, Love Alice."

Accompanying my sister, Alice Carole, to Las Vegas, the first stop on the tour was the first of what would be her four chaperones, my beloved mother, Sara Jane Grant. The next two chaperones were my sister's lovely dance teacher, Vicky Paige and my beautiful Aunt Hattie Belle Potter. My mother and Vicky Paige were with her when she performed in Las Vegas and Los Angeles. My Aunt Hattie Belle went with her on the Midwest tour including Chicago, Illinois and I was with her on the west Coast and western Canada tour. The Pearl Bailey show was described as Pearl Bailey with a cast of fifty. It included Louis Bellson, Pearl's husband, and his orchestra. The acts were listed as The Seven Moroccans, Mr. Wynn, Alice Grant, The Ambassadors and The Tapeteers. Alice Carole danced a solo ballet dance to the music of "Around the World in Eighty Days." She also danced with Mr. Wynn who had to lift her from time to time when they danced together. He would always call her "Potatoes" after she returned to the tour after a vacation. It seems as though 105 pound Alice Carole would put on an additional five pounds while vacationing at home.

In a review by Variety dated October 12, 1960, the following was written about the show: "Pearlie Mae's International House bowed as a

133

legit attraction here and it comes as close as possible to a top Broadway musical revue without having the label. Staged originally for Las Vegas as a nitery turn, the show was at the Twin Coaches and in a last minute switch moved downtown to the Nixon to take advantage of the World Series influx. A serious appraisal of the star herself must show that she is one of today's top talents, and she has surrounded herself with a cast that belongs in her league. Every act is sock, although ballerina Alice Grant is the most outstanding. The 16 year old ballerina, doing amazing work, is the highlight of the first part of the show."

I remember being so proud of her when I saw her dance at the Geary Theater which was built in 1909 in San Francisco, California. Although I had seen her dancing many times in recitals and other performances, I had never seen her dance in a professional show. I don't remember how long the show played at the Geary Theater but I believe that it was at least two weeks. As my sister's chaperone, my parents expected me to function as a parent for her instead of a big brother. When we would eat in the evening, she would always order a hamburger for part of her meal. One time, I told her that she would have to order something different because she was eating too many hamburgers. When the waitress came to get our order, I expected her to order something other than a hamburger. She did, much to my surprise, she ordered a cheeseburger. Needless to say, I didn't think it was funny. In looking back, it was very funny. She would always make fun of me when I ordered pumpkin pie for dessert. I had a slight stutter back in those days especially when I ordered my dessert as I would say give me a piece of pum pum pumpkin pie. One time she disagreed with me on something I told her to do and she tried to exercise her authority by telling me that she writes my check. She got this phrase from Pearl Bailey who would say from time to time to her staff that she writes their check.

I think that Alice forgot one important thing and that is Miss Bailey wrote my check even though my pay came out of what would have been her money if she had been an adult. At that time she was receiving $400.00 per week and I was getting $100.00 a week to be her chaperone. That was very good money back in 1960. At the end of my tour with my sister, I returned home and my sister went to visit Miss Bailey at her Apple Valley California Ranch. Miss Bailey always took good care of Alice Carole and brought her, a few years later, to Broadway to serve as her dance captain in the musical "Hello Dolly"

In August 1964, the day of my graduation from Ohio University in Athens, Ohio, Miss Bailey was performing at the Tommy Heinrich Steakhouse in Columbus, Ohio. The site of Tommy Heinrich Steakhouse later became famous for being the first Wendy's Hamburger restaurant. She introduced my sister and me to her audience and she told them that I had just graduated from college. Miss Bailey went on to receive her Bachelors Degree and served in the United Nations as an Ambassador of Love appointed by President Nixon. She sadly died on August 17, 1990 in Philadelphia, Pennsylvania of coronary heart disease. Just as her character was described in "Hello Dolly," She was a wonderful wonderful woman. One of her favorite quotations is: **"You never find yourself until you face the truth."**

For the law was given through Moses, but grace and truth came through Jesus Christ. John 1:17

TRAINS AND PLANES

Previously I have talked about riding the train from Columbus, Ohio to Indianapolis, Indiana and back when I was a young boy to visit my relatives in the summer. I always loved to take that two and one half hour train ride, although the return trip seemed like only a half hour. I guess I was more excited about getting there than returning home. I can remember riding the train to Louisville, Kentucky to visit my Shobe relatives. Once we arrived in Cincinnati, Ohio, we would have to board a segregated railway car because we were about to travel to Kentucky, a Southern State. If we had been riding on a bus, we would have to take a seat in the back of the bus. Since we were on a train, we would have to get in a car close to the engine. This is because in the summer, the railroad car had to have its windows open in order to provide air to passengers. This was before the days of air conditioning. If the windows were opened, the soot from the locomotive would come into the railroad car closest to the locomotive. Since we were black, we would have to take the most undesirable railroad car.

Aside from this indignity, I always look back on my train rides with fondness. I have had the opportunity to travel to California and back several times by railway coach. The trip usually took about two and one half days but I enjoyed every mile of it. The train would stop periodically to give us passengers a chance to stretch our legs. I loved to watch the country rolling by and seeing the cities, people, farmland and animals. Sometimes in traveling by train, you could see telephone poles moving up and down as they change sizes and locations on the ground right before your eyes. My next to last train ride was in 1960 when I accompanied my sister to San Francisco, California. She was a featured act for The Pearl Bailey Revue. Pearl Bailey was a famous entertainer in the last century who died in 1990. Pearl Bailey was a star of stage, movies and television. She performed as Dolly in the Broadway show of "Hello Dolly" and appeared in movies such as St. Louis Blues and

Carmen Jones. She also appeared on numerous television variety shows in the nineteen sixties and seventies.

Pearl Bailey and my sister along with other performers had performed in places like Las Vegas and Chicago and were scheduled to open up in San Francisco, California at the Gerry Theater. I was traveling with my sister as her chaperone because she was under age. This was in 1960 about a year after I was discharged from the Marine Corps. Pearl Bailey arranged for us to travel from Columbus, Ohio to Chicago, Illinois by railroad coach and then by railroad sleeper car from Chicago to San Francisco. This was my first and only time to travel on a railway sleeper car. I am still so thankful for the opportunity to have had this experience. The ride was very enjoyable and I loved being able to go to sleep in a bed while traveling across country. I can still remember hearing the train making its ding ding sound as I was drifting away to sleep. I also rode the train when I traveled with Pearl Bailey and her cast from San Francisco throughout western Canada and back down to Seattle, Washington and Portland, Oregon.

The show ended and my sister went with Pearl Bailey to visit her at her Ranch in Apple Valley, California. I was given a plane ticket to fly back to Columbus, Ohio. This would not be my first plane flight. I had flown from Cincinnati, Ohio to Chicago, Illinois and then to San Diego, California when I joined the Marine Corps in 1957. While in the Marines I had flown in a helicopter and had also flown home when I was discharged in 1959. These planes were all propeller driven airplanes. The airplane that I flew home on after the show ended was a jet airplane. This was my first time in a jet. I had known about them but had never had the chance to fly in one of them. When the plane took off and began to level once reaching the desired attitude, I saw a sight that I could have only imagined. And what a beautiful sight it was. I could see nothing but clouds and the curvature of the earth below. It was like I imagined heaven to be.

Even though the airplane is a comfortable, fast and efficient way to travel, I still prefer and miss riding on the train. My last train ride was in the late nineteen sixties when I traveled to New York, New York because of my nephew, Robert's illness. The train rides were part of my past and that time like my youth is gone forever. However, God does not want us to live in the past. He wants us to live in the present and prepare for the future. **God will bless our future.**

And my God shall supply all your need according to His riches in glory by Christ Jesus. Now to our God and Father be glory forever and ever. Amen. Philippians 4:19-20

PAY FORWARD

U pon completing my active duty service with the Marines my family would give me another chance to achieve my college education. When I look back and think about all the help that I received along the way, I know that except for the grace of God, I wouldn't be where I am today. I was fortunate and blessed that I was born into the Sara Jane and Marshall Grant family. Both of my parents believed in education as a way of improving your way in life. They moved to Columbus, Ohio from Indianapolis, Indiana in order to seek a better life for themselves and their future children. What they found was some of the same segregationist practices here that they had encountered in Indiana. Even though my father had a law degree, he could not obtain a job equal to his education. His first job was shining shoes at a shoe repair shop. He finally got a job as a janitor at a factory that made refrigeration parts and he stayed there until he retired over thirty years later. At the time of his retirement, he was a supervisor in the machine shop. Over the years, my mother had encouraged him to seek government work but he did not want to take the chance of losing the security that his present job provided him and his family.

His sacrifice did not go in vain because he was able to give his children an education and other opportunities that provided a fulfilling life for them and their children. I have often thought of my parent's sacrifices and I wish that they were still alive so I could pay them back. But they are not alive and I am unable to pay them back. There are also other people who have helped me along the way such as teachers, friends and relatives who are now gone. I also owe these people a debt of gratitude that can never be paid back. But there must be something I can do to settle this debt that I owe. Woody Hayes, the great football coach from The Ohio State University would often say that you can't pay back but you can pay forward. That is what I have tried to do with my children and especially my grandson. At an early age, he showed an interest in music so my wife and I decided to give him piano lessons. He started taking lessons at age three and is now fifteen years of age. He says that he wants to major in music in college and he is preparing so that this dream can become a reality.

I tell my grandson, Kai, that if he is successful, he need not worry about paying me back but he should think about paying forward and helping someone else. There are so many ways that we can do this. Our tithes and offerings at church can be used to help those in need in the community. My church, the Vineyard built a community center a few years ago that is providing a place where children in the neighborhood and city can go for all kinds of services such as health, fitness, recreational and spiritual needs. This center was built with the understanding that it was not just for the church members but for the community in general. Some other churches are doing similar things. My brother's church, St. Philip Lutheran, has an outreach program that is helping the students at Columbus East High School. They are in the process of attempting to send some students on field trips to such places as Washington D.C. They are also working to provide a mentoring program for the students at East High School and Trevitt Elementary School.

My brother and sister believe in helping their children and others develop into productive citizens. All of their children have their college degrees and are doing very well in their chosen professions. They all contribute to their respective communities in many ways such as supporting charities and mentoring to young people. One of my brother's sons, David, has his own insurance business but finds the time to coach the local high school wrestling team. In doing so, he has been privileged to see three of his wrestlers win the high school state wrestling championship. Another son, Tony, sits on the board of several charities and is always trying to raise funds for them. I would encourage other members of my family and friends to get involved in helping someone to achieve some of their dreams. This is the way of following Jesus' second commandment of loving your neighbor as you love yourself. If we can't physically or financially help someone than we can pray for them.

The greatest example that we have of someone paying forward is Jesus' sacrifice on the cross. He paid forward for all of those unborn souls who needed a Savior to reconcile us back to God. He paid our debt.

For there is one God and one Mediator between God and men, the Man Christ Jesus, who gave Himself a ransom for all, to be testified in due time. 1 Timothy 2:5-6

Chapter Six:
RETURN TO COLLEGE

CAN SAUSAGES

Have you ever thought about some of the delicious food that was served to you when you were a child that doesn't seem that great to you now that you are an adult? I remember always loving to eat cheese sandwiches when I was little. These were one of the treats that my parents bought for me when we were traveling on the train to Indianapolis, Indiana during the summer. When I was in high school, my best friend, James Willis and I would go to the bakery and get a bag full of round and stick donuts. We would also buy a quart of chocolate milk and have a party for lunch. I also loved to drink milk by the quart. In fact, I would drink milk like it was water. I still love milk and drink it daily including when it is in coffee. These unhealthy eating habits began to catch up with me in my teens. I have always had a weight problem but since becoming a teenager, I didn't want to be fat. So I started to be more conscious about what I ate but I still enjoyed eating a good meal. After graduating from high school, I went to Ohio University where I stayed three semesters before joining the Marine Corps. I received plenty of good food at the university's cafeteria and continued to have a weight problem. When I joined the Marines, they fed me a lot but they got it all back in sweat because of the hard physical training they put me through.

After leaving the Marine Corps, I returned to Ohio University to finish working on my degree. I had saved some money on a summer job to help finance my return to college. I decided to live off campus because it would be cheaper than living in a dormitory. To pay for my food, I applied for a board job which required me to work two hours a day in the cafeteria. I can still remember being on my board job when John Glenn orbited the earth and when John Kennedy addressed the nation regarding the Cuban missile crisis. Those were exciting times at Ohio University and in the country. One semester I needed more time to bring my grades up so I decided to give up my board job and eat off of a hot plate. Since I had no refrigerator, I would go to the store in the morning and buy can goods and just enough perishable food for the day such as milk for my cereal, and whatever lunch meat I needed for sandwiches. One of my favorite treats was can sausages. At the time, I thought these tasted so good. I would eat these can sausages, along with bread and potato chips. Boy oh boy, what a meal! Many years later, I still remembered those sausages with fondness even though I had not eaten any since my college days.

A few years ago, I was grocery shopping and saw a can of sausages. I decided to buy myself some since it had been over forty years when I had eaten them. I couldn't wait to get home from the grocery store and make myself a meal. I opened the can and prepared to treat myself. I took my first bite and could not believe that they didn't taste anything like I had remembered. I did not finish the can and just threw the sausages away. I guess in some instances, the good old days are not always as good as we thought they were. In looking back, I sometimes wonder how I made it with such limited resources. My brother helped a lot and I am sure my father gave me some money at times. You know I do know how I made it. I made it with God providing for me as He does for the lilies in the field.

Therefore I say to you, do not worry about your life, what you will eat or what you will drink; nor about your body, what you will put on. Is not life more than food and the body more than clothing? Look at the birds of the air, for they neither sow nor reap nor gather into barns; yet your heavenly Father feeds them. Are you not of more value than they? Which of you by worrying can add one cubit to his stature? So why do you worry about clothing? Consider the lilies of the field, how they grow: They neither toil nor spin; and yet I say to you that even Solomon in all his glory was not arrayed like one of these. Now if God so clothes the grass of the field, which today is, and tomorrow is thrown into the oven, will He not much more clothe you, O you of little faith? Therefore do not worry, saying, "what shall we eat?" or "what shall we drink?" Or "what shall we wear?" For after all these things the Gentiles seek. For your heavenly Father knows that you need all these things. But seek first the kingdom of God and His righteousness, and all these things shall be added to you. Therefore do not worry about tomorrow, for tomorrow will worry about its own things. Sufficient for the day is its own trouble. Matthew 6:25-34

THE TRUTH

As a little boy, I can remember believing that telling the truth was important. I must have gotten this value from my parents or maybe I was just born with it. During World War Two, I remember going to the corner grocery store to buy some sugar for my mother. I must have been about seven or eight years old. At that time you needed rationing stamps to buy some products like sugar. I was at the store to buy some sugar and the clerk forgot to take my rationing stamp. I then reminded him that he didn't get my stamp. When I returned home with the sugar, I told my mother what had happened. She asked me why I had reminded the clerk about the stamp since stamps were hard to get. I am sure she did not intend to give me a wrong value but this was World War Two and times for us and others were a struggle.

There were other occasions when I felt compelled to tell the truth. And there were probably many more times where I told a lie without thinking about it. I had returned to college after being honorably discharged from the Marine Corps. In my government class, I received my score back on a test and discovered that my grade should have been a C instead of the B the professor had given me. I took the test back to the professor and told him what happened. He thanked me and changed the grade from a B to C. I was hoping that as a reward for my honesty, he would have let me keep the B grade. But I did not want a grade I had not earned. I feel the same way when I watch professional and college football games and sometimes see the players trying to pretend they caught a pass when they actually trapped the ball on the ground. To me this is a form of cheating.

A few years later as I was getting ready to graduate I received notice that the university had failed me in a correspondence course that I needed for graduation. It seems that I had let a fellow student look at my homework and not only had he copied directly from my work but had sent in some of my papers by mistake. I told the university officials that I was not a cheater but they would not believe me. I became very distraught and began to see how all of my hard work was not going to pay off. I then remembered my honesty about reporting the mistake of receiving a higher grade than I should have. The university contacted my professor and indeed learned that I was an honest person. I thank God for giving me the desire to tell the truth. I did receive credit for this course and I was able to graduate as scheduled.

The question is what is the truth? Is there a constant standard of what is considered to be the truth? If we have to go to court and testify, we are asked to swear on a Bible and agree to tell the truth, the whole truth and nothing but the truth. There are some things called facts that among reasonable people are not in dispute. But there are also principles and concepts that reasonable people can disagree on such as evolution versus creationism and is there life after death. In trying to define the word truth, there is no single definition that scholars and philosophers can agree on.

There are many theories about how truth is defined and this debate goes on today. I was listening to the well known commenter Rush Limbaugh being interviewed and he was asked to give a word association by the interviewer. When given President Barack Obama's name he responded by saying "Disaster" but when asked about President George Bush, he commented "Good Man". To Rush Limbaugh that is his truth. For others, the opposite is the truth. The dictionary defines truth in several different ways: conformity to fact or actuality; a statement proven to be or accepted as true; sincerity, integrity; fidelity to an original or standard. I have accepted Jesus Christ as my Lord and Savior and believe Him when He says:*"I am the way, the truth, and the life. No one comes to the Father except through Me."* John 14:6.

For a Christian, truth lies in the word of God and if we are seeking the truth about life's questions, the answer is contained within His Word. We should study His word constantly in order to live a life of truth as God's word will help us separate the truth from the world's lies. But it is not enough to just read the word as we must also communicate with God through prayer and meditation. We must implant the word of truth in our hearts and be not just a hearer of the word but a doer of the word.

Then Jesus said to those Jews who believed Him, "If you abide in My word, you are My disciples indeed. And you shall know the truth, and the truth shall make you free." John 8:31-32

JOB BEFORE JOB

During my days at Ohio University, I can remember going to church for services only one time. Neither was I an active member of any church when I was home in Columbus, Ohio. I had attended Union Grove Baptist Church Sunday School and sometimes church services when I was a child. I remember my father being baptized at Union Grove sometime before 1950 but I don't know how much he attended If you would have asked me, I would have said that I was a Christian but I really didn't know what it meant to be a follower of Christ. So when I left for college, my spiritual training was lacking. The courses that I took at Ohio University were those offered in the College of Arts and Sciences curriculum. After I had returned from the Marine Corps, I continued working for my Bachelor of Arts Degree. In choosing one of my elective courses, I decided to take a course on Old Testament Survey. Till this day, I still don't know why I ever chose to take this course.

I had no interest in studying religion but I did believe there was a God. I just did not trust in, cling to, rely and depend on Him. A valued possession of mine while I was in the Marines was a New Testament issued to me when I first joined. But I never took the time to read it and I don't remember what happened to it. But again, I don't know why I selected this course on the Old Testament Survey. Maybe I just took it without thinking and only to get credit toward my degree. I can still remember the professor as being thin, gaunt and boring. This course didn't interest me at all. As one of the assignments of this course, I had to write a paper on the book of Job. Job, as I found out, is quite a long book with a special message. In this book, God is having a conversation with Satan about Job and his love for God. Satan is saying that Job only loves God because God has blessed him and Job would not love God so much without God's blessings. Satan wants to test Job's loyalty to God by having God remove his blessings from Job. God agrees to allow Satan to test Job by taking away his blessings.

All of Job's possessions are taken away including his children, animals and other property. Job's friends think Job must have sinned against God to have merited such punishment. Finally Job's health has deteriorated and he is covered with boils. Job's wife tells Job that he ought to curse God and then die. But Job does not listen to his wife. He still loves God but he would like God to explain why He has allowed Job to be attacked like this. God finally talks to Job but doesn't answer his question directly. What God does is ask Job where was he when God created the heavens and earth. Where was he when God created the mountains and hung the moon in the sky? In other words, who was Job to question God? For some reason I never forgot this lesson learned from the Book of Job. Many years later after I had graduated and married, I was blessed to have a son born to my wife and me. He was the joy of my life and I loved him very much. I had adopted my wife's three children from a previous marriage and we seemed to be one big happy family.

About two months before my son's eighth birthday, he became ill and had to be hospitalized. Within two weeks of his illness, his heart stop beating and he went into a coma from which he never recovered. We finally had to make the decision to take him off of life support. An autopsy was performed but a cause of death could not be identified. With his death, the lessons learned in Job came back to profoundly help me with my suffering. My wife had often told me that God's word does not go out in vain and this turned out to be so true for me. Never in my wildest imagination could I have thought that a son of mine would die so young. This was the kind of thing that happens to other people and not to me. It has been over thirty one years since his death and the pain of that tragedy still lingers with me until this day. I know that it is something that I will never get over.

Since my son's death, I have become a Born Again Christian and have confessed that Jesus Christ is my Lord and Savior. **In Matthew 11:28 Jesus says;" *Come to me, all you who labor and are heavy laden, and I will give you rest.*** I am here to tell you that I have found rest in Christ and so much more. He has freed me from the choke hold that sin has had on me. He has given me courage and strength even though I am physically weaker than I have ever been. I pray for His continued blessings and to give me strength in the areas where I am still weak.

I know how to be abased, and I know how to abound. Everywhere and in all things I have learned both to be full and to be hungry, both to abound and to suffer need. I can do all things through Christ who strengthens me. Philippians 4:12-13

THE THREE DOLLAR SHOES

When I was a little boy, it was determined that I had flat feet. My mother would take me to the shoe store and they would put my feet in one of those x-ray foot machines that showed a skeletal picture of your feet. These foot x-rays were taken in the days before the harmful effects of x-rays were fully known. As a result of having flat feet, I had to wear special arch supported shoes. I wore these kinds of shoes for many years and they did help me in my balance and walking. When I was in the Marines I had arch supports put into my boots and it made it easier to walk on those long frequent hikes and marches. During my last six months in the Marines, I was transferred from the infantry to a naval brig where I served as a security guard. Once out of the Marines, I began wearing normal dress shoes and sneakers. I am now wearing special shoes again to protect my feet and provide more balance as I walk. For the most part over the years, I have had to pay special attention to my feet.

I had just returned to Ohio University in February 1964, after being out of school since February 1963 trying to earn the money to return and finish my college degree. During the time I was out of school, President John Kennedy had been assassinated and this country was going through tremendous change. I had money for tuition and food but not for anything else. I had agreed to paint the rooms in my apartment building at the end of the summer semester to pay for my rent. All the money that I had was needed to finance me until August 1964 when I would graduate in summer session with my BA Degree in Political Science. It was probably in late May that I discovered that I really needed some shoes. I just didn't have much money to buy anything else, especially shoes. I expected to graduate soon but unfortunately, I needed new shoes right away. I went to the store to look for some cheap shoes, and I found a pair for three dollars. The soles consisted of foam like material, and the shoes were very uncomfortable. But it was better than walking around in my bare feet.

It is funny that with a lack of money, I couldn't afford to have flat feet. I was grateful just to have some shoes on my feet. During this next couple of weeks, everything was fine with the shoes. I thought that I could probably make it to graduation without buying another pair. But as I found out, this was not to be the case. One day as I was passing by a basketball court wearing my new shoes, I decided to join some of my Kappa brothers and other guys playing basketball. I can't remember the names of those who were playing or if my team won, but I remember having plenty of fun playing the game with them. Once I was finished playing, I noticed that my feet were burning a little. I took my shoes off and saw that the foam soles had almost completely been worn off. Instead of burning up the basketball court with my playing, I had just burned up the soles of my three dollar shoes. These shoes that I had purchased to last until I graduated were now completely destroyed.

Somehow I needed to get me another pair of shoes. I can't remember how I got them. I may have called my brother, Doug, who would help me from time to time. During this period, it was very important for me to show that I could make it on my own. Although, I lived in public housing until I was eleven years of age, I was always well cared for by my father and mother. They gave me plenty of food, clothing, clean housing and good medical care. They also gave me the opportunity to go to college despite the many mistakes I made. But now I was on my own. I wanted to be treated like a man and they did treat me as such, although I knew that they would not let me starve to death or be homeless. Sometimes we parents have to let go and let our children grow up and be independent. I have given all of my children keys to my house and they know that in an emergency they can always come home. But I hope they can continue to make it on their own. I finally graduated from college in August of 1964 and the Lord blessed me with some wonderful jobs since graduating and I always enjoyed what I was doing.

I retired in August 31, 1991 but continued to work part time in our Christian book store. The store closed in June of 2000 and I have not done much work for a salary since that time. The Lord has blessed us with sufficient income to satisfy all of our needs and now it seems so long ago when all I could afford was a pair of three dollar shoes.

And we know that all things work together for good to those who love God, to those who are the called according to His purpose. For whom He foreknew, He also predestined to be conformed to the image of His Son, that He might be the firstborn among many brethren. Moreover whom He predestined, these He also called; whom He called, these He also justified; and whom He justified, and these He also glorified. What then shall we say to these things? If God is for us, who can be against us? Romans 8:28-31

My Brother's Keeper

My mother and father had three children, two boys and a girl. I am the oldest by almost three years ahead of my brother and a little over five years older than my sister. When we were little, my brother and I would fight a lot. Our mother was usually home with us but sometimes, my mother worked as well and we were trusted to take care of ourselves. We were old enough to do so but for some reason a fight would break out among us. My brother had no fear of me and even though he knew that he couldn't beat me, he would fight me anyway. We had tin plated drinking glasses and each one had a dent from where he would try to hit me with them. I would put him out of the house to keep from fighting him and he would push in the front French doors trying to get back in the house. He was younger and shorter than me but he was very strong. He once told me: "I can't beat you but I am going to fight you anyway." When I was almost twenty years of age, I returned from the Marine Corps Boot Camp only to be challenged by him again. We began to argue and wrestle with each other, when he suddenly picked me up and threw me across the bed. He said: "So you have been in the Marines, so what."

One day, years after my college graduation, I was talking to my mother about my brother. And I was complaining about something he allegedly had done to me. She interrupted me, left the room and came back with a letter that I had written to him when I was still in college. In the letter, I asked my brother how he was doing but immediately went to my purpose for the letter. And this was to ask him for money to help me pay my college expenses. My mother reminded me of all the help that he had given me during my college days. It's funny how you forget what someone has done for you when you don't have that need anymore. My brother was three years younger than me with a child to support and yet he always helped me when he could. I will always appreciate

155

what he did for me. This example of helping your family members was given to us by our parents.

My mother and father were both born into families with thirteen children. My father was the twelfth child with eight brothers and four sisters. My mother was the twelfth child with six sisters and six brothers. Each family related lovingly to its family members and to the other family. They would socialize together and help each other financially. Some of the oldest members had children either older or close in age to their little brothers and sisters. I can remember going to dinner and picnics especially with my father's family. I had one uncle who had a five acre estate and we all would get together and have picnics. Every year, during our visit to Indianapolis, we would attend a party for my father's mother on her August the thirteenth birthday at my uncle's estate and this continued long after her death. My birthday was on August the twelfth one day before hers so we celebrated our birthdays together. My father's family was a very close knit family. My mother's family was close also but they lived in multiple locations and didn't see each other as much.

Both of my parents passed on this value of loving your family members to us and we are passing it on to our children. One day my wife gave me a compliment I think. She said that my brother, my sister and I were thicker than thieves. We do spend a lot of time with each other and even have a weekly home bible study together. My brother still helps me out by taking me to the doctor and gym when I need him to do so. My health has been a problem for me for some time and he along with my sister and my wife have stepped in to give me a helping hand. Not only has he been a good brother to my sister and me, he has also been a good father to his five sons. Along with his wife, Addie, they have provided the right leadership for their boys. Of course they are not boys any longer but grown men with children of their own including nieces and nephews.

When I think of the relationship between my brother and me, I remember the time when he wasn't my best friend. He had his friends and I had my friends over the years. I always knew that I loved him but we didn't want to pal around with each other. I still have close friends that I see and talk to from time to time but there is nothing like the relationship I have with my wife, sister, brother and sister-in-law. We are all very close and stick up for each other. When I think of the relationship between my brother and me, I think of the relationship between Cain and Abel. Cain hated his brother, Abel and eventually killed him. When asked where Abel was, Cain said: "Am I my brother's keeper." The relationship with my brother is based on love and mutual respect. If asked, he would have never said "Am I my brother's keeper." He truly was and still is his brother's keeper and I love him very much.

If someone says, "I love God," and hates his brother, he is a liar; for he who does not love his brother whom he has seen, how can he love God whom he has not seen? And this commandment we have from Him: that he who loves God must love his brother also. 1 John 4:20-21

BLACK IS BEAUTIFUL

As a little boy, I would hear this saying from black folks which went as follows; "If you're white you're all right, if you're yellow you're mellow, if you're brown stick around but if you're black stay back." I remember going to the movies and cheering Tarzan and booing the black natives. We would always cheer for the cowboys and boo the Indians. One time a light skin girl moved into Poindexter Village and a bunch of us boys followed her around because of her looks which was based on her light color. I was probably seven or eight years old at the time. On another occasion, when I was about eleven years old, I was walking down Champion Avenue in Poindexter Village and I asked myself why was I born black? Why was I born into a race considered to be inferior by the white Population? As I think about this now, I am reminded about Fats Waller's song titled "Black and Blue." Louis Armstrong did a very good rendition of it when he sang "What did I do to be so black and blue. I'm white inside but that don't help my case." That is the way I felt walking down Champion Avenue. I didn't feel inferior but I believed that the white majority looked and treated me and people like me as being inferior

Segregation and racial prejudice was wide and deep in the United States of America when I was a little boy. Because I lived in a segregated housing project, I didn't come into contact with the out and out racists who could inflict bodily harm on you. For the most part, everything I needed was located within a few square miles of where I lived. I went to African American doctors, dentists, barbers, pharmacies, churches and schools. My first experience with white people was when I attended Franklin Junior High School in 1949 at the age of eleven years old. And I don't remember encountering any racial prejudice at Franklin Junior High School or later at East High School. Almost all of my friends at these schools were black, but I did have some white acquaintances that I talked to on occasion. But for the most part, my world was a black world. Later on, when I attended Ohio University in Athens, Ohio the friends that I made and still have until this day were black. When I applied to Ohio University, I was asked to send in my picture. I later learn the reason for this was because the university administration wanted to make sure that I got black roommates.

In looking back, I suppose that I could be ashamed about the way I felt about being colored, which was what we African Americans were called at that time. But I am not because of the efforts by some of the majority to keep African Americans as close to slavery conditions as possible. This was purpose of the Jim Crow system. In 1954, When the Supreme Court ruled against the "Separate but Equal' doctrine in Brown versus the Topeka Board of Education, I probably began to think for the first time that I had equal value also. I remember being ashamed to eat free watermelon served after the movies on the Ohio University Campus because I didn't want to fall into the stereotype of the watermelon eating Negro. I joined the Marine Corps in 1957 only eight years after President Truman had desegregated the armed forces, and I was treated equally with other Marines including whites, blacks and Hispanics. Jokingly, we were all treated like dogs. Seriously, I don't remember any incidents of racial prejudice. We were and acted as one band of brothers. That is why I am and will always be proud of my service in the United States Marine Corps. After my honorable separation From the Marines, I returned to Ohio University to continue work on my college degree.

Upon my return, I noticed a change in the thinking and behavior patterns of the African American students. We were about making changes in racial policies and not satisfied with just maintaining the status quo. There was a sense of I am somebody and I want my rights now. The Black is Beautiful movement began in earnest in the nineteen sixties with people like Stokely Carmichael, H. Rap Brown and Malcom X. Before, when we called ourselves colored and Negro, many of us believed that the darker the skin one had, the less valuable he or she was. The lighter skinned blacks were deemed to be smarter and superior to dark skinned blacks. When I was attending Ohio University in the early nineteen sixties, I met a young man who looked as white as any white person I knew. In talking to him, he told me that he was really a member of the black race. He said that he would never deny his black racial background if asked but he did not volunteer to tell people either.

Legally, he was classified as black because of the one drop rule which stated that even the smallest amount of black ancestry or drop of black blood made him black.

For many years, African Americans spent a lot of money on creams to lighten their skin and hair products to straighten their hair. Although this still occurs; with the election of an African American president, more African Americans understand that God made them the way they are and He didn't make any mistakes. We are beautiful in His sight whether we are yellow, black, brown or white. There were so many African American and other leaders who helped fight the civil rights battle that it would be impossible to mention them all. However, it would be very negligent if I didn't mention Rosa Parks, Reverend Ralph Abernathy, and Dr. Martin Luther King Jr. who led the Montgomery Bus Boycott in Montgomery, Alabama and the Civil Rights Revolution in the United States of America.

And finally, the Reverend Robert Graetz, a white minister and Pastor Emeritus of my brother's church, St. Philip Lutheran Church in Columbus, Ohio also was a leader in the Montgomery Bus Boycott and has written books about his experiences in the fight to overcome discrimination and segregation. Christ Jesus does not discriminate between us regardless of who we are and He was really the leader of this peaceful revolution. It was not by coincidence that the Christian church played such an important non violent role in the struggle. In a speech given to the full Congress on March 15, 1965, President Lyndon Baines Johnson said "We shall overcome." He had borrowed this phrase from civil rights leaders. **And overcome, we did.**

For you are all sons of God through faith in Christ Jesus. For as many of you as were baptized into Christ have put on Christ. There is neither Jew nor Greek, there is neither slave nor free, there is neither male nor female; for you are all one in Christ Jesus. And if you are Christ's, then you are Abraham's seed, and heirs according to the promise. Galatians 3:26-29

BORN AGAIN

The first African American, Ernie Davis of Syracuse University, was selected as the 1961 winner of the Heisman Trophy. This trophy has been presented by the New York's Downtown Athletic Club to the most outstanding college football player since 1936. However it was first awarded in 1935 to Jay Berwanger under the name of the DAC trophy but the name was changed the following year to honor football pioneer, John Heisman. In all that time since and up to 1961 only white football players had won the Heisman Trophy. Even the great Jim Brown did not win the Heisman Trophy, although many believe it was because he was an African American. One voter, Dick Schaap, for the Heisman Trophy was quoted as saying "I will never vote for the Heisman Award again since Jim Brown was clearly the best player." In 1961, not only did an African American win but another African American, Ohio State's Bob Ferguson, was a very close second. So Ernie Davis' winning of the Trophy was a big deal. He was drafted by the Cleveland Browns and projected to play in the same backfield as Jim Brown. But before he could play for the Browns, he was diagnosed with leukemia. I remember seeing a video of Ernie Davis lifting weights and looking so strong and healthy. I could not believe that he was sick and dying. In 1963, Ernie passed away at age 23.

This was the first time that I came to grips with my own mortality. I realized that I too would have to die some day and the thought of it frightened me. When I thought about it, a sick feeling would come over me. These thoughts became much less over the years but never completely went away. They would come back periodically to frighten me once again. Then something gradually happened to me. I accepted Jesus Christ as my Lord and Savior. Once I accepted Christ, I began to read and study His word. I learned that because of God's love for me, Christ was sacrificed on the cross. With His sacrifice, I was given eternal life with Him if I believed in Him. Christ also told me that perfect love for Him would cast out fear. I went through what Jesus calls being **Born Again**. Many years earlier, I had attended a funeral for a cousin of mine and another cousin, Joanne Russell Ussery, asked me "What did "Born Again mean?" She knew that my wife and I owned a Christian bookstore and maybe I could answer her question. She truly did not understand how a person could be born a second time. I had heard of the phrase "Born Again" but I could not explain the meaning of it to her. I had not yet truly accepted Jesus as my Lord and Savior and therefore was not reading His word.

It wasn't until a few years later when I began to study God's word in the Bible that I began to learn about what it means to be "Born Again." In the third chapter of the Book of John, Jesus discusses with Nicodemus, a Pharisee and ruler of the Jews, the issue of the New Birth. Nicodemus begins to praise Jesus but instead of responding to the praise, Jesus tells Nicodemus that he must be born again to see the Kingdom of God. Nicodemus then asks Jesus, **"How can a man be born when he is old? Can he enter a second time into his mother's womb and be born?"** Jesus answered, *"Most assuredly, I say to you, unless one is born of water and the Spirit, he cannot enter the kingdom of God. That which is born of the flesh is flesh, and that which is born of the Spirit is spirit. Do not marvel that I said to you, "You must be born again." The wind blows where it wishes, and you hear the sound of it, but cannot tell where it comes from and where it goes. So is everyone who is born of the Spirit"* John 3:4-8

Nicodemus answered and said to Him, "How can these things be?" Jesus answered and said to him, *"Are you the teacher of Israel, and do not know these things? Most assuredly, I say to you, We speak what we know and testify what We have seen, and you do not receive Our witness.* **If I have told you earthly things and you do not believe, how will you believe if I tell you heavenly things?** *No one has ascended to heaven but He who came down from heaven, that is, the Son of Man who is in heaven. And as Moses lifted up the serpent in the wilderness, even so must the Son of Man be lifted up, that whoever believes in Him should not perish but have eternal life. For God so love the world that He gave His only begotten Son, that whoever believes in Him should not perish but have everlasting life. For God did not send His Son into the world to condemn the world, but that the world through Him might be saved.* John 3:9-17

I now know that the first birth is physical but the second is spiritual. **Born once die twice. Born twice die once.** My fear of death has been replaced by my love for and faith in Christ and His promise of eternal life.

"He who believes in Him is not condemned; but he who does not believe is condemned already, because he has not believed in the name of the only begotten Son of God. And this is the condemnation, that the light has come into the world, and men loved darkness rather than light, because their deeds were evil. For everyone practicing evil hates the light and does not come to the light, lest his deeds should be exposed. But he who does the truth comes to the light, that his deeds may be clearly seen, that they have been done in God." John 3:18-21

ELECTION NIGHT

During my days on the Ohio University campus, the sporting event that caught the nation's imagination was the World Series. Pro football and basketball were being played but they did not have the popularity that major league baseball had. The World Series was always played in the daytime and many times people would take off from work or miss classes to watch the games. I remember the first year in 1955 that Jackie Robinson and the Brooklyn Dodgers beat the New York Yankees in the World Series. It was wonderful finally seeing the Yankees get what was coming to them. I missed some classes that I should have attended just to see the games. Brooklyn had lost to New York in 1941, 1947, 1949, 1952 and 1953 before beating them in 1955. But the next year in 1956, the Yankees again beat Brooklyn in the series. The next time the Dodgers beat the Yankees was in 1963 after the Dodgers had moved to Los Angeles. By this time, my allegiance had changed from baseball to pro football.

I started as a Cleveland Browns fan in 1950 when they joined the National Football League. The Browns began as a charter member of the All American Football Conference. They dominated this conference and won all four of its championships. When the league folded in 1950, the Cleveland Browns joined the NFL and won four additional championships before the National Football League merged with the American Football League. As great as they were prior to the merger of the NFL and AFL, they have never qualified for a Super Bowl since the first Super Bowl was played on January 15, 1967. History tells us that pro football got a big push on December 28, 1958 when the Baltimore Colts played the New York Giants for the NFL Championship at Yankee Stadium. This game has often been referred to as the greatest game ever played and signaled the beginning of the National Football League's immense popularity which they enjoy today. The Super Bowl has replaced the World Series as the highlight of the sporting world.

Another sport enjoying great popularity is pro basketball produced by the National Basketball Association. Its popularity began with the Minneapolis Lakers and George Mikan. This popularity continued with the Boston Celtics and its great championship teams with Bill Russell, K.C. Jones, Bob Cousy and John Havlicek That team led by Bill Russell won eleven championships in thirteen seasons. They continued to win championships and increased their popularity again when they drafted Larry Bird out of Indiana State. Along with Magic Johnson of the Los Angeles Lakers, they kept the NBA in the forefront of popularity among sports fans. Then in 1984, the greatest player ever, Michael Jordan, joined the Chicago Bulls and led them to six championships before he retired. He along with, Oscar Robertson, Kareem Abdul Jabbar, Larry Bird, Ervin "Magic" Johnson, Julius Erving and Isiah Thomas made the league what it is today. Sport fans always look forward to the playoffs and the championship event in their favorite sport.

We can't overlook the impact that college football and basketball has had on the sports watching public. It is exciting to follow college football and then watch the best teams compete for the right to play for the national championship. This process of selecting the two teams for the title is very controversial because there is no college playoff system. We don't always know if the best teams are really playing each other. There have been many fans asking that the National Collegiate Athletic Association create a true playoff where the title is decided on the field and not with computers. Even President Obama has commented that we ought to have a playoff system for college football. The NCAA Basketball Championship is truly determined on the basketball court. The only criticism is that some teams on the bubble don't get a chance to be one of the sixty five teams selected to enter the tournament but March Madness remains an exciting time of the year.

My personal favorite event is not any of the above but is the presidential election that comes along every four years. I have been interested in politics as far back as the election of President Dwight D. Eisenhower. This was probably the first time I saw the convention and election results on television. The campaign and election of President John F. Kennedy motivated me to major in political science when I was in college. I loved it when Bill Clinton was elected in 1992 with his defeat of President George H.W. Bush. And I can't begin to express my happiness at the election of President Barack Obama in 2008. Well you have probably guessed by now that I am a Democrat. I am but I respect and admire mostly all of those men who have occupied that high office. For me election night is greater and more exciting than any of the above mentioned sporting events including championship boxing matches. There is nothing more thrilling than to see the peaceful transfer of power from one political party to another in this great country of ours.

Therefore I exhort first of all that supplications, prayers, intercessions, and giving of thanks be made for all men, for kings and all who are in authority, that we may lead a quiet and peaceable life in all godliness and reverence. For this is good and acceptable in the sight of God our Savior, who desires all men to be saved and to come to the knowledge of the truth. 1 Timothy 2:1-4

Chapter Seven:
AFTER GRADUATION

GLORIOUS FOOD

Food and I have had a love affair since I was born and probably before when I was inside my mother. I remember always liking to eat. My mother told me that when I was just a little child, she sent me downstairs from our apartment to get her a glass of orange juice from her neighbor. On my way back upstairs to give the juice to her, I drank the entire glass of orange juice, and than I handed my mother an empty glass. My mother would tell this story every so often for her entire life. When I was a little boy, milk was delivered to our house by the milkman. He would set the bottles of milk on our back stoop. In those days, the cream in the milk would be at the top of the bottle. You would have to shake it up to evenly distribute the cream throughout the bottle. Well I would take the milk and pour the cream on my cereal before my brother and sister had a chance to eat. In effect, they were getting skim milk and I was receiving all of the cream. No wonder, I earned the nickname fat boy when I was little.

As I grew older, I became concerned about my weight and from time to time would attempt to go on a diet. This worked out for me and I was able to somewhat control my weight. But I was never able to entirely control my appetite. I always had a problem in controlling my weight until I joined the Marine Corps. After I entered the U.S. Marines I could eat whatever I wanted and not gain weight. In fact, I lost much weight but gained a lot of muscle. The Marine Corps' boot camp training was so tough that during my sixteen weeks there, I burned off pounds and pounds of fat and turned what was left into muscle. When I completed Marine Corps' boot camp, I was a lean mean fighting machine. I was in the best shape that I have ever been in before or since.

After I was discharged from the Marines, I returned to Ohio University and completed the requirements for my degree. After graduation, I had the occasion to return to the university for the celebration of my fraternity, Kappa Alpha Psi, receiving their chapter charter. It was a long and difficult struggle in getting our fraternity officially established on campus. We started as an interest club named Kappa Psi Phi. Now we had finally obtained the status of a fraternity on campus known as Kappa Alpha Psi. For this occasion, there was some food and the pledges had made us a beautiful chocolate cake. I have always loved to eat and especially sweets. I had a big piece of chocolate cake and it tasted so good that I had another piece. The party of celebration broke up and we finally went to our rooms for the night. I was staying in the dormitory with one of the brothers.

About 5:00 a.m. in the morning, I became sick to my stomach and had to use the restroom. The other brothers in the room were experiencing the same thing. I later found out that brothers in other dormitories were also having the same problem. I discovered that the pledges had put a laxative in the icing of the cake. We looked everywhere for these pledges but we didn't find them. They were somewhere hiding and having a wonderful laugh on us. Today, I am struggling again to control my weight. This time, in addition to the problem of controlling my weight, I am fighting the disease of diabetes.

This is a terrible disease for me because it requires self control. My mother had this disease and she was good at controlling it because she was disciplined about her eating habits. I remember her telling me that she hoped that I would never get diabetes because my eating habits were not good. An older gentleman once told me "It is ironic that when you were young, you can eat all kinds of food but you can't afford it. Now when you are old, you can afford it but you can't eat it." I have a great nephew named Grant Gibson, who seems to have taken after me. He loves to eat but he doesn't seem to be turning into a fat toddler. I pray that he will always enjoy food but will be able to control it better than I did. I know that Christ will help him and us with any problem if we genuinely ask Him.

Do not mix with winebibbers, Or with gluttonous eaters of meat; For the drunkard and glutton will come to poverty, And drowsiness will clothe a man with rags. Proverbs 23:20-21

JOB AFTER JOB

Studying the Book of Job came before I had graduated from college and finally got a real job. Now I want to tell you about the jobs I worked on after my study of the Book of Job. My first job after graduation from college was as a case worker with the State of Ohio's Franklin County Department of Aid for The Aged. This job didn't pay a lot of money but it was a wonderful first job after college. I had an area that consisted of the suburbs in Columbus, Ohio. I enjoyed driving around to see all of the clients on my caseload. This was a program for those in need of financial assistance. But many of my clients lived with well to do children or other relatives. Many of these people lived in better houses than I did. I learned a lot from meeting and talking with these elderly people. Now I am among them having recently celebrated my seventy second birthday. I thank God that I am somewhat financially sound and able to provide for my family and myself through my retirement income.

I stayed with Aid for The Aged for one year and than I decided that I had to make a career move and look for a better job. I found a job which was located a floor above me in the same building where I had been working. This was a job that involved adjudicating social security disability claims for workers that had become disabled and could no longer work. When this Social Security Disability Law was written in the late 1950's, the states retained the right to determine who was disabled under this disability act. My assignment required that I sit at a desk all day making decisions about who was able to return to work and who could not. Many a day while walking during my break time I would wonder whether or not I was going to return to this job when my break ended. I really did not like the confinement of sitting at a desk all day. After three years of doing this, I decided to look for another job and went to the Columbus Urban League looking for assistance in finding another position.

The Director, of the Columbus Urban League's Job Placement Team, Irvin Lowery, interviewed me and asked me if I would like to work for the Columbus Urban League. I said yes and spent the next four years helping people get jobs. One of the people I helped to get promoted on his job through our agency was my brother, Doug Grant. He had trouble getting promoted at AT&T, where he had been a machine operator for nine years. He was also active in his union and had been the first African American elected to its local board. Maybe it was because of his union activity or his skin color but he was not able to get a promotion on his own. My helping him was ironic because my brother had a lot to do in helping me get to where I was at this point in my life. He had periodically sent me money to help with my expenses through out my college years. I told my supervisor, Irvin Lowery about this problem and he was able to influence the plant manager into giving my brother a promotion.

But despite the enjoyable aspects of this job, after fours years, I decided to look for another job. This job didn't offer me the career opportunity I needed which included job security, advancement and retirement benefits. I started searching for another job and found in the newspaper want ads that my former agency had been combined with another agency. This new agency was seeking to hire a training officer and I applied and was hired out of fifty applicants. This job had many creative aspects including writing training programs, creating videos and designing slide shows. This job also involved travel throughout the State of Ohio and the Eastern half of the United States of America. I eventually was in charge of training new vocational rehabilitation counselors and providing training to our management and clerical staff.

This was a wonderful job and I stayed with this agency for the next nineteen years until my agency offered early retirement. I believe that God gave me these jobs and that in spite of me not knowingly working for His glory; He guided and directed me in most of my job activities and decisions. The lessons I learned years ago from the Book of Job continued to help me long after I had graduated from college, got my first real job and through out my life.

And let the beauty of the Lord our God be upon us, And establish the work of our hands for us; Yes, establish the work of our hands. Psalm 90:17

NEAR MISSES

Everyone who has ever lived can probably recount some stories of how they barely missed being killed or seriously being injured. I am no exception. My first recollection of being saved from a serious accident was when I was driving back to California after being on leave from the Marine Corps. My mother had told me to leave my car home and take a train back but I didn't listen to her. This was one of many times that I didn't listen to her to my detriment. I had driven home from the base with a couple of marine buddies who helped me drive. But they canceled out on the return trip leaving me to drive all the way back alone.

I started back towards California but first I had to stop in Indianapolis, Indiana to get some money from my Uncle Everett Shobe, my mothers' brother. He gave me the money I needed and I resumed my trip. When I arrived near Conway, Missouri, I fell asleep at the wheel and awakened to find myself in the grass between the four lane highways with the car out of control. I immediately put on my brakes and the car turned completely around and turned over twice landing on its wheels. When I got out of the car, I saw that I had left my west bound lane, crossed over the grass and drove in the east bound lane still going west. Then I crossed back in the grass medium strip and awakened to find the car out of control. I immediately put on my brakes but the car did an about face and turned over twice landing upright. Because of the damage incurred, I could no longer drive the car.

Within five minutes, a man going to California in a pick up truck stopped to help me and offered to drive me to my barracks if I would help him with the gas and driving. He must have been a brave man or a fool to consider letting me drive him but he did. A tow truck came and took my car away and I never saw it again. It was a nice looking 1951 two door white Buick Special. I was always proud of that car. I don't think that I had any insurance on the car; therefore I lost my investment in it. Well my Good Samaritan drove me back to my Marine Corps barracks so that I could report on time. Years later I know that the Lord Jesus Christ was looking out for me because it was certainly nothing that I did to save myself in that situation.

Another time I was driving with two friends in my brand-new 1964 American Rambler automobile that I had bought after graduating from college. I was driving down a two lane country road when the passenger in the back said "Isn't that car on the wrong side of the road." I was busy talking to my friend, Mike Preston, in the front and I didn't really comprehend what the guy in the back was saying. Then suddenly and loudly, Mike in the front said "He is, he is, he is." I then realized that this car was coming towards us and would probably collide head on. At the last moment, I pulled over to the side of the road and the car coming toward us passed through my lane of traffic. We could have very well been killed but the Lord is good and saved us all that day.

In 1990, I was diagnosed with prostate cancer and the cancer had spread past the prostate into one of my seminal vessels. Because the cancer had spread, my doctor told me that it wouldn't benefit me by having my prostate removed by surgery. He said that he would treat me initially with radiation and then with chemotherapy. For almost nineteen years, I have been treated with chemotherapy and have been able to live an abundant and productive life. I thank God for this blessing of life but I thank Him more for accepting me as his child with all of the benefits of being His heir. Because of my experiences, I was able to influence my brother into getting checked for this terrible disease and God blessed him by giving him the gift of life also after being diagnosed with prostate cancer. He had surgery fourteen years ago and has followed through with specific checkups and is doing very well.

After saying all of this, we know that in the end our body will fail us and return to the earth from where it came. But those of us who have accepted Jesus Christ as our Lord and Savior will live on eternally with Him.

For this we say to you by the word of the Lord, that we who are alive and remain until the coming of the Lord will by no means precede those who are asleep. For the Lord Himself will descend from heaven with a shout, with the voice of an archangel, and with the trumpet of God. And the dead in Christ will rise first. Then we who are alive and remain shall be caught up together with them in

the clouds to meet the Lord in the air. And thus we shall always be with the Lord. Therefore comfort one another with these words. 1 Thessalonians 4:15-18

DOUGLAS GRANT

In the summer of 1967, my sister and mother were living in New York while my sister was trying to build a career in show business. They brought Robert Jr., my brother's son, to New York City for a visit. During the visit, an audition was being held for the musical titled "Maggie Flynn." This musical was about an Irish woman providing care for orphaned children of runaway slaves. She is on the verge of marrying again when her husband who had abandoned her previously returns on the scene. The stars of the musical were Jack Cassidy and Shirley Jones. Not only were they starring together but also married to each other. Robert auditioned for the musical and was selected. At this time for show business purposes, Robert began using his middle name of Douglas. In addition to Robert, some of the other orphans were Irene Cara, Giancarlo Esposito and Stephanie Mills. In the musical, Robert played the part of Walter, one of the orphaned children. I saw the play in Detroit, Michigan while it was in try outs and before it went to Broadway. I never got the chance to see it on Broadway because it was canceled following a ten week production run. Although the play did not survive, the cast album achieved moderate success and can be purchased at music stores, including Amazon.Com.

The canceling of the Musical, Maggie Flynn, was not the end of Robert's theatrical career but just the beginning. He went on to play the part of Walter Gee in a movie titled, "The Landlord." The Landlord was released in 1970, when Robert was eleven years old. Starring in this movie were Beau Bridges, Pearl Bailey, Lou Gossett, Diana Sands, Lee Grant and Mel Stewart. After The Landlord, Robert united again with Irene Cara to star as a member of the Broadway Musical titled "The Me Nobody Knows." This musical opened off-Broadway on May 18, 1970. I had the chance to see the performance and I was not only thoroughly entertained but extremely proud of my nephew. The show closed on November 15, 1970 after 208 performances. It then opened at the

Helen Hayes Theater on December 18, 1970 and closed on November 14, 1971 after 378 performances. The musical won an Obie Award for its off-Broadway performances and received a Tony Award nomination for its Broadway performances. After The Me Nobody Knows, Robert rejoined Irene Cara to appear as a member of the "Short Circus" which was featured in Bill Cosby's, "The Electric Company."

Some great actors in addition to Bill Cosby starring in The Electric Company were Rita Moreno and Morgan Freeman. Robert played the part of Zack in The Electric Company and he was in 260 episodes from 1971—1973. Robert also appeared in many televisions shows including Good Times and What's happening. After graduating from high school, Robert decided to attend college on a fulltime basis. He enrolled at The Ohio State University in Columbus, Ohio where he pursued the study of art among other subjects. In an article published by the Lantern newspaper of the Ohio State University in 1980, Robert described himself as an artist and a scientist. He says that he is a person with a diverse range of knowledge, something he aims for by spreading his academic attention over many areas. In fact, when he graduated, Robert had many courses that he had completed which he did not need for graduation credits. He graduated with a Bachelor of Arts Degree in Art history and subsequently attended Temple University in Philadelphia, Pennsylvania to work on his Masters' Degree in Fine Arts. At Temple, Robert began to seriously study painting at the graduate level.

Robert has been doing art in one form or another for over twenty nine years. He graduated from the Tyler School of Fine Art in Rome Italy, which is a part of Temple University. As early as 1990, he had a show here in Columbus where he presented a number of his paintings for viewing and purchase. At this particular show he had twenty six paintings on display. Since that time, he has had his paintings displayed in various art shows. Painting, music, acting and dance have all played an integral role in Robert's search but painting is his primary focus. In fact, he met his future wife, Eileen Smith at a painting exhibition. Robert's experiences in acting, art, music, ballet and opera have all had a great influence on his work. He views art as a very personal statement and uses a variety of mixed media in his paintings to express a sensibility in which to see the world. Both Robert and his wife, Eileen Smith Grant are professional artists living and working in New York, New York with their little Toy Poodle, Basquiat. Robert has been described as a renaissance man who searches for the truth in artistic expressions. I am here to tell him and you that the search for the truth is over. **Jesus Christ is the way, the truth, and the life.**

Jesus said to him, *"I am the way, the truth, and the life. No one comes to the Father except through Me."* **John 14:6**

THE TEMPTATIONS

I have previously written about my brother Doug's singing group, the Orlandos which were an outstanding local group singing in the nineteen fifties in Columbus, Ohio. I have also talked about my two cousins, Chester Brown and Robert Wesley, who were part of the nineteen fifties national singing group, The Counts from Indianapolis, Indiana. The Counts had two hit records, "Darling Dear," and "My Dear, My Darling." This next group was created in Detroit, Michigan in the nineteen sixties and is still singing professionally today in 2009. They began in 1960 first known as the Elgins and were also known as Otis Williams and the Siberians. The group included singers from two local Detroit groups called the Distants with Otis Williams, Elbridge "Al' Bryant, and Melvin Franklin and the Primes with Eddie Kendricks and Paul Williams. Also joining them were David Ruffin and Dennis Edwards. David Ruffin had replaced original member, Elbridge "Al" Bryant and Dennis Edwards eventually replaced David Ruffin.

Well if you haven't guessed by my title, they were the fabulous Temptations, a Motown legend. They had only minor success until 1964 when they recorded a song written by Smokey Robinson titled "The Way You Do the Things the You Do." Eddie Kendrick sang the lead on this song and it was their first big hit and then, they scored another big hit in December of 1964 when they recorded; "My Girl" with David Ruffin as the lead singer. They continued to have hit records such as; "Since I lost My Baby," "Get Ready and "Beauty's Only Skin Deep." In 1968, David Ruffin left the Temptations for a solo singing career and was replaced by Dennis Edwards. In 1969 their hits continued with "Cloud Nine" and "I Can't Get Next To You." In 1971, they had a hit titled "Just My Imagination" and that same year, Eddie Kendricks left for a solo career and Paul Williams left due to poor health. In 1972, they recorded their hit titled "Papa Was a Rolling Stone."

In the years that followed, David Ruffin, Eddie Kendricks, Paul Williams and Melvin Franklin all passed away but the Temptations have continued along with original member and leader Otis Williams remaining to sing with, and lead the group. In 1988, Otis wrote his autobiography and in 1998, his book was made into a television mini series titled appropriately, The Temptations and it is an outstanding account of the story of The Temptations. This group gave plenty of fans including me a lot of enjoyment and pleasure in being entertained by them over the many years. Otis Williams summed up the success of The Temptations when he said; "The Temptations still stand today, not in spite of those who left us, but because of them."

As good as these Temptations have been as a positive influence in our lives; there are other temptations that have had a negative influence. Food has been always a temptation for me and just last night I ate something that I shouldn't have. Now, what I ate was some delicious homemade chili, my wife had made. But I am on a special diet and should not have eaten the chili. I did anyway and paid the consequences the next day because I woke up tired. I am a diabetic and have to watch closely what I put into my mouth. Living with diabetes has been the hardest thing for me to do. My mother had diabetes and she was very good at controlling what she ate. She once told me that she hoped that I would never come down with this disease because I was not as disciplined as her. I am ashamed to say that she was right and I am asking God to give me the strength to deal with this temptation of food. I know that I can look into His mirror of truth so that I can really see what I look like to Him.

There are other temptations that we as human beings have to deal with such as anger, sexual lust, lying, dishonesty, alcohol and the use of illegal drugs. These are just some of the temptations that we face as Christians and non Christians. There is no sin in being tempted. The sin is giving in to the temptation. Even Jesus was tempted by the devil in the wilderness. In the Book of Luke chapter 4 verses 1-13 Jesus full of the Holy Spirit was led by the Spirit in the desert and for forty days, He was tempted by the devil. In verse 3, the devil said to him; "If you are the son of God, tell this stone to become bread." Jesus answered in verse 4 by saying, "It is written; "Man does not live by bread alone."

The devil in verse 5, then took Jesus up to a high place where He could see all the kingdoms of the world and the devil said in verses 6-7 that he would give Jesus authority over all of these kingdoms if Jesus would only worship the devil. In verse 8, Jesus said; "It has been said, worship and serve the Lord God only." In verse 9, the devil led Him to Jerusalem and had him stand on the highest point of the temple and then told Him to throw himself off onto the ground. The devil said His God would send His angels to protect Jesus. But Jesus 'answer in verse 12 was not to put God to a test. The devil then gave up and left Jesus alone. Jesus has given us the example of how to resist temptation and **God will also protect us from the temptations of the devil.**

No temptation has overtaken you except such as is common to man; but God is faithful, who will not allow you to be tempted beyond what you are able, but with the temptation will also make the way of escape, that you may be able to bear it. 1 Corinthians 10:13

ALIVE OR DEAD

The year was 1966 and I met my future wife Delores through my cousin who had tried to set us up on a date. My cousin had arranged for us to meet at a local night club. We met and later I took Delores back to my apartment where I had some friends over for a small party. We danced a few dances and then I took her back to her apartment. I probably told her that I would be calling her but I never did. About two weeks later, I was in the bed resting on a Friday night as I was going out of town on Saturday. The phone rang and it was my cousin who said she had a message from Petie. This was the childhood nick name for Delores and my cousin said that Petie wants to know if I was alive or dead. Well, I thought that was a cute question and I immediately went over to my cousin's house to let Petie know that I was still alive. I never made that trip out of town on Saturday, as I had planned and have been with Petie ever since, which is over forty three years and still counting.

When we think about how our lives have turned out, we have a tendency to think it was all chance. But in looking back, maybe it was not chance at all. Before I met Delores, I knew of Jesus Christ but I didn't know Him in my heart. Over the years and through many experiences I was gradually shaped and molded by Him to be what I am today and the shaping and molding continues. A day doesn't go by when I do not get a new revelation or inspiration from Him through the Holy Spirit. When I first entered the Marine Corp Boot Camp, The drill instructors' goal was to tear us down and then build us up in the image of a Marine. Jesus through the Holy Spirit has done that to me spiritually by giving me a new birth. He has made me a new creature with a new nature. I was dead to His nature and He has given me a new life. So when Petie asked me whether I was alive or dead, I went immediately to see her and let her know that I was alive.

The most important question was not whether I was physically alive but rather was I spiritually alive. Unfortunately at that time when I first met her, I was not spiritually alive but I had experienced reading the word when I took that Old Testament survey course in college with its focus on the Book of Job. The lessons learned from reading Job stayed with me and when I needed its wisdom, the message reappeared in my heart. My wife was very influential in me becoming a Christian and as she would put it, she was used as an instrument by God to reach me. When I became ill with prostate cancer, my wife said that this was not a fight against cancer but rather a fight against Spiritual Warfare. The answer for me was not to read and learn everything that I could find on prostate cancer. The answer would be found in Jesus Christ and His healing powers. This was not a physical battle but a battle for my mind, soul and spirit.

The truth is, when I met my wife, I was not spiritually alive but dead in sin and didn't even know it. I had no idea how abundant my life could really become if I would turn my life over to Jesus Christ. With Christ's death and resurrection, those of us who have accepted Him as our Lord and Savior have died to sin and been reborn with Him into a new life. When my wife opened our Christian book store she decided on the image of a butterfly as our logo. The change from the Caterpillar into a Butterfly represents the change from a spiritually dead person into an alive Born Again Christian. What I want to say about this transformation from death to life was said to me by the Apostle Paul in the sixth chapter of the Book of Romans

"What shall we say then? Shall we continue in sin that grace may abound? Certainly not! How shall we who died to sin live any longer in it? Or do you not know that as many of us as were baptized into Christ Jesus were baptized into His death? Therefore we were buried with Him through baptism into death, that just as Christ was raised from the dead by the glory of the Father, even so we also should walk in newness of life. For if we have been united together in the likeness of His death, certainly we also shall be in the likeness of His resurrection, knowing this, that our old man was crucified with Him, that the body of sin might be done away with, that we should no longer be slaves of sin. For he who has died has been freed from sin. Now if we died with Christ, we believe

that we shall also live with Him, knowing that Christ, having been raised from the dead, dies no more. Death no longer has dominion over Him. For the death that He died, He died to sin once for all; but the life that He lives, He lives to God. Likewise you also, reckon yourselves to be dead indeed to sin, but alive to God in Christ Jesus our Lord. Therefore do not let sin reign in your mortal body, that you should obey it in its lusts. And do not present your members as instruments of unrighteousness to sin, but present yourselves to God as being alive from the dead, and your members as instruments of righteousness to God. For sin shall not have dominion over you, for you are not under law but under grace." Romans 6:1-14

MY CHILDREN

April 1966 was the month and year that I met my future wife, Delores, and I liked her from the beginning. She had been married with three daughters and was now divorced. I began seeing her on a regular basis, like every day; and I started a friendship with the children also. They were six, eight and ten years of age at the time. However, I had no plans of getting married to her. I don't know what I was thinking. I did know that I was attracted to her more than anyone else that I had ever known. She was smart, appealing and seemed to have values similar to mine. As I learned later, she came from a close knit family with good family values; and I began to develop a good relationship with the kids also. The children seemed to like me too including the oldest, Charissa, who since I married her mother has always called me daddy. She was a very loving child and it is hard to believe that she is now a mother with four children and nine grandchildren.

The middle daughter, Renita, asked me one day to be her father. She is the mother of Kai Lee, about whom I have written several stories. Renita and the youngest, Kathy, have always called me dad since I married their mother. Almost a year had passed since I first met Delores and the issue of marriage started coming up. I was trying to fight this urge of wanting to be with her forever but I was losing the battle. Finally, I decided to ask her to marry me and she accepted my proposal. We were married on May 27, 1967, which is over forty two years ago. Over the years, our relationship has not been perfect, but it has been pretty good through the grace of God especially working in her life. She helped to bring Jesus Christ into my life and I accepted Him as my Lord and Savior. I adopted the children and my relationship with them was good except there were certain areas where I could have been a better parent.

I believed that for the most part, I always got along with the older two daughters very well. But I didn't seem to have as close of a relationship with the youngest one. Also, my wife and I had a son together, who unfortunately died when he was almost eight years old. It was after his death that the oldest two children moved out of the house to be on their own. The youngest daughter, named Kathy, was now eighteen years old and we didn't seem to be close at all. Then two incidents happened between us that caused me to think about the quality of our relationship. One time, she wanted to give me a compliment and she said" Dad the one thing that I can say about you is that you have been good provider." Another time we both met by accident at the bus stop and I got on the bus first and found a seat for both of us. She then boarded the bus but she found a seat with a perfect stranger on the bus. This bothered me a lot as I thought that she should have come and sit with me.

I began to think about my role as the adult and parent in our relationship. I realized that I had not given her the love and attention that I should have given. I then made it a point to show her my love and one of the ways to do this was to give her my most prize possession, my college degree. Our relationship is now excellent and we are very loving and affectionate toward each other. And this is all because of Jesus Christ in both of our lives. Just as Jesus reconciled us back to God, He also will reconcile us to each other if we will only follow His commandments. I was forced to look at my behavior in relationship to what Jesus would have me do. Jesus wants us to love one another as He has loved us. During this time of the incident between Kathy and me, we were both undergoing a grieving process for my son's passing. As the adult in this situation, I should have been held to a higher standard of conduct and leadership. I finally recognized my responsibility as the parent and asked the Lord for the ability to change my behavior and become a more loving and caring parent. **I thank God for His transformation.**

Therefore, if anyone is in Christ, he is a new creation; old things have passed away; behold, all things have become new. Now all things are of God, who has reconciled us to Himself through Jesus Christ, and has given us the ministry of reconciliation, that is, that God was in Christ reconciling the world to Himself, not inputting their trespasses to them, and has committed to us the word of reconciliation. Now then, we are ambassadors for Christ, as though God were pleading through us: we implore you on Christ's behalf,

be reconciled to God. For He made Him who knew no sin to be sin for us, that we might become the righteousness of God in Him. 2 Corinthians 5:17-21

GRANDPARENTS

B oth my father's father and my mother's father were born in the State of Kentucky before the end of the Civil war. Therefore they were both born into slavery even though Kentucky, along with several other border slave states, was under Union control. The Emancipation Proclamation did not apply to the slaves in Kentucky and these other border states. My grandfathers and others like them were freed by separate federal and state actions. My mother's mother, Alice Cooke, was only twelve years old when she married my grandfather, Ben Shobe. She went on to have thirteen children with eleven reaching the age of maturity. My father's mother, Lucy Mitchem was eighteen years of age when she married my father's father, Bob Grant. in 1885. They went on to have thirteen children with eleven living to maturity. Both of my parents had some siblings old enough to have been their parents and I can remember seeing the respect that they had for these older brothers and sisters.

Only one of my four grandparents was alive when I was born. That was my beloved and beautiful grandmother, Lucy Grant, who was born in 1867. She lived until age eighty three dying in 1951. She was loved and respected by all of her family. She gave birth to nine boys and four girls. My father was the second from the youngest. Eight of the boys and three of the girls lived to maturity. Unfortunately, one of the grown sons suffered from mental illness and died in a mental institution. My grandmother was seventy years of age when I was born but I still was a witness to her beauty and charm. Every Christmas, she would send us a big box of goodies and we always looked forward to getting it. I don't know if she ever received any government money for her old age but I do know that her children took very good care of her. My father was asked periodically to contribute for some kind of maintenance or other household expense. And every time that he visited her, he would always give her some money when he departed. When she died, I was hurt deeply and until this day, I miss her and think of her often.

I married my wife in 1967, a hundred years after my grandmother's birth. My wife was fortunate to have all of her grandparents alive when she was born with the last one dying just before the turn of the century in 2000. Her first grandparent to die was her grandfather on her mother's side named Ralph Waldo Alston, who died in 1945. Her grandmother on her father's side was named Lillian Parks and she was affectionately called Mom Parks. Mom Parks loved to shop and her apartment was filled with bargains that she had picked up along the way. Her husband, John, was a strong and yet gentle man who was a strong follower of Jesus Christ. My wife says that she received some of her earliest Christian instruction while sitting on her grandfather's knee and listening to Christian radio. She has continued to attend church and study the Bible through out her life until this very day. Both Mom Parks and Grandpa Parks died leaving my wife with one grandparent left alive.

This last grandparent was her grandmother on her mother's side. She was named Bessie Alston and she was born in the late eighteen nineties. Bessie Alston was a remarkable woman. She had five children to live to maturity and along with her husband had done a good job in raising them. She was known for loving God, being frugal and saying exactly what was on her mind. She would always comment on the price of goods and services in comparison to the time when she was young. She didn't understand why a house and loaf of bread would cost so much today. Another source of her comments was my weight. It seems as though every time I saw her she would start out by saying "Sonny you are just getting too fat." This never bothered me and I would always look forward to seeing her again even though I knew that she would probably talk about my weight.

She always called me Sonny and never by my real name of Marshall. I supposed I should be honored because I never heard her call her own son by his name of Richard or Dick. She would always call him "Sonny Boy." I remember her as being very strong willed and opinionated. She had accomplished a lot in her lifetime. She lived through world wars, depressions, and civil rights struggles and the death of four of her children. One day she came over to my house and, as usual, began to talk about how fat I was getting. I had an answer for her that day, which I thought would get her off my back. I told her that if I was not overweight, the women would not leave me alone. I explained that as it is, the women don't bother me. As she looked at me, beginning from the bottom and slowly working her way to the top, she said "I can certainty understand that." She died in 1999 at the age of 101 after having confessed Jesus as her savior for most of her life. And we miss her very much. We thank God for the grandparents' presence in our lives and the Christian legacy they left.

Peace to the Brethren, and love with faith, from God the Father and the Lord Jesus Christ. Grace be with all those who love our Lord Jesus Christ in sincerity. Amen. Ephesians 6:23-24

Chapter Eight:
WORK YEARS

REUNIONS

My first high school reunion was in 1974 and it seemed like I had been out of high school forever. It had only been twenty years but twenty years in those days was a long time. This past June it has been fifty five years since I graduated from Columbus East High School. Now that is a long time. But thirty five years ago in 1974, I thought I was getting old. I was a married man with three adopted daughters and one four year old son. I had a good job, nice home and three cars. I was doing pretty well for somebody who wasted about four years between high school and graduation from college. At this 1974 reunion, I had a chance to renew some old acquaintances with friends that I had not seen for twenty years. There was Betty and Gail Rucker who lived in Poindexter Village and also went to East High School. Howard Ransom, Jon Austin and the actor, Hal Williams from Los Angeles, California also attended. Of course my friend, James Willis and his wife, Fredericia Bates Willis were there. There have been East High School reunions since but I have only attended that first one in 1974. The next high school reunion was in 1989 but eleven years earlier my son had died and I suppose I was still grieving and didn't want to look back in time. The last East High School reunion that I know of was held in 2004, fifty years after I had graduated.

The next reunion that I remember fondly is the Poindexter Village reunion held in 1975. I was the leader of the group that brought that reunion about. The other members were Howard Tidwell, Roy Houpe, Lucille Cherry and my brother, Doug Grant. The idea of the reunion started out with a way to honor Doug Comer, who was our beloved recreational leader when we were children living in Poindexter Village. But in order to assure the necessary turnout needed to make the event a success, we decided to focus around a reunion of former Poindexter Village residents. I had been working as a training coordinator for about three years and had gained experience in putting on large events.

193

I obtained photos from my childhood friends and made slides which also included pictures of the Poindexter Village being built. We decided to have a free bar which probably helped to get the turnout we wanted. I was against it but the other group members were for it including my own brother. We wanted the Reverend Jack Watkins to participate but he refused because we were having liquor at the event. I did then and still admire him for following his principles. As a Christian, sometimes you have to take a stand against what you think is wrong. I have taken a drink on occasion but very rarely. The New Testament doesn't have a lot of do's and don'ts. **"Therefore, whether you eat or drink, or whatever you do, do all to the glory of God." 1 Corinthians 10:31**

In 1991, my wife and I attended a reunion of African American Alumni of Ohio University in Athens, Ohio. I was now almost fifty four years old and one month from retiring from my job as a training officer with the State of Ohio Rehabilitation Services Commission. I knew about the upcoming reunion but wasn't planning to attend. I received a telephone call from one of my best college friends, Rita Osborne Lewis and she said: "you are coming aren't you?" And I answered: "yes of course." I haven't seen or talked to Rita for over twenty five years but it was just like yesterday when she called me. Rita faithfully wrote to me while I was in the Marines from 1957 through 1959 and I have always appreciated her kindness. I went to the reunion because I knew that I would get a chance to see her again. I had a wonderful time especially knowing that I was going to retire in another month. I had struggled to get through college, mostly my own fault, but now I was a success. I owed it all to God's grace and mercy.

The last reunion that I attended was in May of 2009, when I was reunited with my Kappa Alpha Psi Brothers at Ohio University in Athens, Ohio. The reunion was designed to honor those brothers who founded our Epsilon Lambda chapter of Kappa Alpha Psi at Ohio University. I was able to again see people like Ron Holman, Leon Chapman and Dr. Martin Tyler who were my close friends and fraternity brothers back in the day. I also met for the first time brothers like Dwight Washington and Alan Seifullah who had organized the reunion. The Epsilon Lambda chapter received its charter in 1966, two years after I had graduated. I am proud to be included in the list of brothers that were instrumental in founding the Epsilon Lambda chapter of Kappa Alpha Psi at Ohio University. My nephews Tim and Chris Grant were also members of the Epsilon Lambda chapter. They followed me there but became much better students. I thank God for them and their families. My last reunion is yet to come because that is the reunion that God is calling his own to be with him. The only thing that I have to do to register for that reunion is to declare that I have truly accepted Jesus Christ as my Lord and Savor and when I have passed away, He will come and take me to where He is.

That if you confess with your mouth the Lord Jesus and believe in your heart that God has raised him from the dead, you will be saved. For with the heart one believes unto righteousness, and with the mouth confession is made unto salvation. For the Scripture says, "Whoever believes on him, will not be put to shame." Romans 10:9-11

ALI VS. SPINKS

February 15, 1978, was the night when Muhammad Ali fought his first fight with Leon Spinks and this is a date I will never forget. I don't remember that night because of the fight but rather because my little son was hospitalized and I was watching the fight from his hospital room. At the time, I knew that my son's condition was serious enough for him to be in the hospital but I never imagined that it was life threatening. As I watched the fight, I could not enjoy it because of seeing my son in that hospital bed. Muhammad Ali was one of my favorite celebrities and I was very disappointed when he lost his heavyweight championship that night to the young upstart Leon Spinks. I had admired Leon for being a great Olympic champion but I didn't want to see him beat Muhammad Ali. Little did I know at that time how insignificant a boxing match could be. My son's condition gradually grew worse and the doctors did not know what was causing his problems. They gave him a number of tests but could not come up with a diagnosis. One day, while I was with him, his heart stopped beating. The hospital staff revived him but he remained in a coma and could not breathe without a ventilator.

A few days passed, and we were advised that he had no brain function. He was taken off the ventilator and he passed away very peacefully. Before his death, he had been in some pain but now he was free and I was glad that he did not have to suffer any longer. The pain of losing him was almost unbearable but I knew that he was now with his Lord and Savior Jesus Christ. You see, just two weeks before he became ill, he had accepted Jesus as his Lord and Savior and was baptized. He was two months shy of being eight years old when he died. Shortly after his death, I had a dream that I was trying to help him but in my dream he told me to leave him alone and let him go. I took this dream as a message from God that my son was in safe hands. In the meantime, Muhammad Ali had signed to fight a rematch with Leon

Spinks although I did not have much interest in the upcoming fight or other sporting events. I was still grieving for my son and life did not seem to be that important to me any more. I can remember going to see the doctor for a nodule in my abdomen and not caring whether it was cancerous or not; however it was benign and easily removed.

Some months passed and it was now September 1978. My wife and I along with our friends, James and Fredericia Willis decided to travel together to New Orleans Louisiana to attend the National Baptist Convention. Coincidently, the Ali vs. Spinks rematch was going to be held in New Orleans a week after the convention but the fighters were already in town training for the fight. The convention was being held in the Louisiana Superdome which is where the fight was going to be. I had never seen any stadium like the Superdome which some people have called the eighth wonder of the world. Many years later this would be the site of so many people trying to survive after the disastrous results of Hurricane Katrina. But now it was the joyous site where so many Christians came to meet and worship God. In addition to attending convention activities, we enjoyed sightseeing in New Orleans including going to the French Quarter, viewing the above ground cemeteries and eating at the wonderful New Orleans restaurants. We also took rides on the famous New Orleans Trolleys.

One day while sightseeing, we decided to attend Muhammad Ali's training camp. We paid a few dollars to watch Ali shadow box, jump rope and spar a few rounds. After this was over and Ali headed back to his dressing room, my friend James told us to hurry and follow him because we were going to be able to see Ali in his dressing room. I didn't know why we were selected to go to the dressing room but I ran along with my wife, James and his wife Freddie. I later found out James knew Ali's barber and the barber got us in. The reason why James knew the barber was because James owned a beauty supply business and had met many barbers and beauticians over the years. Not only did we meet Ali during our New Orleans visit but our wives later met Dick Gregory and Leon Spinks and took pictures with all of them including our earlier visit with Ali. We also had an extended conversation with Angelo Dundee and former Champ, Jimmy Ellis. I remember talking to Angelo Dundee and Jimmy Ellis was like talking to a friend back home. They were so gracious with their time that it is still hard to believe.

I returned home from the convention and the next week I watched the fight on television. I was happy Ali won his title back but I still wished the best for Leon Spinks. As I was watching the fight, I could not help but remember how short of a time had passed since I lost my beautiful son. The one thing that I know for sure is that life goes on and waits for no person. I also learned that God will not give you a greater burden than you will be able to bear.

"Come to me, all you who labor and are heavy laden, and I will give you rest. Take My yoke upon you and learn from Me, for I am gentle and lowly in heart, and you will find rest for your souls. For My yoke is easy and My burden is light." Matthew 11:28-30

FRIENDS

During the 1980's, my church's Sunday school class presented lessons on how to be a friend with others. I remember that the lessons taught you could either be a friend of someone or a friend to someone. But you should be friendly toward everyone. There are some people that you are able to develop a close relationship with and this allows you to share intimate thoughts and feelings such as each others joys and burdens. There are others you cannot get close to but you can be friendly toward them by showing them the Fruit of The Spirit, described in the 5th chapter of Galatians. And for all of your friends, you can pray for their well being regardless of whether you are a friend to or a friend of.

Over the years I have had many friends. Some I haven't seen in years and others I still talk to from time to time. Some of my friends I have known since childhood. Others, I met in public school, college, the Marine Corps, church and on my job. My first best friend was a boy named Samuel A. Cherry, who was known by the nickname of Little June. We were both born in 1937 a few months apart. He has remained a lifelong friend as we still talk by telephone. My other child mates were Bobby Martin and Newton and John Foster. We have been friends since I moved into Poindexter Village in 1940 where I met them and Little June. Some of my other early close friends are Paul and Billy Shearer, Luther Guynes, Herb Foster. and James Willis.

There is a special friend that I met on the job. His name is Mike Sheets and we were different in many ways. He is white and I am black. He is a Republican and I am Democrat. But he had a special gift which is a Christian love for others and he was always talking about his love for his wife and children. He was a staff trainer like me and he seemed to put so much of himself into his workshops. He really wanted people to benefit from the training that he was presenting. It wasn't just a job to him; he really cared about the people he was serving.

When my son died, he was right there to console me. He had never met my son but he took his passing very personal. Other friends were trying to cheer me up with jokes or telling me that I could get another son but Mike Sheets was different. He had the empathy to see what I was going through. We both cried together about my loss and just writing this now makes me want to cry again. The last time that I saw him, I told him that if we never see or talk to each other again, to remember that I loved him as a friend.

One of my other work related friendships involved a guy, named Charles Parish, who I initially met as my supervisor on my job. I knew him for almost 33 years until his death. He was a person who did not get close to other people but for some reason, we had a good working and personal relationship. He would always say that we weren't friends but companions of circumstance. He would always encourage me in whatever positive thing I was trying to do. He would say "Marshall, You can do that" or "Marshall that was a great job." Although he was only nineteen months older than me, he acted as my mentor.

One time our supervisor, Ronn Perrin, came and asked us to do a very difficult job. Our agency was changing physical locations and we had to be out of our old building two days before we could move into the new building. The question arose as to what could be done with our 1500 member staff during this period. We thought about it for maybe ten or fifteen minutes and came up with a solution. The solution was to contract with a local community college to provide a two day training session for our staff. I wanted to immediately tell Ronn that we had solved his problem. But my friend said lets wait and tell him in a few days because we didn't want to make it seem too easy.

Charles and I would frequently go to lunch together and although we came from different backgrounds, we had many things in common. We went past the stage of being friends to each other and became friends of each other. We would share feelings, thoughts and each others' burdens and joys. We would often talk about traveling, after we retired. He retired two years before me and bought a recreational vehicle. His wife went with him on his first trip to Alaska but she didn't want to go on other trips. He asked me, after I had retired, if I would travel with him but I turned down the offer since I didn't want to spend any time away from my wife and family.

We would periodically meet for lunch over the years and one Saturday we all watched the Ohio State vs. Michigan football game together. I had not seen him for six or more months before his wife called to tell me that he was terminally ill with cancer. She said that he didn't want anyone to know about his illness. She asked me to give him a call since I probably would never get the chance to talk to him again. I called him and we had our usual conversation talking about old times. Then shortly after, I read in the newspaper that he had passed away. I still miss him and his friendship and I did love him as a friend. In the beginning we may have been companions of circumstance but in the end, we had become good friends. Ralph Waldo Emerson put it very well when he said. **"The only way to have a friend is to be a friend."**

Two are better than one, because they have a good reward for their labor. For if they fall, one will lift up his companion. But woe to him who is alone when he falls, For he has no one to help him up. Ecclesiastes 4:9-10

My Best Friend

Remembering the night my son, Little Marshall, was born brings back memories of my wife moaning with pain in the delivery room at the hospital. Finally the doctor came out and told me that I had a little boy. I first saw him as he and his mother were leaving the delivery room and going to their hospital rooms. He was such a beautiful little boy and I, like other parents, had immediate love for him. We brought him home from the hospital and began to watch him grow. He was very fortunate in that he had three older sisters who adored him and looked after him. As a little boy my wife took him to church and Sunday school. Unfortunately, I was not attending church at the time. One time he came to me and asked "daddy why don't you go to church." I can't remember how I answered him. I know that I really didn't have a good answer. But fortunately, his mother set the example and introduced him to Christ. I always tell my wife that she has been a wonderful mother to all of her children, grandchildren and great grandchildren.

My son was a smart little boy and began to read at an early age. I remember him being able to read the book titled "Roots" when he was about six. He was a good child and for the most part, he always obeyed his mother and me. I only remember having to spank him one time for misbehaving in school. One of my fondest pictures of him is when he was waiting in line with his mother to see Santa Claus. The picture tells the story of the love between my wife and her son. I can remember taking my son with me on an out of town business trip one day. We had lunch in a restaurant and he met my co-workers. In looking back, this has been a wonderful memory. If you haven't already guessed it, my little boy is no longer with us. He passed away from a mysterious illness when he was just seven years old. This was the worst thing that I have ever experienced. Even though I had not accepted Christ in my heart, I remembered reading about Job in college. God allowed Job to be tested by Satan who took away Job's children and possessions. But

Job continued to love God despite the pain and suffering allowed to be inflicted on him.

A few weeks before my son passed away, he chose to be baptized. As usual, I did not attend. Then he became ill from this mystery illness that the doctors could not provide a diagnosis. I remember my son being very brave in spite of the pain he was going through. When asked how he was feeling, he would always say "I am feeling fine." I was in the room with him when he stopped breathing. My wife had gone home to take a well deserved break. I had to call and give her the bad news. We then had to make the decision to take him off the breathing machine since he had no brain function. In the past, I would ask my son who do you love the best. He would point to me but sometimes point to his mother. One time just before his illness, I asked him this same question. He gave me an annoying look and replied that **Jesus was his best friend**. A few weeks after his death, I had a dream in which my son told me to leave him alone and let him go. I let him go and took my burdens to the Lord. A few years later, I also accepted Jesus Christ as my Lord and Savior.

The story doesn't end there. It has been over thirty one years since my son passed away and I still miss and love him very much. I don't know what kind of man he would have become but based on what I saw, I believe that he would have been able to make a difference in this world. The effect of his death and other experiences has had a tremendous effect on me. Instead of becoming depressed and hopeless, I turned to the Lord from whom my help comes. I gave my burdens and sorrows to him knowing that He is in control and my faith in him is stronger than ever. The tears still come when I think of my son and other loved ones that I have lost over the years but God through His Son Jesus, is able to wipe away all of my tears.

You have turned for me my mourning into dancing; You have put off my sackcloth and clothed me with gladness, To the end that my glory may sing praise to You and not be silent. O Lord my God, I will give thanks to You forever. Psalm 30:11-12

Glorious Work

The celebration of Teddy Kennedy's life and a sermon by my pastor, Rich Nathan, on the role of Christianity in the workplace helped me to look back at my own work history. Although I believed my job performance was good to excellent, I never thought of myself as a worker who was working to glorify Christ's holy name. On these jobs, I had no sense of a goal or mission. For example, one of my earlier jobs as an employment interviewer required initiative especially since there was no one constantly telling me what to do. I would sit around when I was not interviewing clients and try to figure out how to pass my time. In looking back, there were a lot of things that I could have done to help people that I was suppose to be serving but I didn't have the insight to know that then.

In my last job before retirement, I did a lot of assignments that I took pride in and found rewarding. Although they were successful, I was not doing it for the glory of God. When I first started this job I was assigned the task of writing in basket problems for Vocational Rehabilitation Counselors, who helped disabled people get back to work. This was my first major training session which was designed to get the counselors to look in their casework manual instead of calling up the central office when they needed to solve a problem. Another major program I was in charge of was the New Counselor Training Program where we would bring in newly hired counselors for a four week period and give them basic training in doing their jobs as Vocational Rehabilitation Counselors.

Another important program that I had the opportunity to work in was The Management Resource Bank. This program was designed to help all staff members who wanted to advance in the agency. We would assess their potential for jobs on the promotional ladder and then provide training to help them achieve their goals. I was just doing my last follow-up interview on those who had been assessed when I found out this program had been eliminated. The agency had begun a freeze on jobs without telling me. This caused me to be somewhat disillusioned about what I was doing. From that time on, I never had enthusiasm for my job again until about three years later, when a friend, Charles Parish, that I had closely worked with retired and a new person was hired to take his place.

This new person was a Palestinian Arab named Suhail Zidan, who was very bright and energetic. He was very motivated to do high quality work but I wasn't about to join him. He would keep trying to motivate me and I would keep saying that the agency doesn't appreciate my efforts citing the situation regarding the Management Resource Bank. We had often talked about our faith and he knew that I professed to be a Christian. He then asked me the ultimate question. He said "You say you are a Christian." I replied "Yes I am." He then said "Wouldn't Jesus want you to do your very best? What could I say? He had me there. I answered "Yes you are right." I then changed and tried to do my very best.

The last three years of my career were the most productive. In fact, I presented a seminar on communication two days before I retired. With my old attitude, I would have slowed down or stopped working much earlier. However, even with the change in my attitude, I was not knowingly working for the glory of God but I believe that the Holy Spirit was involved in my daily job activities. It was years later after retiring, when I truly began to worship and praise God that I understood what it means to work for the glory of God.

Since I have been writing about my life memories, I have been working harder than I ever did before I retired in 1991. I look forward to beginning my day at the computer and writing about my experiences and the importance of Jesus Christ in guiding and directing my life. Jesus is indeed providing me with an abundant life.

Therefore, whether you eat or drink, or whatever you do, do all to the glory of God. 1 Corinthians 10:31

GUIDING VALUES

Have you ever thought about the values that guide and direct you when you are making decisions and choices in your life? Why do you do the things that you do? What do you value most in this life? Is it money, good looks, sex, tasty food, power and strength? Is freedom and being independent one of your values? What motivates you to get up in the morning and then go to work? You know we all have values even though we haven't sat down and thought them out. When I was a little boy, I had a value of wanting to tell the truth. I had this value even though I didn't always follow it. Another one of my values was not to use profanity in everyday conservation; however, I would say bad words if I was angered. These were all values of mine but I could not always keep them. When I was working for the Ohio Rehabilitation Services Commission in the 1980's, my agency decided to develop a set of written values. My director, Ronn Perrin believed that as an agency we had values whether they were documented or not. Our values may have been imperfect but in actuality were there. Ronn wanted to write a set of good values and then implement them in our agency. One of his values was that each and every employee should be valued as an important member of the team.

Over the years I have thought about what he was trying to do and I have thought about other values such as American, Family and Christian values. Many of our American values are contained in our nation's Constitution and Declaration of Independence. For example, the Declaration of Independence states the following; **"We hold these truths to be self evident, that all men are created equal, that they are endowed by their creator with certain inalienable rights that among these are life, liberty and the pursuit of happiness."** Unfortunately when Thomas Jefferson wrote this, he did not include slaves in his definition of all men. In fact, Thomas Jefferson owned slaves himself. There are many other American values contained in other documents like the Constitution, legislation and speeches by our nation's leaders. We often hear politicians talking about family values when they are running for office. Some of them have been caught violating their stated values. When I was growing up, my father would really get upset if one of us called someone a liar. I grew up knowing that I should not call anyone a liar and this has been a value of mine all my life.

Another value I learned was to love and have a good and close relationship with other members of my family. Both of my parents came from large families and they were all close to each other. There are other values that I have such as believing in pro life, opposite sex marriage only and getting a good education. Many of us get our values from our parents, peers, movies, television, recorded music and words such as rap. One of the values I received as a child from the movies was not to let anyone pick on you without retribution. The old cowboy movies were about the bad guys versus the good guys with the good guys winning in the end. We were always surprised to find out that sometimes the movie actor with strong positive values is really someone in real life with weak values contrary to what he or she portrays on the movie screen. To me, the most important values come from my Lord and Savior, Jesus Christ. Jesus summed up the Ten Commandments into just two commandments which are to love the Lord God with all your heart, soul, strength and mind and to love your neighbor like yourself (Luke 10:27). **The Apostle Paul says that whatever you do, you should do it for the glory of God (1 Corinthians 10:31).**

In Matthew the fifth chapter, Jesus lists some of His values in what is called the Beatitudes. He begins by describing those who are blessed which include those who are poor in spirit and those who mourn. There are many more listed including; "Blessed are the peacemakers." As individuals, families, organizations and countries, we all have values whether they are written down or not. For example, the United States of America's written values did not coincide with its practiced values regarding its African American citizens. This is what Martin Luther King Jr. was talking about when he said that African Americans had received a check promising our acceptance as Americans but this check had been returned for insufficient funds and could not be cashed. The Civil Rights Revolution was all about cashing that check. We Christians must understand that just saying we are Christians doesn't make us one. We must be followers of Christ, obey His commandments and through Him become righteous. Just following the law does not make us righteous but becoming righteous through Christ makes us follow the law. **If we love Him, we will obey Him by following His Commandments. He will make us righteous.**

For I am not ashamed of the gospel of Christ, for it is the power of God to salvation for everyone who believes, for the Jew first and also for the Greek. For in it the righteousness of God is revealed from faith to faith; as it is written, "The just shall live by faith." Romans 1:16-17

KUM BA YA

Kum Ba Ya is the title of an African inspired Christian song which literally means to come by here. This was the name my wife decided to name her Christian bookstore in 1980. There were other Christian book stores in the city but this was the first one owned and operated by an African-American. This had been a dream of my wife to start a Christian book store for many years but it was never realistic. Then our son died at almost eight years of age from an unknown illness. Two years later my wife again expressed an interest to start a Christian bookstore and I decided to go along with her. My wife quit her job and used her retirement money along with a loan from her grandmother to begin the business. I also gave her some money to add to this venture. We opened for business on November 1980 in 1200 square feet of retail space in a medium sized neighborhood shopping center. In looking back, it took a lot of nerve opening that store with so little merchandise to sell. Of course my wife would say that it took a lot of faith in God. For her this was not a business venture but a stewardship and her goal was not to make money but to be an instrument in saving souls for Christ.

In our first year, we only grossed about $95,000.00 but because our expenses were so small, we actually made a profit. My wife didn't receive a salary and our only expenses were rent, utilities and purchasing inventory. Because we had made a profit, the tax bill was $4500.00. Our business was considered a sole proprietorship and my wife and I had to pay the taxes ourselves. I spent several nights worrying about where I was going to get the money to pay this tax bill. Finally I decided to turn this problem over to the Lord. This was something new for me because even though I was a partner in a Christian bookstore, I was not yet a Born Again Christian. Remember this was my wife's venture and I was just being a good husband and supporting her. Well when the time came to pay the taxes, we had made enough money so that I could pay myself back $4500.00 of our original $15,000.00 investment.

I don't remember where the money came from. It was probably from the sale of choir robes to a church. I remember my wife telling me that God had provided us a ram in the bush.

For the first three years, my wife was the sole unpaid employee and I would report there after I finished my day job. Than we hired our first employee, Patty Solis, who stayed with us for about sixteen years. Two years after hiring our first employee, our daughter, Renita, came to work for us. She worked for us for over ten years until she took a job with an automobile manufacturing company. Over the years, we had other people work for us on a full time and part time basis such as Bernice Lewis, Mary Jo Booth, Frank Barnes and one of my co-workers, Zelpha Rinehart, from my day job. Another daughter of ours, Kathy Grant, also worked part time for us. Three of my nephews, Tony, Tim and Chris Grant worked for us during their college break. About five years into the business, we started selling office supplies which greatly helped to finance my wife's Christian book store stewardship. Our business flourished for many years and then we began to lose business selling office supplies. We finally had to close our business but it really was the right time. We were ready to retire from working and we were able to pay all of our debts from the business. It is very hard to imagine how many people benefited from the presence of Kum Ba Ya, but I am sure that there were many times my wife helped people in need and would pause during her busy day to pray with those needing or requesting prayer.

Owning this store benefited us in so many ways that it is impossible to list all of them at this time. We were able to meet and spread the message of Jesus Christ to a lot of people. I had an unbelievable opportunity to grow and develop as a Christian through the use of all of the Christian material being written and produced. My wife and I had the opportunity to travel to Christian book store conventions and visit different cities and meet many other Christian book store owners. We also had problems like a couple of armed robberies; and people who would shop lift our merchandise. One time a young man stole some bible covers and my wife took after him. I don't know what she was going to do if she had caught him. Knowing her, she probably would have offered to give him some money and pray for him too. I mentioned earlier that my wife's goal was to be an instrument in saving souls. Well it was a few years into her stewardship that I accepted Jesus Christ as my

Lord and Savior. Her Christian behavior over the years and her fulfilled dream of owning a Christian bookstore help lead to my salvation.

Beloved, I beg you as sojourners and pilgrims, abstain from fleshly lusts which war against the soul, having your conduct honorable among the Gentiles, that when they speak against you as evildoers, they may, by your good works which they observe, glorify God in the day of visitation. 1 Peter 2:11-12

THE FOLLOWER LEADER

As a training officer for the State of Ohio, I had the responsibility to present leadership training for our managers and supervisors. The age old question then and to this day is whether leaders are born or made. In trying to answer this question, I turned to such management experts as Warren Bennis, Burt Nanus and especially William D. Hitt Ph.D., who was the Director of Management Development at Battelle Memorial Institute in Columbus, Ohio. In reading Dr. Hitt's books and leadership books by other authors, I often asked myself what Jesus would have to say about this issue of whether leaders are born or made. There have been many leadership books written to advise those seeking leadership and management skills on how to develop themselves into leaders but this question of whether leaders are born or made remains.

Many leadership experts say that leadership is a skill that can be learned. But how much can a person improve his or her leadership or management skills? Dr. Hitt in his book, The Leader Manager, says that there can be some improvement but don't expect on a scale of 1 to 10 that a person who is a "1" can become a "10." He further states that it would be difficult for a "3" to become a "7." However Dr. Hitt says that he believes that a manager who is a "4" can become a "6" or a "5" can become a "7". Dr. Hitt claims that based on his research and knowledge this two point improvement can spell the difference between "Fair" and" Good" or between "Good" and "Excellent." Dr. Hitt further states that he promises no miracles, but does promise realism.

As a Christian, I have in the past been looking for miracles and have received at least one that I know of for sure. I was diagnosed with prostate cancer over twenty years ago and at that time; my cancer had spread past my prostate. Since initially receiving radiation, I have also been receiving chemotherapy every three months. A few years ago, my doctor, Erroll Singh, examined me and kiddingly asked "What are you still doing here?" He has called me his miracle patient. Neither Dr.

Singh nor Dr. Hitt can produce miracles but God has and still does. For example in John 20:30-31 the author, The Apostle John, explains that Jesus performed miracles so that people would believe in Him and in believing they may have life in His name.

So the question for those of us who believe in miracles from God is whether He can change a person's leadership skills from a "1" to a "10" or a "2" to a "9" or a "3" to a "7." There is a saying that I read recently that says: **"God doesn't call the qualified, He qualifies the called."** There are many examples in the Bible where God takes someone with limited leadership skills and transforms him or her into a great leader. But the common thread that binds all of these biblical leaders together is their tremendous faith in God. Beginning with Abraham, we see that he had great faith in God and where He was leading him. God promised Abraham many descendents who would carry out God's plan and provide a blessing for the entire world. But before any of this could happen, Abraham had to obey and follow God in faith.

Another example of biblical leaders who were unqualified but God called and qualified them were Moses and the Apostle Paul. God called Moses to lead the Israelites out of Egypt in Exodus 3:11, Moses said to God: "Who am I, that I should go to Pharaoh and bring the Israelites out of Egypt?" God qualified Moses by preparing him to be the leader of his people and empowering him to succeed. The Apostle Paul is most responsible than any other person for spreading the gospel around the world. But before his conversion on the road to Damascus, he was the greatest oppressor of the Christian Church. He took delight when he heard that Stephan, the first deacon of the church, had been stoned to death. Yet when he was blinded by Jesus on the road to Damascus, His first reply was: "Lord, What do you want me to do?" Paul went on to write many books of the New Testament including 1 Corinthians Chapter 13, which describes unconditional love.

Now getting back to whether leaders are born or made, I believe that there are all kinds of leaders but only God makes authentic Christian leaders. The Declaration of Independence states: "We hold these truths to be self-evident, that all men are created equal, that they are endowed by their Creator with certain unalienable rights that among these are life, liberty and the pursuit of happiness.' But God does not create people equally with the same talents and gifts. However, He can indeed take someone with the leadership skills of a "1" and transform him or her into a "10." **God Transforms.**

I beseech you therefore, brethren, by the mercies of God, that you present your bodies a living sacrifice, holy, acceptable to God, which is your reasonable service. And do not be conformed to this world, but be transformed by the renewing of your mind, that you may prove what is that good and acceptable and perfect will of God. Romans 12:1-2

Chapter Nine:
SPIRITUAL CHALLENGES

FEAR

SIN AND FORGIVENESS

TWO NATURES

SPIRITUAL WARFARE

STICKS AND STONES

SICKNESS AND HEALTH

WEAK BUT STRONG

MONEY HONEY

DREAM BABIES

FEAR

This is an issue that I find some difficulty in writing about. Since we were little we were taught to be brave and not to be fearful. Movies and television programs would often depict people of courage as being the heroes. Books like "Profiles in Courage" became best sellers. The highest honor for bravery a soldier can receive is the Congressional Medal of Honor. But fear is such a dominant factor in our life that many movies and stories are also shown and written to take advantage of our weaknesses. Michael Jackson used this fear factor when he wrote and starred in his video Thriller. This video played on all of those horror movies we would watch. Even though they scared us while we were watching them, we could always walk out of the movies knowing that it was make believe. However, there were some movies that left us fearful for some time. For example, there was Alfred Hitchcock's Psycho, starring Anthony Perkins. Who can ever forget the shower scene of Janet Leigh being stabbed to death by Anthony Perkins?

Well I have had my share of fears over the years and I can't say that they have all gone away. I will talk about three primary fears that I have had to deal with since my teenage days. The first is my fear of being inside enclosed places which translate primarily into not wanting to ride in elevators. I have never been stuck in an elevator but I don't like to ride in them. I can remember years ago as a teenager, I would accompany my mother when she was applying for a government job as a typist. In those days when taking a typing test, you had to bring your own typewriter. Instead of me carrying the typewriter in the elevator to the examination site, I would carry the typewriter up flights of stairs no matter how many. My mother would laugh at me for doing this and she could not understand why I did not like riding in elevators. Many years later my mother had a doctor's appointment and she was accompanied by my sister and my sister's son. It was a cold and snowy day and they had to ride an elevator to get to the doctor's office.

Well guess what happened. The elevator became stuck between floors. My sister began to panic but my mother remained quiet although she was fearful of being stuck in the small dark cramped elevator. They shouted for help and someone came and told them not to worry because help was on the way. My sister's little boy, who was attending a Catholic Elementary School, told my mother and sister that what they should do is pray. After this incident, neither my mother nor my sister teased me about my fear of riding in an elevator again. A few years later, I took my mother to the doctor and discovered that we had to ride an elevator down one floor to get to the doctor's office. I didn't want to do this but I didn't have any choice. This was my mother and I am not a coward. Much to my surprise, my mother said that she didn't want to ride the elevator and she would prefer to walk down the stairs. I was delighted but was still concerned about her walking back up the stairs. When the time came for us to leave the doctor's office and walk back up the stairs, she didn't hesitate and started back up.

A second fear of mine has been the fear of flying. I have flown many times but still feel uncomfortable when I am on an airplane. One time my wife and I were returning on a flight from Minneapolis, Minnesota to Chicago, Illinois when the pilot told us that we could not land because of an obstruction on the runway. I was becoming increasingly uncomfortable the longer we had to circle the airport. I later learned that this was the pilot's way of saying that there had been an air crash. While we were circling over the airport, I looked over at my wife and she was reading a Christian book about how temporary the flesh is. This did not help me at all since I was not yet a Born Again Christian. After we had opened our Christian book store, we were going to attend a Christian book seller's convention in California and I wanted to drive but my wife wanted to fly. Well she won and we scheduled our plane flight. I told my children that if the plane crashes and our bodies were not recognizable, we would be the couple with one skeleton having his hands around the other skeleton's throat. Of course, I was only kidding.

My third fear has been the fear of having medical procedures and surgery done on me. Over the years, I have undergone many medical procedures and at least two surgeries. I have found out there is nothing as bad as you imagine it to be. This has been true for me although I am sure this may not be the case with everyone. The ultimate fear we have all faced is the fear of death. But I am here to tell you that our Lord,

Jesus Christ can handle all of your fears through faith and perfect love in Him.

Whoever confesses that Jesus is the Son of God, God abides in him, and he in God. And we have known and believed the love that God has for us. God is love, and he who abides in love abides in God, and God in him. Love has been perfected among us in this: that we may have boldness in the day of judgment; because as He is, so are we in this world. There is no fear in love; but perfect love casts out fear, because fear involves torment. But he who fears has not been made perfect in love. We love Him because He first loved us. 1 John 4:15-19

SIN AND FORGIVENESS

For all have sinned and fallen short of the Word of God according to the Apostle Paul in Romans 3:23. There are no exceptions except for our Lord and Savior, Jesus Christ. The Lord's Prayer given to us by Jesus in the Gospel of Matthew 6:9-13 and in the Gospel of Luke 11:2-4 includes asking God to forgive us our trespasses as we forgive those who trespass against us. God does not want our sins to keep us from Him. That is why He sent His Son, Jesus Christ to earth so He could serve as a sacrifice and reconcile us back to God. The origin of sin is described in the Bible as Adam and Eve disobeying God and eating the fruit from the tree of knowledge. From that time on, we have had to pay the price of that original sin. We have the tendency to think that we are good when we compare ourselves to some other person who is considered by most people as a bad person. We want to use the standard of behavior listed in the Ten Commandments or laws enacted by our legislature but there is no law that can measure up to what Jesus wants us to be like. **Jesus wants us to love one another as He first loved us.**

When asked to give the greatest commandment, Jesus said that in Matthew 22:37-39 that the Ten Commandments could be summed up into Two Commandments. You shall love the Lord your God with all of your heart, soul, and mind and you shall love your neighbor as you love yourself. Jesus knows that we are unable to strictly follow the law so that is why He sacrificed Himself on the cross. Our standard of perfection is through Him and His love for us. He gave us the Fruit of His Spirit described in Galatians 5:22-23 and by this we shall be known as belonging to Him. We want to believe that our little sin like lying or putting money ahead of God is not as great as murder or committing adultery. The Bible doesn't differentiate between big sin and little sin. Sin is sin and any sin without repentance will separate us from Christ Jesus. We are too weak to stop sinning on our own. But as we are weak,

He is strong and in Philippians 4:13, we read that through His strength we can do all things.

The Apostle Paul was converted by Jesus Christ on the way to Damascus and from that time on, he began to live his life for the Lord. But even Paul could not stop sinning on his own power. In the book of Romans 7:20, Paul says the following: "Now if I do what I do not want to do, it is no longer I who do it, but it is sin living in me that does it." In Romans 7:25, Paul says that in his mind he serves the law of Christ but in his flesh he serves the law of sin. So if we think that we can stop sinning on our own without Jesus, we can forget it. In 2 Corinthians 7:8-12, Paul describes our sorrow of being sinners as godly sorrow because this kind of sorrow leads to repentance and salvation. And the other kind of sorrow, worldly sorrow, leads to death. Just like the Apostle Paul, I know that I am a sinner saved by grace and not by anything that I have done. The good news is that we have someone who can save us from our sinful nature and that is our Lord and Savior, Jesus Christ.

The Lord Jesus Christ served as a sacrifice on the cross so that we might be forgiven for all of our sins. This is His grace given to us which we did nothing to deserve. Not only does Christ forgive our sins but He also forgets them. We have people who have sinned against us and we say that we can forgive them but we can't forget what they did to us. If Christ can forgive and forget, then why can't we. Well I know who Jesus is and we are not Him. Some say it is impossible for us humans to forget unless we develop amnesia. My Pastor, Rich Nathan of the Vineyard Church, gave a sermon one time in which he discussed the issue of forgiving and forgetting. Pastor Nathan said that maybe we can't forget but we can choose not to remember. The following prayer of forgiveness by an unknown author can be used by any of us seeking forgiveness for our sins and asking Christ's salvation "Father I know that I have broken your laws and my sins have separated me from you. I am truly sorry, and now I want to turn away from my past sinful life toward you. Please forgive me, and help me avoid sinning again. I believe that your son, Jesus Christ died for my sins, was resurrected from the dead, and is alive and hears my prayer I invite the Lord Jesus to become the Lord of my life, to rule and reign in my heart from this day forward. Please send your Holy Spirit to help me obey You, and to do Your will for the rest of my life. In Jesus' name I pray, Amen."

If we say that we have no sin, we deceive ourselves, and the truth is not in us. If we confess our sins, He is faithful and just to forgive us our sins and to cleanse us from all unrighteousness. If we say that we have not sinned, we make Him a liar, and His word is not in us. 1 John 1:8-10

TWO NATURES

Did you know that as Born Again Christians, we are living with two natures inside of us? They are the old and new natures. The old nature represents the side that was present in us before we accepted Jesus Christ as our Savior. And the new nature is what God gave us through The Holy Spirit after accepting Christ. Remember **2nd Corinthians 5:17** which says**: "Therefore, if anyone is in Christ, he is a new creation; old things have passed away; behold all things have become new."** Even though we have a new nature, we still have the old nature to deal with. The old nature is called the sin nature, sinful nature or flesh and it is still with us even though we now have a new nature. Even as I write my stories with a Christian influence, I am dealing with negative thoughts in my head which reflects the presence of that old sinful nature. As a believer, I have the ability to resist what the old nature would have me do. But when I was an unbeliever, I didn't have the ability to resist the urge to sin although I basically was a good person and did good things at times.

Have you ever asked yourself why you, me and others continue to sin after accepting Christ as our Lord and Savior. Why do we have negative thoughts about ourselves and other people? Why do we continue to exhibit the characteristics of someone who has not been saved? Why do we lose our focus on Christ when we are saying our prayers or singing Christian music? The Apostle Paul dealt with this issue in the Book of Romans. Paul says that he is inherently a sinful person. He wants to do the right thing but he doesn't do it. He doesn't want to do the wrong thing but he does it anyway. Paul says that since he doesn't do what he wants to do but does what he doesn't want to; then it is not him doing it, but the sin inside him doing it. I can remember going to a restaurant and wanting to order a healthy meal. But as soon as the waitress came to take my order, I instinctly ordered the unhealthy meal as though I had no control. I wanted to order the healthy meal but I didn't. I didn't want to order the unhealthy meal but I did anyway.

The question is who is in control of me. Am I under the control of the new nature or still dominated by the old nature. The Bible talks about us being slaves of sin before our conversion to Christ. After accepting Christ we are supposed to be liberated from sin and become new creations. The end of slavery in the United States did not solve all of the former slaves' problems. After the Civil War in the United States, former slaves had to decide if they were going to strike out on their own or continue to work for former masters. Some former slaves who decided to go on their own were dragged back into a form of slavery by being forced to work as share croppers for former owners. Then there was the enactment of the Jim Crows laws which was an attempt to keep the former slaves as close to their former conditions of slavery as possible. As a Born Again Christian, we are told by the Apostle Paul the following in **Galatians 5:16 "I say then: Walk in the Spirit, and you shall not fulfill the lusts of the flesh."** The old sinful nature is still in us but we are now no longer slaves to it. We are still slaves but we are now slaves to Jesus Christ. We are now free to choose Him as our Lord and Master.

Another question is why the word of God isn't more widely accepted by people who have heard it. The answer may lie in a discussion of The Parable of The Sower. In the Parable of The Sower, Jesus talks about seed being planted in different types of soil and what results from it. When seed is sown on the road, it is stepped on and eventually the birds eat it. The seed sown on rocky ground has no water to nourish it and it dries up and blows away. Seed sown among thorns is choked and killed by the growth of the thorns. But seed sown in good ground grows and multiplies many times over. In this parable, seed is the word of God. When the word is given along the road, Satan may come along and take it away by putting doubts in your mind. Just like seed sown on the rock, people receive the word but it is not deeply planted in their heart and they continue to sin. Others receive the word, but like the seed sown among thorns, have too many choices competing with it such as money, sex and other pleasures of life. Then there are some people who receive the word of God and plant it deep within their heart and from those roots grow the fruit described in Galatians 5:22-23. We must understand that Jesus has set us free from having to sin and we are now His slaves to righteousness. **Praise God.**

But now having been set free from sin, and having become slaves of God, you have your fruit to holiness, and the end, everlasting life. For the wages of sin is death, but the gift of God is eternal life in Christ Jesus our Lord. Romans 6:22-23

SPIRITUAL WARFARE

The first time I remembered hearing about the term," Spiritual Warfare" was when I was diagnosed with prostate cancer. My wife said we were going to fight this cancer with spiritual warfare. We immediately begin to immerse ourselves in reading the Bible and listening to sermons on tape. This was an enlightening period in my life from a spiritual point of view. I began to look at my problems and confrontations with other people differently. My wife informed me that our battles are not with other people but rather against negative powers around us. We can't fight these battles on our own because we need God to fight them for us. The Bible speaks on this subject as follows: **"For though we walk in the flesh, we do not war according to the flesh. For the weapons of our warfare are not carnal but mighty in God for pulling down strongholds, casting down arguments and every high thing that exalts itself against the knowledge of God, bringing every thought into captivity to the obedience of Christ, and being ready to punish all disobedience when your obedience is fulfilled." 2 Corinthians 10:3-6**

Sometimes it is painful in looking back at some of my past behaviors, which were made with guidance from the old nature. There was a man that I hired to do some work for me who I trusted with $400.00 to buy materials for the job. Well, he never bought the materials and refused to give me my money back. I finally went to his job to confront him about the money he owed me. He was angry at me for coming and he threatened me with bodily harm. He was a number of years younger and probably in much better shape. But I foolishly called his bluff. He then backed off and said that he would make amends. At that particular time, I really disliked that guy and wanted to put a hurting on him. I was on the road to being a Born Again Christian but I was unable to use the powers that Christ gives those who believe in and rely on Him. I have a better understanding today of those people who don't think and just act emotionally. I really wanted to hurt that guy. But the Lord is good and worthy to be praised. He saved me from my foolish self.

This battle with the man who took my money is an example of spiritual warfare. Jesus gives us clear directions on how we are to behave in these kinds of situations. In Matthew 5:38-48, Jesus says that you should turn the other cheek when slapped on the right cheek and if someone steals your tunic, then let him have your coat also. He wants us to love our enemies and pray for those who despitefully use and persecute us. I had a history of fighting as a child and was always taught to fight back and give more than you got. When I enlisted in the Marines, I was again taught to fight and given training in the use of weapons. I carried loaded weapons when I was transporting prisoners from one location to another. As a human being, I don't have all the answers to every question, but for us believers, we have a source that we can go to for directions on how to fight our battles here on earth. The source that we can go to is our Lord and Savior Jesus Christ, for His word and the Holy Spirit. In the Book of Ephesians, the Apostle Paul tells us how to put on the whole armor of God in order to prepare for spiritual warfare:

"Finally, my brethren, be strong in the Lord and in the power of His might. Put on the whole armor of God, that you may be able to stand against the wiles of the devil. For we do not wrestle against flesh and blood, but against principalities, against powers, against the rulers of the darkness of this age, against spiritual hosts of wickedness in the heavenly places. Therefore take up the whole armor of God that you may be able to withstand in the evil day, and having done all, to stand. Stand therefore, having girded your waist with truth, having put on the breastplate of righteousness, and having shod your feet with the preparation of the gospel of peace; above all, taking the shield of faith with which you will be able to quench all the fiery darts of the wicked one. And take the helmet of salvation, and the sword of the Spirit, which is the word of God; praying always with all prayer and supplication in the Spirit, being watchful to this end with all perseverance and supplication for all the Saints"—Ephesians 6:10-18

Regardless of what battles we faced or trials we have to go through while we are here on this earth, we are secure in the knowledge that as Christians, we have already won and the game is over. We should live our lives as if this is true.

For whatever is born of God overcomes the world. And this is the victory that has overcome the world—our faith. Who is he who overcomes the world, but he who believes that Jesus is the Son of God? 1 John 5:4-5

STICKS AND STONES

S ticks and stones can break my bones but words will never hurt me. I am rubber. You are glue. What bounces off me, sticks to you. Do you remember hearing or saying that when you were a child? We wanted to believe that was true but we found out that it wasn't. Of course sticks and stones can break your bones but words can break your spirit if you let them. Kids can be so mean especially in using words against each other. Some kids would call me fat boy when I was little because I was overweight. But it was very rare and I don't remember calling other kids names very often. It probably happened but so infrequently that I can't remember any specific incidents. I do remember that as kids we would play the Dozens with each other. This is where you talk about somebody's mother in a derogatory way with each person trying to out do the other. The Dozens was just a game as understood by all participants and it usually did not lead to arguments or fights.

I grew up in a family that liked to tease each other. This was especially true in my father's family of originally thirteen children. I have always looked on the family teasing as harmless fun but if I had a choice as an adult and I do, I would prefer to use words in a positive way. When my grandson, Kai, was little, he was having problems with some of his classmates in elementary school. I thought that it would be a good idea to toughen him up by teasing him and if it bothered him, I would continue until it didn't bother him any more. I figured that when he was teased for real, he could resist the teasing. In looking back, I should have explained to him that words can hurt other people and that he should never say harmful words. And if someone says bad things about him, he should pray for them and remember it is not them but spiritual warfare that he is dealing with.

I remember when I was thirty five years of age and just starting a new job, I was introduced by my supervisor, Evert Strickland PhD, to the staff as someone who comes highly recommended. Dr. Strickland further stated that he knew that I was going to do a fine job for the agency. After hearing those words about me, I tried to live up to his introduction of me and I believe my good work performance was motivated by his words. He only supervised me for one year of the nineteen years that I spent in that agency but those wonderful words of introduction stayed with me for my entire career there and motivated my performance. Another time when I was working in the same agency but for another supervisor, Ronn Perrin, I was given a great written compliment by Ronn. In fact, I have been retired for over nineteen years and I still pull out that compliment and read it from time to time.

Words, good or bad can be written or spoken but mainly they are spoken. In this country we have freedom of speech and we can say anything we want within certain limitations. We can't yell fire in a crowded theater or other public gathering unless there really is a fire. We can't libel someone, writing untruths or slander a person, speaking untruths but just about anything else we can say. I am focusing here on using oral communication to hurt another person. For this, you need to have a tongue. Now Wikipedia encyclopedia describers the tongue as a muscle on the floor of the mouth that manipulates food for chewing and swallowing. It is the primary organ for taste. A secondary function of the tongue is for speech in which the organ assists. In addition to eating and speaking, the tongue is used in expressing sexual affection. The tongue is indeed a very important member of the human body.

But just like almost everything in life, the things we have can be used for either positive or negative objectives. In the Book of James in the Holy Bible, the tongue is described like the rudder of a ship; which is so small but yet so powerful that it can change the direction of a very large ship. James also talks about the fact that speaking good and evil can come from the same mouth. He compares it to a fountain that gives forth both fresh and salt water from the same spring. The problem isn't with the water but from that spring inside of us that is providing the water. That is why it is so important to stock our spring with the living water that our Lord and Savior Jesus Christ can provide us. Therefore, when we give forth water, it will be living water. Jesus has ordered us to follow His commandments and if we do, the words that come out of our mouths will reflect our followership. I have learned over the years that we can never be a whole Christian until our hearts have changed. Then our behavior will mirror what Christ would have us do. Maybe as Christians, people would listen to us if our behavior was not so loud and un Christ like.

For every kind of beast and bird, of reptile and creature of the sea, is tamed and has been tamed by mankind. But no man can tame the tongue. It is an unruly evil, full of deadly poison. With it we bless our God and Father, and with it we curse men, who have been made in the similitude of God. Out of the same mouth proceed blessing and cursing. My Brethren these things ought not to be so. James 3:7-10

SICKNESS AND HEALTH

When I was young and getting married, I didn't think much about the wedding vow of keeping each other in sickness and health. It wasn't that I had never experienced sickness because I had. Before I met my wife, I had hurt my back and until this day, I don't know how. My back would bother me sometime to the extent that I could hardly walk. I was in my middle twenties and I knew that I could not choose a job that involved any kind of labor. That is why I was motivated to finish college and find a sedentary job. When I graduated, I applied for a job as a caseworker for Aid for the Aged in the State of Ohio. This job had no physical demands but after working for about a couple of weeks, I came down with the flu. I have never been so acutely sick before or since. I was having tremendous night sweats and had to be off work for several days. I became concerned about my job security but in fact, I had nothing to be concerned about. Even though I was still on probation, I had a legitimate illness and had a doctor's excuse to give to my supervisor, Mrs. Redman, who I remember with much fondness as a very nice person.

When I was married about two and one half years later, I had forgotten all about that period of sickness and when I took those vows about sickness and health, I didn't think about ever being sick again. Before I married, I would watch what I was eating and periodically try to exercise. During this time, exercise was not as popular as it is today and if you were running on the public street, someone might make fun of you by calling you by the name of some famous athlete such as Jim Brown. After I married, I stopped eating healthy and quit exercising. My wife was built on the slender side and she ate healthy foods like plenty of green vegetables and fruits. I remember that when we popped popcorn, I would take fistfuls and she would take one kernel at a time. She finally had to take fistfuls of popcorn to be able to get her share. It has been said that when two people marry, they begin to share habits and they become more alike. It is true that my wife grabs more popcorn and makes sure she gets her half of the pizza, but for the most part she kept her good eating habits. And unfortunately, I did not develop her good habits, but rather my bad habits became worse.

She has one habit that I gradually adopted over the years which was to develop a faith in my Lord and Savior, Jesus Christ. I thank God for her witness to me especially through her behavior over the years. But I could not follow her direction in developing good eating habits. My inability to do this finally caught up with me and I was first diagnosed with high blood pressure, later with diabetes and then prostate cancer. I have been hospitalized three times over the past ten to twelve years. During this time my wife has faithfully watched over and cared for me. It has been difficult for her because my health conditions became chronic rather than acute. At times, she has even had to bathe me because I didn't have the energy to do it myself. She has prepared my meals and even brought them up to my room. She has done all of this while having to attend to her ninety year old mother who lives nearby. In addition, my brother and sister have taken me to the doctor and gone with me to assist in my exercise program.

In looking back, I wonder if my wife knew what she was getting into. I began to look at her as indestructible and expected her to be there when I needed her. She was telling me that she wasn't Superwoman but I just didn't listen. Last week, I noticed her sitting in the living room when I thought that she had gone to her mother's apartment. I asked her why she was still here and she responded by saying that she felt a little ill. I went upstairs to my bedroom to watch television and the next thing I heard was her telling me that she had to go to the hospital. I drove her to the hospital and this was unusual because she always drives me when we travel. When we got to the hospital, she needed a wheelchair to go to the emergency room. Her heart was beating at an unusually fast rate and it could have caused a possible stroke if not treated. The hospital administered treatment and fortunately her heart returned to its normal beat. She was examined thoroughly while being hospitalized for two nights and two days.

I am so grateful to God for allowing her to come home from the hospital in better condition then when she entered last week. I am trying to do more things for myself and for her when I can. I do love her very much.

Husbands, love your wives, just as Christ also loved the church and gave Himself for her, that He might sanctify and cleanse her with the washing of water by the word, that He might present her to Himself a glorious church, not having spot or wrinkle or any such thing, but that she should be holy and without blemish. So husbands ought to love their own wives as their own bodies; he who loves his wife loves himself. Ephesians 5:25-28

WEAK BUT STRONG

When I was in the Marines, I was strong, trim and fit. I have walked one hundred miles in five days with a full pack including rifle and sleeping bag. I have unloaded railroad cars filled with ammunition loaded in crates. We Marines would stand shoulder to shoulder with our bare chests and unload these crates of ammunition by passing them along at shoulder level from one marine to another in a rapid and competitive manner. I was strong physically but never as strong as my brother, Doug. This guy was born naturally strong and didn't need the Marines to build him up. When I was home on my first furlough from the Marine Corps, We got into our usual argument and he picked me up and threw me across the room. I had forgotten that I had lost weight while in boot camp training and I was now easier to pick up and throw. After being discharged from the service, I could walk over five miles at a time easily and could jog three or more miles without getting tired. Shortly after that, I remember that back pain gave me the first notice that my body was headed down hill. I don't recall any particular incident that contributed to my back pain; it just began to bother me.

I could be lying in bed, knowing that I could not get up immediately even if the house was on fire. I never complained or saw a doctor about it but just took the pain for granted. However, one time I went to my brother and told him that maybe I had cancer in my back. I don't know why I said this. Maybe it was the pressure I was feeling in trying to graduate from college. Over the years, as I became older and gained more weight, I started to feel weaker. I couldn't jog as fast anymore and I couldn't lift heavy objects like I could in the past. One time I was at church helping to set up chairs and tables and forgot that I should not be doing that. The next day, my back began to hurt badly and I realized what I had done to cause the pain. In 1991, I was diagnosed with prostate cancer and began treatment with radiation and chemical therapy. This treatment was successful in dealing with the cancer but caused my body to feel weaker. I was also dealing with high blood pressure and diabetes and these conditions affected my ability to do the physical activities that I was previously able to do, such as playing basketball and walking two or three miles at a time. I am sure that others have also experienced this problem.

We all get older and weaker in time but not at the same time in our lives. Some people take better care of themselves and the Lord's grace and mercy extends to each of us in different ways. But knowing that I am weaker than I previously was, I believe that I am stronger in some ways than when I was young. **In 2 Corinthians 12:7-8,** the Apostle Paul talks about the thorn that has been given to him and he asked three times that it be removed. **In verse 9,** Paul receives his answer from Jesus; **"My grace is sufficient for you, for My power is made perfect in weakness."** This verse sums up exactly how I feel about my physical condition. Our strength doesn't come from us being in excellent physical condition or being young, pretty or handsome. Our strength comes from the power inside of us given by a gracious, merciful and loving God. Remember the story about Samson and Delilah that was portrayed in Cecil B. DeMille's movie titled Samson and Delilah released in 1949 and starring Victor Mature and Hedy Lamarr. This story of Samson and Delilah was adapted from the Book of Judges in the Holy Bible. This movie was highly successful but to understand the real story about Samson and Delilah, you should read the account of it in the Book of Judges Chapters 13-16.

Samson was born with the gift of strength given by God as long as he never cut his hair. He was an Israelite born into Israel dominated by the Philistines. As Samson grew older he became a threat to the Philistines, eventually killing many of them in battles. In the 16th chapter of the Book of Judges, Samson meets and falls in love with Delilah, a Philistine. The Philistines wanted to find out the secret of Samson's strength and used Delilah to help them in this effort. After many attempts, Delilah finally finds out the secret, which is in Samson long hair. After she entices him to fall asleep, she has someone come and cut off his hair. When he awakens, he is bound like in previous attempts; but this time he is unable to free himself. He is blinded in both eyes and forced to work as a grinder in the prison. During his imprisonment, his hair begins to grow back. The Philistines were celebrating the capture of Samson and rejoicing to their gods; and during their celebration, they called for Samson to perform for them. They stationed him between the pillars that hold up the temple and Samson prayed for God to give him his strength back so he could take vengeance on the Philistines. God gave him his strength back and that day Samson was able to kill all of the Philistines in the temple and himself by pushing these supporting pillars down and destroying the temple.

As I look back over the years, the weaker my body, the stronger my spirit. **My strength lies in God and not in me**

And lest I should be exalted above measure by the abundance of the revelations, a thorn in the flesh was given to me, a messenger of satan to buffet me, lest I be exalted above measure. Concerning this thing I pleaded with the Lord three times that it might depart from me. And He said to me, "My grace is sufficient for you, for My strength is made perfect in weakness." Therefore most gladly I will rather boast in my infirmities, that the power of Christ may rest upon me. Therefore I take pleasure in infirmities, in reproaches, in needs, in persecutions, in distresses, for Christ's sake. For when I am weak, then I am strong. 2 Corinthians 12:7-10

Money Honey

W ell the landlord rang my front door bell. I let it ring for a long long spell. I went to the window and peeped through the blinds. I asked him to tell me what was on his mind. He said money honey, money honey, money honey if you want to get along with me. These are the lyrics from an early 1950's song by Clyde McPhatter and the Drifters titled Money Honey which focused on the importance of money in our society. There have been many things said about money and one is that money is the root of all evil. In truth, the correct quotation is from the **Holy Bible, 1st Timothy 6:10** and it states; **"For the love of money is a root of all kinds of evil, for which some have strayed from the faith in their greediness, and pierced themselves through with many sorrows."** Money itself can be a very useful tool to provide for our needs and the needs of others. When money is loved for it's sake only then it becomes an idol. The Bible states that you can't have two masters at the same time; **"No one can serve two masters; for either he will hate the one and love the other, or else he will be loyal to the one and despise the other. You can not serve God and mammon."** Matthew 6:24

Money is very important to most human beings but to some, it is the number one thing in their life. Some people will rob and kill other people, including their relatives for money. They will lie, con and scheme others to obtain as much money as they can. Husbands, wives, brothers, sisters, parents, children and friends have been known to fall out over money and develop irreconcilable differences with each other. There was a carpet installer who took $400.00 dollars of my money as a down payment on new carpet but he failed to deliver the carpet. When confronted about this, he promised to get the carpet but he never did. I didn't pursue the matter in court and finally gave up trying to get my money. As I am writing this, I do not remember his name. I am grateful to God that He has given me the ability to forgive and forget this injustice. When my father died in 1973, he did not have a will so my brother, sister and I completed the necessary legal papers to assure that my mother retained possession of the family home. At that time, I told my mother that she ought to make a will and ultimately leave her house to my sister, Alice, because both my brother and I had a house. My sister had continued to live off and on with my mother and had never bought a house. My mother asked me at the time; "Did I think my brother, Doug, would mind." I boldly answered for him by saying; "You know Doug wouldn't mind since he has always been so generous to all of us."

As it turned out, my sister moved back home with my mother and became her primary caregiver. When my mother died in 1994, my sister found her will and she had left everything to her. I remember my sister saying that the house belonged not only to her but to my brother and me. I told my sister that I appreciated her feelings on this matter but this house belonged to her alone. The relationship between my sister, brother and me is priceless and there is no amount of money that could ever come between us. Although most of my wife's and my income come from my retirement, my wife has possession of our checkbook. A few years ago, after retiring from the bookstore, she started working on an intermittent basis for the Ohio Department of Taxation. She earns a salary and deposits it in her own checking account in which I am listed as a co-owner. In other words, she has two checkbooks, ours and hers. We have no problem about how money is spent. I am boss as everyone knows but what she says always goes. Over the years, I have learned to trust in my wife's judgment. She has saved me a number of times from making a bad decision. In fact, she advised me against giving the carpet installer the $400.00 dollars but I decided not to listen to her. I did take her advice when I decided to put the matter behind me and I have never regretted doing so.

Money is a wonderful tool to have if we use it for the glory of God. When we are providing for our family and supporting various charities and contributing to a church practicing Christ's values, we are using money in a way that is consistent with Jesus' commandment to love God and each other. But when money and its pursuit comes between our relationship with God, this is when we are worshipping an idol and not our Lord and Savior, Jesus Christ. In **Matthew 19:24,** Jesus says *"And* *again I say to you, it is easier for a camel to go through the eye of a needle than for a rich man to enter the kingdom of God."*

"Do not labor for the food which perishes, but for the food which endures to everlasting life, which the Son of Man will give you. Because God the Father has set His seal on Him." John 6:27

DREAM BABIES

D ream Babies was the title of a song in a Broadway musical that my nephew, Douglas Grant was in when he was eleven years old in 1970. The show was titled "The Me Nobody Knows," based on a book with the same title, edited by Stephen M. Joseph with music by Gary William Friedman and lyrics by Will Holt. The Dream Babies' song lyrics ask the question of "What do you do in your dreams? Do you fly?" Are you trying to reach the sky? I have had dreams of being able to fly and was quite disappointed when I awakened and realized that I could not fly. When I sleep, I have a tendency to dream quite a lot. Unfortunately, when I wake up I am sometimes unable to remember what my dream was all about. I would dream in the past about not being prepared for my upcoming college tests. And in my dream, I am starting out at the beginning of the semester and I plan to keep up with all of my assignments and not fall behind. But something prevents me from going to class and the test is coming up soon and I am not prepared. Then I wake up to find that not only have I graduated from college but I have been retired from my job for over eighteen years. This same dream would occur periodically but I haven't had it in some time.

The fact that I did not do as well in college as I should was something I needed forgiveness. The Lord had already forgiven me but I could not forgive myself. I prayed to the Lord to allow me to forgive myself and my dreams about failing in school have stopped. Another dream I had was about getting into an argument with someone and would wake up with a headache and my heart beating fast. The further I grew in my Christian walk, the less I experienced these dreams where I had confrontations with some imaginary person or persons. Sometimes I would have negative dreams trying to appeal to my old nature but my new nature is now beginning to dominate my spirit and save me from the effects of the evil one. I have spoken before about grieving over the passing of my little son, I dreamed that my son told me to let him go

241

and stop grieving over him. I believe that this was a message from God and I did obey the recommendations in my dream.

If I could have only written down what all my dreams were about, I might have been able to write some good stories about them since I have had some very interesting dreams. On one occasion, I dreamed that I had broken up with my girl friend and now wanted to get back together with her but she didn't want any part of me. I was very sad in my dream about our breakup and thought I had lost her forever. Well much to my surprise I awoke to find my girlfriend next to me in bed and she had been my wife for over thirty five years. This was one dream that had a happy ending. I have no idea of why people dream a lot and others barely dream at all. I do know that I find I have a tendency to dream more if I have eaten than when I go to bed on an empty stomach. Also, I generally dream about a subject that is on the television, when it is kept on while I am sleeping.

Sometimes I have a difficult time in keeping my mind focused on things above in God's Kingdom rather than on things below of this world. And these negative thoughts pop into my head not only while I am awake but also when I am sleeping. I know it is always a spiritual battle for my mind but I realize that I can't have two thoughts in my mind at the same time. Here is a scripture that has helped me to focus on Christian thoughts: **"Finally brethren, whatever things are true, whatever things are noble, whatever things are just, whatever things are pure, whatever things are lovely, whatever things are of good report, if there is any virtue and if there is anything praiseworthy— meditate on these things." Philippians 4:8**

There are also dreams that we have while we are awake. When Martin Luther King Jr. gave his "I have a dream" speech he was talking about a vision of everyone respecting and honoring the diversity in this country. I was recently talking to my grandson, Kai, and I told him don't ever let anyone tell you that you can't achieve your dreams I told him to aim high because as the Christian author, Chuck Swindel says: **"Your attitude determines your altitude."** I told my grandson that he has to have a goal or dream. Then he has to develop a plan to acquire it. And finally, he has to work as hard as he can to achieve it. Once he has done all of this, **God will do the rest.**

Therefore we also, since we are surrounded by so great a cloud of witnesses, let us lay aside every weight, and the sin which so easily ensnares us, and let us run with endurance the race that is set before us, looking into Jesus, the author and finisher of our faith, who for the joy that was set before Him endured the cross, despising the shame, and has sat down at the right hand of the throne of God Hebrews 12:1-2

Chapter Ten:
SPIRITUAL GROWTH

Faith

Grace and Mercy

Mirror, Mirror

Jesus is Love

Perfect Peace

Half and Half

Praise and Worship

Extra, Extra

FAITH

Today is October 8, 2009 and I have just left my urologist, Dr. Errol Singh, who has treated me for prostate cancer since November, 1990. Back then, Dr. Singh told me that it was unnecessary to remove my prostate because my cancer had gone past the prostate. He said that he would treat me initially with radiation and then with chemotherapy. A couple of years ago, Dr. Singh informed me that the chemotherapy did not seem to be working as well as it had in the past. He thought that it would be a good idea for me to be seen by an oncologist. And he referred me to a doctor that I had met years ago when he was just getting ready to enter medical school. In 1971, this future doctor was interning at my place of employment for the summer and would be entering medical school in the fall. He subsequently graduated and then over the years received training in internal medicine, hematology and oncology. His name is William J. Hicks M.D. and I went to see him at The Arthur James Cancer Center of The Ohio State University. He examined me and decided to give me a cat scan and a bone scan. He also scheduled me for a scan of the prostate, a test which was not available when I was first diagnosed.

The test results came back negative for any cancer spreading in my body. I have continued to see both my urologist and my oncologist about every three months. About six months after my P.S.A. had continued to rise, both of my doctors decided to take me off of the chemotherapy I was receiving and see if my P.S.A. would fall. During this period, I was given another set of scans and again the results came back negative for any spread of cancer. During today's visit, Dr. Singh gladly informed me that my P.S.A. blood test had fallen to within normal limits. He then looked me in the eyes and said that it must be God. During my initial diagnosis in November 1990, I had informed Dr. Singh that I was putting my cancer problem in the hands of God. Many years later, which was a few years ago, he had put his arm around my shoulder and asked me what was I still doing here? But as I told him today, God does the healing but he uses wonderful doctors like him to perform his miracles. Dr. Singh like all of us has a great opportunity to work for the glory of God through healing and comforting those in need.

When I was initially diagnosed, my wife ministered to me and said that we were going to attack this problem from a spiritual point of view. She called my diagnosis "Spiritual Warfare." This was the beginning of putting my faith into practice. Unlike the Apostle Paul who was converted on the road to Damascus, my conversion was a gradual process. It started in earnest after my seven old son died in 1978 of unknown causes. I started listening to gospel music and attending bible study. In 1980 my wife and I opened a Christian book store which was her idea but I was her helper whose faith was still developing. I kept growing as a Christian and I believe that I still have a long way to go. But I firmly know who my Savior is and where my help comes from. I never thought that I would get to the point that I would think of cancer as a blessing. But in the Book of James, the writer talks about considering it all joy when you undergo trials and tribulations. He says that you are being tested and that the testing will perfect you.

I know that I have been tested and my faith in God and Jesus Christ as my savior is very strong. **"Now faith is the substance of things hoped for, the evidence of things not seen." Hebrews 11:1** The dictionary talks about faith as being a firm belief in something for which there is no proof. My faith in Jesus Christ has been a gradual process. I have been attending church on and off since I was a child. I joined church in 1967 and was baptized a few months before I was married over forty two years ago. I first began to deal with my mortality in 1963 after the death of Ernie Davis, the first African American Heisman Trophy Winner from Syracuse University. I thought that if this guy so young and strong could get sick and die than so could I. During all of this time I still attended church but did not consider myself a strong believer. After my son died, I began to remember the story of Job that I had studied in college so many years ago. God agreed to let the devil test Job's faith for God. Despite being stripped of all of his possessions and children, Job kept his faith for God.

The Bible talks about the faith of Abel, Enoch, Noah, Abraham, Sarah, Isaac, Jacob, Joseph, Moses and others in Hebrews and other

Books of the Bible. They were all tested and able to accomplish impossible tasks that could only be achieved through faith in God.

Jesus said to him, *"If you can believe, all things are possible to him who believes."* Immediately the father of the child cried out and said with tears, "Lord, I believe; help my unbelief!" Mark 9:23-24

GRACE AND MERCY

O ver the years, I have asked myself, what is the difference between grace and mercy. I have heard the terms used especially in religious conversations but I really could not distinguish between the two. I just recently saw a Christian quotation that briefly defined and compared the two words as follows: **"Grace is getting what you don't deserve and mercy is not getting what you do deserve."** Remember the famous hymn titled "Amazing Grace." It was written by John Newton on May 10, 1748. In the lyrics, he describes himself as a wretch who was saved by grace: "He once was lost but now is found. He was blind but now can see."

I can especially understand what it means to be physically blind. Well maybe not completely blind but blind in one eye. For years I never had my eyes examined and when I finally did, I discovered that I was losing sight in my left eye. This condition persisted until I was completely blind in that eye. I could not see anything but only distinguish between light and darkness. My ophthalmologist, Richard Lembach M.D. suggested that I undergo a cornea transplant and removal of a cataract. I had the surgery in 2006 and the vision in my left eye is now excellent. From a physical standpoint, I can truly say that I was blind but now I can see. From a spiritual point of view, the cataract blinding my heart and separating me from Jesus was removed by grace in the early nineteen eighties.

But getting back to John Newton, he had endured many trials and tribulations as a youth, before becoming the captain of a slave ship. One time when traveling home, the ship encountered a violent storm and it seemed that it would sink. John prayed for mercy from the Lord and the storm subsequently subsided. John believed that the Lord had saved him through grace. From that time on, John Newton always thought of the day of the storm as the day he came to Christ. He still continued in the slave trade for some time after but he began to treat the slaves under his control more compassionately. His conversion was gradual and eventually he became a minister after educating himself. It took about forty years before he directly opposed the slave trade. In 1780, at a church he was serving, he met and had the opportunity to influence William Wilberforce, who became a leader in the battle against slavery. In fact, Wilbeforce University in the State of Ohio is named after him.

The origin of Amazing Grace's melody is not known for sure. But it is highly speculated that it may have come from a tune the slaves were singing. When I would sing this song in church before I had truly accepted the Lord as my Savior, I always thought that I am not a wretch like that described in the lyrics. But in looking back I realized that I was a lost blind wretch who through God's grace, I was now saved. I needed God to clean me up and make me presentable in his sight. Sometimes we don't come to God because we want to try and clean ourselves up or we have a value standard that says we are ok. There was a self help book written in 1969, by Thomas A. Harris M.D. titled I'm Ok, You're Ok, which in 1972 became a best seller. However, the Bible tells us we are not ok because all have sinned against God and fallen short of His law. Jesus Christ came to be a sacrifice to atone for our sins and to reconcile us back to God. We Christians look to Jesus as the standard of perfection on which to guide us in making life decisions. **Jesus Christ is indeed the way and the truth and the life.**

The Old Testament was originally written in Hebrew and the New Testament written in Greek. When looking for the meaning of words in the Bible it is advisable to go to the Hebrew or Greek translation of the word you are looking up. Both grace and mercy are legal terms found throughout the Bible. Generally speaking, grace means doing something for others when they don't deserve it and mercy means holding back the judgment that one does deserve. God extends grace and mercy to us each day by continuing to give us life and everything we need to sustain that life. I have been in pain from a headache or a stomach problem and have asked the lord for relief from my pain and he has always answered my prayers. Do I deserve relief from my pain? If I do, what have I done to deserve it? What the Lord does for me is always through grace and mercy. His gift of salvation to me is because of His grace toward me and not because of anything that I have done.

My father always said that he didn't believe that God made a man just to destroy him. One of the big unanswered questions for non believers is what happens to us after we die. The Bible gives those who have accepted Christ as our Lord and Savior the answer. Christ has gone to prepare a place for us and when it is our time, He will come and take us to be with Him.

"Let not let your heart be troubled; you believe in God, believe also in Me. In my Father's house are many mansions; if It were not so, I would have told you. I go to prepare a place for you. And if I go and prepare a place for you, I will come again and receive you to Myself; that where I am, there you may be also. And where I go you know, and the way you know." Thomas said to him, "Lord, we do not know where You are going, and how can we know the way?" Jesus said to him, "I am the way, the truth, and the life. No one comes to the Father except through Me." John 14:1-6

MIRROR, MIRROR

When I was a little boy, I remember watching the movie called Snow White and the Seven Dwarfs. Snow White's mother, the queen dies and her father, the king remarries a beautiful woman who becomes Snow White's stepmother. The new queen was very wicked and jealous of Snow White's beauty. Snow White was indeed a beautiful child and continued to grow more beautiful as time passed. A handsome young prince was riding by the castle one day and saw her and fell in love. This angered the stepmother and she went to a special mirror in her house that would tell only the truth. The increasing beauty of Snow White, prompted the stepmother to periodically ask the mirror the following question: "Mirror, mirror on the wall. Who is the fairest of them all." The mirror always answered back that the stepmother was the fairest of them all and this was true because at that time the stepmother was prettier than any other in the Kingdom.

Snow White continued to grow and she finally reached the age of eighteen. After Snow White's eighteenth birthday, the queen again asked the mirror; "Mirror, mirror on the wall who is the fairest of them all." This time the mirror replied; "You are fair my queen. Yet fairer still is Snow White. She is fairest of them all. "The stepmother became angry and arranged to have Snow White killed but the person assigned the job could not do it. He told Snow White to run away and hide. She found a cottage where seven dwarfs lived and moved in with them. The stepmother asked the mirror again who was the fairest but the mirror repeated that Snow White was the fairest. The stepmother now knew that Snow White was still alive and she decided to find and kill her. She found the cottage and disguised as an old woman she gave Snow White a poisoned apple to eat. Snow White ate the apple and was apparently dead when the prince found her in a coffin at the dwarfs' cottage. The prince kissed her and she awakened. They were married and lived happily ever after.

When I was a young man attending Ohio University in 1955, I would go and meet friends at the John C. Baker Student Center on Friday and Saturday nights. Sometimes I would have a date or go there with a buddy of mine. I would always go to the bathroom first to see how I looked. As usual, I thought I looked pretty good. I was eighteen years of age when I entered Ohio University. If I was with a buddy, he would admire himself in the mirror as well. Years later in 1991 I returned to the University for a reunion of the African American alumni. As I did in the old days, I first went to the bathroom but this time because I needed to. As I was washing my hands, I looked in the mirror and saw that not only had the mirror itself aged but I looked a lot older than I looked back in 1955. Of course I already knew this but looking into this particular mirror had a great impact on reinforcing the fact that I had also aged a lot.

This reminded me of a scripture in the Book of James that states: **"But be doers of the word and not hearers only, deceiving yourselves. For if anyone is a hearer of the word and not a doer, he is like a Man observing his natural face in a mirror; for he observes himself, goes away, and immediately forgets what kind of man he was. But he who looks into the perfect law of liberty and continues in it, and is not a forgetful hearer but a doer of the work, this one will be blessed in what he does." James 1:22-25** I know that this scripture speaks loudly about me and my behavior. I am often reminded of my shortcomings and the areas where I can improve upon in my life. I just heard a sermon yesterday by my pastor, Rich Nathan that tells us Jesus wants us to help the poor. The message was that instead of buying that $40,000 automobile, we should maybe spend less on a car and give some of our money to help the poor in this country and around the world. The example of Mother Teresa was given when she said: "If you can't feed a hundred people, then just feed one." **We can all do something to help.**

A lot of us think that we are good persons and according to this world, we probably are. We aren't killing or robbing anyone. And we aren't beating people up or lying all of the time when we are asked questions. We think that we are probably good in God's sight. But the Word of God surpasses all understanding and while we can admire the honesty in the Snow White fable's mirror of truth, the mirror was limited in the truth it could tell (who is the fairest). Unlike this fable,

Christ is the complete truth teller. He is the way, the truth and the life and His sacrifice on the cross gives eternal life to those who have accepted him as their Lord and Savior. Our prince is not an ordinary prince but the Prince of Peace or the Word as described in John 1:1. Jesus Christ through the Word tells us what He expects from us and through prayer and listening to the Holy Spirit, we can find the truth.

In the beginning was the Word, and the Word was with God, and the Word was God. He was in the beginning with God. All things were made through Him, and without Him nothing was made that was made. In Him was life, and the life was the light of men. John 1:1-4

Jesus Is Love

On December 29, 1993, my wife and I were at Doctors Hospital North awaiting the birth of our grandson, Kai Lee. The doctors decided to do a C Section so we had an idea when he would be born. We were down in the cafeteria when we received the message to come back up to the waiting room. Then the little fellow entered this world. The next thing we saw was his father carrying him across the hall where they dressed him in a blue outfit with a little blue munchkin cap. The nurse rolled up his pants leg and gave him a shot which caused him to give out a big yell. We took him home to my house while his mother recuperated. Everybody wanted to hug and hold him. I went out and bought a movie camera so I could take pictures of these precious moments. He was a good eater and would always open his mouth when food was placed in front of it.

At an early age, he seemed to be musically inclined. He loved to dance, act and sing. He would imitate the characters in the Barney and Psalty videos. My wife had bought him a toy piano which he loved to pretend that he was playing. I had also begun to teach him the lyrics of some of the great music written prior to World War Two. We then decided to give him piano lessons at the age of three and he has been taking them for over twelve years. He also loves to sing and I taught him the lyrics of many songs including "After You're Gone." He then recorded the song on cassette tape. He says that he wants to major in music when he goes to college. He has always seemed to have a love for singing and the ability to play the piano. He has performed in school plays, musicals, piano competitions and his church choir. He is doing very well as a student in school and hopefully will have a number of options when he chooses a career.

One day, when he was about ten years and I was picking him up from school, he had an angry expression on his face. I asked him what was wrong and he told me that he hated one of his schoolmates. I guess this particular boy had been giving him some problems from time to time. I told him that he should not hate anyone but love everyone. I informed him that Jesus Christ had summed up the Ten Commandments into Two Commandments. The first was to love The Lord God with all your heart, soul and mind and the second was to love your neighbor as you love yourself. My grandson then asked me "What if you don't love yourself?" The question initially caught me by surprise but I was able to respond quickly. I told him that if you love God with all your heart, soul and mind then you will love yourself.

In a book titled The Four Loves, the famous Christian writer, C.S. Lewis, writes about the Christian view of the use of the word love. He lists the four types of love as affection (storge), friendship (phila), Eros (erotic) and Charity (agape). The first three loves all have conditions for the love being given or received. The first two words, "affection and friendly" love is between family and friends who share a strong interest between each other. The city of brotherly love, Philadelphia, Pennsylvania, received its name from the word "Philia." "Eros" is erotic or sexual love between two human beings. This love can be good or bad depending on how it is used. The love that I was talking about with my grandson is Charity as described in 1 Corinthians Chapter 13 of the King James Version of the Bible. This love is called **"agape"** in the Greek language. Agape is unconditional love that one person has for another and C.S. Lewis describes this love as the greatest of all the loves.

My grandson was told about the different kinds of love and seemed to understand that of all the loves compared above, unconditional love (agape) is the love the Apostle Paul was describing in 1 Corinthians Chapter 13. There is a Christian song, written some years ago and recorded by Lionel Ritchie and the Commodores, titled "Jesus Is Love." This song accurately describes who Jesus is. Jesus, himself, summed up the ten commandments into two.

But when the Pharisees heard that He had silenced the Sadducees, they gathered together. Then one of them, a lawyer, asked Him a question, testing Him, and saying, "Teacher, which is the great commandment in the law?" Jesus said to him, "You shall love the Lord your God with all your heart, with all your soul, and with all your mind. This is the first and great commandment. And the

second is like it: "You shall love your neighbor as yourself. On these two commandments hang all the Law and the Prophets." Matthew 22:34-40

PERFECT PEACE

This morning I awakened to the startling news that President Barack Obama had won the Nobel Prize for peace. He is the third sitting American president to win the peace prize. The other presidential Nobel Peace Prize winners were President Theodore Roosevelt and President Woodrow Wilson. President Jimmy Carter won the prize as an ex president. Obama is the third African American to win the peace prize. The first was Ralph Bunche who won it in 1950 and Martin Luther King Jr. won it in 1964. President Obama has only been in office for about nine months so his selection was a complete surprise. I thought he had a good chance of eventually wining the peace prize someday but I didn't think that it would be this soon. How wining the Nobel Peace Prize will help President Obama with his political agenda is still a mystery but I don't believe that it can hurt him. The President is currently being advised by his staff on what strategy to use in the Afghanistan war.

Ever since Barack Obama came on the scene, he has been an outspoken supporter of peace. In fact, he was against the war in Iraq, when he was still a state legislator in the State of Illinois. He spoke about diplomacy as an alternative to war during the presidential campaign. There is no doubt there has been a change of tone in Washington since the last President, George W. Bush, was in office. Perhaps this was the Nobel Peace Prize Committee's method of trying to support and encourage President Obama's efforts to bring peace to the world. The question is why we as human beings always seem to want to fight each other. From the time of our birth, we are in conflict with others. As toddlers, we are sometimes involved in fights with other toddlers. When I was a youngster, my mother said that she could not travel a block without me getting into a fight. I would pick on other kids and other kids would pick on me. My brother and I would fight each other after our parents had gone to work.

I have been hit in the head with rocks a couple of times when I was a child. As children growing up in Poindexter village, we were always getting into fights. When I was a teenager, there would be fights after high school sporting events. Everyday we read in the newspaper about fights and killings in our communities and throughout the world. In all parts of the world there is always one group of people warring against another. Violence is often portrayed in movies, books, television, and videos because it sells. Unfortunately peace is not a natural characteristic of ours but it seems that violence is. That is why we will honor the peacemakers when we can. Even this award to Obama is bringing out negative comments from some of his political opposition.

In commenting on the award, President Obama is accepting it with humility by saying that he doesn't deserve it in comparing himself with some past peace prize winners. He looks upon this award as symbolically being awarded through him for other people desiring peace including peace dissidents and soldiers fighting in Afghanistan and Iraq. In theory, most people probably want peace but the question is how do we achieve it or can it ever be achieved here on earth. One thing I believe is that human beings are incapable of ever achieving peace without help from our Lord and Savior Jesus Christ. In **Galatians 5:16-26**, the Apostle Paul talks about the Fruit of the Spirit that characterizes a Born Again Christian. Paul tells us to walk in the Spirit because the flesh lusts against the Spirit and the Spirit against the flesh. Since these are contrary to each other, you won't do the works of the flesh if you walk in the Spirit.

The Apostle Paul lists the works of the flesh as: adultery, fornication, uncleanness, idolatry, sorcery, lewdness, hatred, contentions, jealousies, outbursts of wrath, selfish ambitions, dissensions, heresy, envy, murders, drunkenness and revelries. Paul goes on to say that the Fruit of the Spirit is: love, joy, peace, long suffering, kindness, goodness, faithfulness, gentleness, and self control. **In 2nd Corinthians 5:17 Paul tells us: "Therefore, if anyone is in Christ, he is a new creation; old things have passed away; behold, all things have become new.** Peace is one of the fruit of the Spirit. And I believe Christ is the only answer to achieving peace on earth. Jesus said in the Beatitudes: **"Blessed are the peacemakers, for they shall be called sons of God." Matthew 5:9** Our mission as Christians is to spread the word of the gospel as Jesus commanded us to do in Matthew 28:18-20

And Jesus came and spoke to them, saying, *"All authority has been given to me in heaven and on the earth. Go therefore and make disciples of all the nations, baptizing them in the name of the Father and of the Son and of the Holy Spirit, teaching them to observe all things that I have commanded you; and lo, I am with you always, even to the end of the age."* Amen. Matthew 28:18-20

HALF AND HALF

O n Saturday evening November 14, 2009, I was channel surfing
on the television and I turned to the channel where Dr. Charles
Stanley was giving his weekly message. Dr. Stanley is an outstanding
pastor in Atlanta, Georgia and I had listened to his messages many
times in the past. But since I have been attending the Vineyard Church
in Columbus, Ohio where Rich Nathan is the senior pastor, I have not
watched many sermons on television. At first, I thought I would turn
to another channel as I usually do when I see a preacher on television.
It is not that I have anything against watching a television preacher,
it is just that I am satisfied with the messages I am receiving from my
own pastor. But for some reason, I could not change the channel. I
believe the Lord was telling me if I wanted to write about Him, than
I should listen to His word that day. Pastor Stanley began his sermon
by speaking about the expression that sticks and stones can break your
bones but words can never hurt you. He said of course that was not true
because words can hurt you a lot. Pastor Stanley then went on to explore
how we Christians can never be a whole Christian until we are truly
following Christ and His commandments. I received an idea for two
stories, "Sticks and Stones" and "Half and Half." from Pastor Stanley's
message that evening.

I have written "Sticks and Stones" and now I'm in the process of
writing "Half and Half. As I write, the Lord is convincing me to do my
best in becoming a whole Christian person for Him. The more I write
my stories, the more I realize how far I have to go to live my life as He
would want me to live it. In the past, I would have admitted that I am
not the person that Christ wants me to be, but I would have also said
that I am going to work on my faults and try to improve. Today, I still
admit that I am not spiritually where Christ wants me but I now know
that it is impossible for me to improve on my own. I don't have that kind
of strength to do it on my own. I truly need a Savior and that Savior

is Christ Jesus. The flesh that I live in fights against doing what Christ would have me do. That is why I have to give up and give in to Christ Jesus. This is not easy for me or others in my same position; however; **Christ tells us in Philippians 4:13 that we can do all things through Him who gives us strength.**

I remember "Half and Half" from my childhood days as being a creamer used in coffee being one part milk and one part cream. This was a way to cut down on calories when using cream in your coffee. I am also reminded of the old days when milk was delivered in bottles with the cream on top. You would have to shake the bottle so the cream would be distributed evenly throughout the bottle. I would often get the bottle of milk before the cream had been distributed and use the cream for my cereal. Other beverages and food products use the term: "Half and Half" to name their products. Generally, half and half can be a good thing such as the Arnold Palmer drink of half lemonade and half ice tea. There are many examples of many food selections being described as half and half such as Fish and Chips. But half and half is not a good thing to be when describing a Christian. Jesus doesn't want half of us. He wants all of us. He doesn't tell us to half love but to love completely. He doesn't say have some faith. He says to have complete faith. Jesus wants to completely take control over our physical, mental and spiritual life.

Jesus addresses this very issue of lukewarm Christians in The Book of Revelations chapter 3:14-19. He is talking to a financially prosperous group of people who are unfortunately spiritually impoverished. Jesus describes them as neither cold nor hot but lukewarm and says He will vomit them out of His mouth. Unfortunately, many people who described themselves as Christians go to church on Sunday and that is it until next Sunday. They think just because they give to charities and don't sell drugs or rob others, they are good Christian people. Other people tell themselves that they are not perfect but they are better than some other persons. This reminds me of people caught for speeding and complaining to the police officer that there were other drivers speeding faster than them. I remember hearing the testimony of a former pastor when I attended a Christian bookseller's convention one time. The pastor had been caught in adultery and was very remorseful about his act of infidelity. He made a statement about those who profess to be Christians that I have never forgotten. He said that a better name for

Christians should be to call them followers of Christ. Christ wants us to obey His commandments and if we don't than how can we truthfully call ourselves Christians. **In John 14:15,** Jesus says *"If you love me, keep my commandments."*

"I know your works, that you are neither cold nor hot. I could wish you were cold or hot. So then, because you are lukewarm, and neither cold nor hot, I will vomit you out of My mouth." **Revelation 3:15-16**

PRAISE AND WORSHIP

When I first attended the Vineyard Church, I noticed we were spending about thirty minutes before the church sermon on praise and worship. This was new for me as part of a church service. In the past, at other churches, I would hear a church choir sing and listen to a lot of announcements before the sermon began. I could see that this praise and worship service was helping me to focus on my relationship with God. Praising and worshipping God has a way of humbling you by showing you are the clay and He is the Potter. One of the worship songs that I sing is about coming to the Lord unformed and lonely asking Him to form me. If you sincerely ask the Lord to shape and mold you as He wants you, then He will do it. I have enjoyed gospel music for some time but now I also listen to praise and worship music. In the past. I probably placed my emphasis on the music but now my focus is on the lyrics.

It is special to begin your day with praising your Lord and Savior, and reading His Holy Word. This makes your whole day start out on a positive note. When situations arise during the day, you are ready to deal with them on a spiritual basis. Remember, even though we may be Born Again Christians, we still have to deal with the old nature that is trying to pull us down. Our new nature should dominate our thinking and behavior but it needs to be charged and strengthened in the morning after we awaken. Like our cell phones, in order to use them without any problem, they must be charged during the night so they will work properly during the day. Just as I sometimes forget to charge my cell phone, I forget to do my praise and worship. And as my cell phone doesn't always work, my day does not always go as well as it should. This act of beginning my day with prayer, praise, worship and then reading God's word will help me to walk in the Spirit and not fulfill the lust of the flesh.

The question that I have asked myself is what is the difference between praise and worship? According to Webster's Dictionary, worship is paying religious reverence, as in prayer and praise is expressing adoration of and glorifying God. Praise is a part of worshipping God. The Strong's Concordance defines worship as to prostrate oneself before God, bow down, humbly beseech and do obedience or reverence. Praise is defined to revere (with extended hands), laudation, specifically a hymn, to kneel and to bless God. Like love and marriage, praise and worship go together like a horse and carriage. It is only natural that we as human beings offer praise and worship to someone or something we think as being higher than ourselves. The origin of life and its final destination can be a mystery to those who have not accepted Jesus Christ. Of course this is my opinion as a Christian who believes in searching the Holy Bible for answers about the mysteries of life and death.

Another question is why should we do praise and worship? We should do it because we are commanded to do it. **"Oh, worship the Lord in the beauty of holiness! Tremble before Him, all the earth" Psalm 96:9.** Not only in this passage from the Old Testament but throughout the Bible the command is given to worship and give praises to God. In the New Testament, when Satan was trying to get Jesus to worship him instead of God: **Then Jesus said to him, *"Away with you, Satan! For it is written, "You shall worship the Lord your God, and Him only shall you serve." Matthew 4:10*** The Lord wants us to have an abundant life and the way to achieve this is to begin our day by praising and worshipping the Lord. We don't have to spend a long time, maybe just a few minutes. But the main thing is to acknowledge who He is and who we are in relation to Him. **He is in control**. How should we worship God? The Bible tells us that we should worship Him in spirit and truth.

Jesus said to him, *"I am the way, the truth, and the life. No one comes to the Father except through Me." John 14:6* We must first develop a relationship with Jesus Christ by repenting our sins and accepting Him as our Lord and Savior. Then we will be able to worship God in spirit and truth and the evidence of this will be shown in what we say, think and do.

Then Peter said to them, "Repent, and let every one of you be baptized in the name of Jesus Christ for the remission of sins; and you shall receive the gift of the Holy Spirit. For the promise is to you and to your children, and to all who are afar off, as many as the Lord our God will call." Acts 2:38-39

EXTRA EXTRA

As a teenager living on East Long Street in Columbus, Ohio, my parents had the opportunity to subscribe to two daily newspapers. One was the Columbus Citizen formed in 1899 and the other was the Columbus Dispatch with its first issue published on July 1, 1871. The Columbus Citizen was delivered in the morning and the Columbus Dispatch was delivered in the evening. I was a newspaper carrier as a young teenager and I carried both papers at different times during my high school years. During the year I was discharged from the Marines, The Columbus Citizen Journal was formed in 1959 by a merger of the Columbus Citizen and the Ohio Journal. The Ohio Journal had been formed in 1809 and was acquired by the Columbus Dispatch owners at the beginning of the twentieth century. The newly formed Citizen Journal shared printing facilities and all other staff with the Columbus Dispatch. Then after 25 years, The Citizen Journal went out of business with its last paper being printed on December 31, 1985. This occurred, after negotiations for a new operating agreement between the Citizen Journal and the Columbus Dispatch failed. On January 1, 1986, the Columbus Dispatch changed from an evening publication to a morning publication.

The way news is gathered and printed has also changed over the years since I was a little boy living in Poindexter Village. The news stories in the past had to be telephoned in or brought in manually by a reporter. Then it was typed and sent over news wire service or it was set in type with all the other stories and printed for edition. Today our news comes by way of many sources. There are traditional broadcasting companies like NBC, ABC and CBS and also cable outlets like MSNBC, Fox and CNN. "Breaking News" is such a common term because all of the television stations use it. Many times when watching a television program, you will see breaking news scrolled at the bottom of the television screen. Back in the days when newspapers were the primary source of delivering the news, breaking news stories were given to the public by special newspaper editions. These special editions were sold by newspaper boys who attracted buyers for these extra paper editions by shouting:" **Extra! Extra! Read All About It.**" This was their way of letting the public know that something big had just happened.

There are all kinds of news, good and bad. It you want to know what sin is, just pick up a newspaper to read or turn on the radio or television. If you have the internet, you will see many examples of sin even as or shortly after it occurs. But these media outlets also give us some good news from time to time. Just the other day, I was watching Kareem Abdul Jabbar, the great former college and NBA basketball player. Kareem talked about recently being diagnosed with leukemia. Now, this was bad news but when he said this condition was manageable through medical treatment, this was good news. In fact, Kareem said that he was happy to receive this good news. He said that his son Amir is a medical student and has been helping him understand this disease. I was sorry to get the bad news about his illness but was happy to receive the good news that he wasn't in imminent danger of losing his life. As I listened to Kareem's news, I thought back to the time when I was diagnosed with prostate cancer over nineteen years ago. I was given my bad news on a Friday night just before leaving work and I didn't have any good news at that time of being able to survive physically. **But I did have the good news of surviving spiritually**

But about ten years before my diagnosis, I had begun the process of turning my life over to Christ and had received the greatest **"Good News"** that could be given to anyone. This is the news that I would like to share with anyone else willing to listen. This news is about the free gift of salvation given to us by God and paid for by the sacrifice of the body and blood of His Son, Jesus Christ, over two thousand years ago on a cross at Calvary. The first man, Adam, did not obey God and through his disobedience, caused his descendents to be separated from God. As a result of this separation from God, man has been doomed to suffer and die in this world ever since. From the moment of being conceived, man has a sinful nature as the Bible says:" **For all have sinned and fall short of the glory of God."** **Romans 3:23** But there is yet breaking good news for us all. **Extra Extra read all about it:**

"For God so loved the world that He gave His only begotten Son, that whoever believes in Him should not perish but have everlasting life. For God did not send His Son into the world to condemn the world, but that the world through Him might be saved. He who believes in Him is not condemned; but he who does not believe is condemned already, because he has not believed in the name of the only begotten Son of God." John 3:16-18

Chapter Eleven:
SPIRITUAL BLESSINGS

DARKNESS AND LIGHT

When I was a little boy, people were still using the horse and buggy as a means of transportation and to deliver goods in this country. Our milkman delivered milk to our apartment in Poindexter Village in a horse and wagon. Commercial aviation was still in its infancy and the radio was used widely throughout America for information and entertainment. Instead of using the internet to send messages, we had to write letters and send telegrams. There were telephones and electric refrigerators but we didn't have them. We had an icebox that was kept cool by a block of ice delivered by the iceman. There was no television but we would watch cartoons and Joe Louis' fights with an 8 millimeter movie projector using the icebox and later the refrigerator as a movie screen. There were very few automobile owners that lived in Poindexter Village and we didn't get one until 1949. Although, it sometimes seems like I was born in the middle ages compared to today with all of our electronic marvels, we did have the electric light bulb. Our apartments, workplaces and streets were all lighted up for our use and enjoyment.

Before the invention of electricity, we people have always had the sun, moon and the stars to provide us with light. This was God's gift to us. **"In the beginning God created the heavens and the earth. The earth was without form, and void; and darkness was on the face of the deep. And the Spirit of God was hovering over the face of the waters. Then God said, "Let there be light;" and there was light. And God saw the light that it was good; and God divided the light from the darkness. God called the light day and the darkness He called night. So the evening and the morning were the first day." Genesis 1:1-5**

For practical purposes the history of modern lighting can begin with Alva Thomas Edison. The invention of the electric light bulb is credited to him in 1879 and it functioned as an electric lamp in which an electric current is used to heat a filament in a light bulb to incandescence. Thomas Edison was of course not the only person involved in inventing artificial light but he is given the credit for inventing our modern lighting system. Before Edison's electric light bulb, gas was used to light our way at night. Remember the movies showing lamplighters moving through the town lighting the lamps on the streets so people could find their way in the darkness. There were others involved in the power struggle to control the use and spread of what we now know of as modern electricity but Thomas Edison and his companies became the dominant figures in developing electric lights and electricity.

Edison did more than just invent the electric light bulb; he was able to deliver this system of electricity from power stations to homes, government and business in a way that enables us to live as we do today. Today, the incandescent light bulb is being replaced by fluorescent lights and other improvements to improve conservation and efficiency. Alva Thomas Edison also had over 1000 patents with the first in 1868 which was a vote counter to speed up proceedings in congress. His first successful invention was the stock ticker and he also developed the first phonograph. Remember that movie projector that our family used to watch cartoons and Joe Louis' fights; Edison was also instrumental in its invention. In 1928, Edison received the Congressional Gold Medal for his inventions that have provided so much use and service to United States citizens in the nineteenth and early twentieth centuries. Alva Thomas Edison was born on February 11th 1847 and died at age 84 on October 18th 1931.

I have always known light as I know it today or have I? The Light that I know today is not the electric light I knew since my birth. Instead it is a spiritual light. This Light that I did not know in the past but I know today is the Light of the World as Jesus describes Himself in John 8:12. In the Book of John chapter 3 verses 19 through 21, Jesus speaks about a situation that is still with us today. Evil people love darkness rather than light because their deeds are evil; *"For everyone practicing evil hates the light and does not come to the light, lest his deeds should be exposed. But he who does the truth comes to the light, that his deeds may be clearly seen, that they have been done in God."* **John 3:20-21**

Then Jesus spoke to them again, saying, *"I am the light of the world. He Who follows me shall not walk in darkness, but have the light of life."* John 8:12

MY HELP

As a child, I can remember my mother taking us to Children's Hospital in order to receive medical check ups. We would put on the little white gowns before being seen by the doctor. She would also take us to The Ohio State University Hospital to receive medical check ups. I don't remember going for these medical visits because we were sick. In fact, I don't remember ever being sick but I probably had my normal childhood illnesses. I believe my brother had pneumonia and one time he had cuts around his eyes because of a broken glass. The only time I remember receiving medical treatment was when I had my tonsils taken out and I believe, I was in my early teens. I did receive a thorough medical and dental check up when I was in the Marines and had work done on my teeth that are still in my mouth today, fifty two years later.

When I was in high school, a friend and classmate of mine, James Willis, had to have an operation. Because of this, it was advisable that he have routine medical checkups. Some years later, after I had finished my military enlistment and graduated from college, we started hanging out together again. It was during this time that he encouraged me to find a physician and start getting yearly checkups. He referred me to his doctor and I started to see a doctor again on a routine basis. Well over the years, I changed doctors and started to see my mother's doctor. It was during one of these checkups, that I discovered that I had high blood pressure. I was thirty six years old at the time. Years later, I was still getting my yearly checkups; however in 1989, for some reason, I missed getting one. Late in 1990, I was working on an important project at my job, but I told myself that I would schedule an appointment with my physician as soon as the project was completed. I had no new medical issues that I knew of but I also knew that I should be receiving yearly medical checkups. When my project was completed I scheduled and kept my appointment.

The doctor examined me thoroughly including an examination of my prostate. This was my first prostate exam and I had just turned fifty three. As he was examining my prostate, he said "This feels like a lump on your prostate." He told me, "It is probably nothing serious and you shouldn't be alarmed." He said that he would refer me to Dr. Errol Singh, a urologist, who would probably give me a blood test called a PSA and after receiving the results Dr. Singh would decide on further action if necessary. It was my first time ever to see a urologist and I was somewhat concerned about the examination. Dr. Singh again felt my prostate and based on what he had examined, he decided to give me a PSA blood test. The PSA results came back abnormal, so the doctor decided to do a biopsy on my prostate. The biopsy is a simple procedure and involves snipping off a small sample of prostate tissue so it can be evaluated to see if cancer cells are present in the sample.

I remember being at work late with everyone in my section gone when the phone rang one Friday evening. On the line was Dr. Singh with the results of my biopsy. He said that my test was positive and I had cancer. He then said that if I needed to talk to him over the weekend I should feel free to call. I asked him why should I call him. He said that I may be upset about what had just happened to me and might need someone to talk it over with. I told him I appreciated his kindness but I would be calling on Jesus Christ in prayer to address my concerns. It has been almost nineteen years since I was first diagnosed and not only have I continued to live but I have lived an abundant life through Jesus Christ. About a year ago Dr. Singh put his arm around my shoulder and asked me "Marshall what are you still doing here?" He has called me his miracle patient. I am here to tell him and everyone else that God is indeed still working miracles. I just recently had my three month check up and my PSA blood test was within normal limits. When giving me the results, Dr. Singh explained what was happening by simply saying that it was God who was doing the healing. I agreed with him but added that God works through wonderful physicians like him who are dedicated to healing the sick and injured. In fact, God can work through us all if we would just make ourselves available.

I will lift up my eyes to the hills—From whence comes my help? My help comes from the Lord, Who made heaven and earth. He will not allow your foot to be moved; He who keeps you will not

slumber. Behold, He who keeps Israel shall neither slumber nor sleep. The Lord is your keeper; the Lord is your shade at your right hand. The sun shall not strike you by day, Nor the moon by night. The Lord shall preserve you from all evil; He shall preserve your soul. The Lord shall preserve your going out and your coming in from this time forth, and even forevermore. Psalm 121:1-8

BIBLE STUDY

My first experience with Bible study began many years ago when I took a course on Old Testament Survey at Ohio University. In this course I studied the Book of Job whose wisdom ministered to me greatly when my son died in 1978. The next time I was in a Bible study class was when my wife and I joined the Rock of Faith Baptist Church. It was there where I first memorized First Corinthians Chapter Thirteen, the love chapter. I also dealt with my son's passing in one of the Bible classes I attended there. While at Rock of Faith, my wife, Delores, started a Bible study group in our home. She had been attending Bible classes for some years at another church in the city and she wanted to share that experience with others. The first book of the Bible we studied was the book of James. I learned so much from James that helped to change my life for the better.

My first experience in teaching a class came after we joined New Salem Baptist Church. A group of senior citizens asked me to be the teacher for their Vacation Bible School class. I was not sure that I could adequately teach the class since my knowledge of the Bible was limited. But I did work as a staff trainer for my agency and was experienced in training adults. But this wasn't work related training, this was Bible study. I prepared as best as I could and then presented the lesson each week for the period assigned for Vacation Bible Study. This class not only helped those in the class but I was able to benefit so much by preparing and presenting the lesson. Well, the seniors enjoyed the class very much and gave me some money to buy ice cream for my family. I donated the money back to the church since I didn't want to profit in any way from my service to the Lord. But I did feel much appreciated.

The next time I taught Bible study was to assist my wife in presenting training for the new members of our church. I assisted her for a couple of times and then was given my own class. I taught new members class for a few years and developed many wonderful relationships with the people in those classes. During this time, I became interested in starting a family Bible study and approached my sister and my brother about doing this. They were not interested initially but later decided to do this with me. My wife suggested that we do the study that I had presented in my new members class. Initially, I didn't want to do this study because I had done it many times. Once we started this study, I realized that I was getting so much more out of it than I had expected. It is amazing how God's word continues to feed us as our appetite for His word grows. We have now been having weekly Bible study together for over two years and our lives have been immensely changed by the Holy Spirit working in our life.

My brother is especially enthusiastic about learning what the Bible tells us. He is always questioning what he reads and will search the Bible, concordance or the internet for answers. He always comes to class with handouts that he has prepared from the internet. He is becoming quite a Bible scholar. He is looking forward to our next topic of study. We are presently studying the Book of Galatians in a detailed manner which tells us that Jesus has set us free from the law to follow Him in spirit and truth. My sister also has benefited from our Bible study. She is now trying to live her life based on the commandments laid down by Jesus Christ. When she is listening to the sermon at church she is amazed at how many times she has already read the passage of scripture the pastor is talking about.

As for me, I continue to benefit greatly from reading my Bible, attending my new church, Vineyard Columbus, participating in my small church group and worshiping God. The Lord Jesus Christ promises us an abundant life if we would just give Him control over our lives. I am living an abundant life and I love it. I thank my wife for being the main instrument used by God to witness to me and others. She always told me that the Lord's word does not go out in vain. My life is living proof that what she said and what the Lord Jesus promised to us believers is so true.

Be diligent to present yourself approved to God, a worker who does not need to be ashamed, rightly dividing the word of truth. 2 Timothy 2:15

I AM FREE

The freedom that we enjoy here in the United States of America can be traced back to the Magna Carta that was developed and written in the year of 1215 in England. The Magna Carta required that King John of England give freemen certain rights and that he understands his power was limited by law. Among these new rights was the writ of habeas corpus which prohibits unlawful imprisonment. This is an important right that we as Americans enjoy today. The Magna Carta had a direct impact on what we call the common law. The common law is defined as case law which comes from judges and court decisions and not from the legislature. When judges are searching how to apply the law to cases that they are presiding over or reviewing, they look to previous case decisions for precedence. They determine how the law was applied to similar facts in other cases. This principle is called "Stare Decisis" and decisions made creating this principle are binding on lower courts. Generally appellate court decisions are binding on lower courts in their jurisdiction. The United States Supreme Court decisions are binding on all courts in the United States because of the principle of Stare Decisis.

The Magna Carta is one of the most important documents in the English speaking world and it led to the principle of constitutional law enjoyed by United States citizens today. Another essential document in our country's history that gave us the freedom we have today is the Declaration of Independence. It was written by Thomas Jefferson, our future third President, and adopted by the Continental Congress on July 4, 1776. The Declaration of Independence stated that the thirteen colonies were now free and independent states and no longer a part of the British Empire. This is why we celebrate the fourth of July as Independence Day in the United States of America. The Declaration of Independence listed the reasons why we were no longer part of the British Empire by stating our grievances and our natural right to revolt against them. The second sentence of the Declaration of Independence has received the most notice as a broad statement on human rights: "**We hold these truths to be self-evident, that all men are created equal, that they are endowed by their Creator with certain unalienable rights that among these are Life, Liberty and the pursuit of Happiness.**"

It is ironic that Thomas Jefferson could so eloquently talk about all men being created equal when he owned people of color as slaves and is thought to have fathered children by his slave, Sally Hemings. But it is evident that he and others of that time did not think of people of color as being human. Despite this irony, the Declaration of Independence has been used as a foundation for the freedom of all people. I understand that President Abraham Lincoln used the Declaration to guide him as he presided over our country during one of its most difficult times in our history. The United States Constitution is the supreme law of the land and was adopted by the Continental Congress on September 17, 1787 in Philadelphia, Pennsylvania and ratified by conventions in each of the states. The Constitution lists the three branches of government as the legislature branch with a House and Senate, the judicial branch led by the Supreme Court and the executive branch led by the President of the United States. The constitution has been amended twenty seven times and the first ten amendments are known as the Bill of Rights. The second amendment is being discussed today by those who don't want any restrictions on their right to bear arms. The amendments all deal with freedoms that we take for granted today.

As an African American, this next document is very important in giving my descendants and me freedom from the evils of slavery. I am talking about the Emancipation Proclamation which was issued by President Lincoln in two executive orders beginning on September 22, 1862. The first order gave freedom to all slaves in any state of the Confederate States of America that did not return to union control by January 1, 1863. The second order was issued to ten specific states on January 1, 1863. Although most slaves were not freed by this proclamation, it did provide the framework for eventually freeing all slaves. When I think about the freedom I have from living in this great country, I want to give all the praise and thanks to God. But the greatest freedom that I have is not man made freedom. It is the freedom of being set free from the law of Moses and Abraham because of Jesus' sacrifice on the Cross over 2000 years ago. We once were imprisoned by sin and even though the law was there to be a guide, it was impossible for us to completely follow it. But we are now free to follow Christ and glorify Him. He has given us the promise of an abundant life on earth and eternal life when our earthly days are over. **Christ has given us the freedom not to sin.**

Stand fast therefore in the liberty by which Christ has made us free, and do not be entangled again with a yoke of bondage. Galatians 5:1

THE GIFT

Do you remember what it was like the night before Christmas as you waited for Santa Claus to put your gifts under the Christmas tree? I remember being hardly able to sleep until morning. Finally I awoke and immediately ran to the Christmas tree to see what I had gotten for Christmas. They say that it is better to give than to receive and I believe that now. But when I was a little child there wasn't anything better than receiving gifts on Christmas. Of course, I always loved celebrating birthdays, especially my birthday. But I don't remember the birthday gifts as much as I remember the Christmas gifts. When I became a father I received so much joy from giving my children gifts on Christmas and their birthdays. This is when I fully began to understand that it is more blessed to give than to receive.

My wife is someone who likes to give to others. She is always buying small gifts and sending cards to family members and friends. One day a lady that I knew called on the telephone to thank us for a card sent and signed by my wife for both of us. My wife was not at home but I pretended that I knew that my wife had sent her the card and I accepted her thanks. It is always nice to get gifts that we like but sometimes we get gifts that we don't want or we may receive something of value that we don't open. A couple of years after we had closed daily operations of our business, I found an unopened letter from the Ohio Bureau of Workers Compensation. This letter had been in our possession for over a year. Inside the letter was a refund check for $1400.00 but the date for cashing it had expired. I called the bureau about this and fortunately they agreed to issue me another check which I immediately cashed. This was an example of a gift that I had but knew nothing about.

During my nephew Robert and his wife's annual August visit to Columbus, Ohio in 2009, he became ill and had to be hospitalized. My wife wanted to give him something spiritual to read and she found a small Christian book dealing with the issues of faith and communion with God. This book was written over three hundred years ago by a Monk named Brother Lawrence. My wife found this book on our bookshelf and discovered that she had given it to me over twenty four years ago on Valentine's Day. As I looked in the book, I saw the inscription that she had written to me, using my nickname, which stated the following: "Junebug, Happy Valentine's Day, love, Delores 2-15-85." I don't remember ever having received this gift. I know that I never read this book.

I began to read it and discovered that I have been dealing with many of the issues over the years that Brother Lawrence is writing about. For example, Brother Lawrence tells when he is praying or praising God, his attention leaves God and goes to other thoughts. Then he again focuses on God. This has happened to me a lot and it was somewhat troubling to me. Brother Lawrence's main theme is that his communion time with God is not limited to a set aside time for prayer, praise and study. Communion with God should be constantly throughout the day and night. Our daily activities should reflect the presence of God in our lives. Whatever we do we should do for the glory of God.

As I continued to read this book, I questioned why I never read it when my wife originally gave it to me. There is so much wisdom in this book that would have benefited me greatly. But I never took the time to read it. Maybe I had to go through more life experiences before I was ready to receive the benefits from reading this book. This story didn't begin twenty four years ago when I received this gift. It began over two thousand years ago on the cross at Calvary when Jesus Christ died for our sins. This is the greatest gift that man could ever receive and was given by our Lord and Savior, who sacrificed His blood and body to reconcile mankind to God.

As I was thinking about writing this story of the gift, I wanted to immediately go to the computer and write my thoughts down because I might forget what I wanted to say. But then I instantly realized that I should do my worship and praise time first. Fortunately I remembered, and this is what the story is all about, giving honor and praise to God first. This message is for all of us who may not realize the importance of this gift that we received before we were born and before the beginning of the world. This is the precious gift of Christ's sacrifice on the cross; an abundant earthly life and His promise of eternal life knowing that Christ will come again to receive us unto Himself.

For by grace you have been saved through faith, and that not of yourselves; it is the gift of God, not of works, lest anyone should boast. Ephesians 2:8-9

COMMON SENSE

We often talk about the necessity of using common sense in making the right decisions but for some reason, we seem at times to do the wrong thing. It would seem that our common sense would keep us on the right path. First of all, how do we define common sense? According to the Merrian-Webester Online Dictionary, Common Sense is defined as follows: sound and prudent judgment based on a simple perception of the situation or facts. Another definition is the ability to make sensible decisions. Today we are seeing people buying houses they can't afford and using credit cards without concern about the tremendous debt they are creating. A former pastor, Keith Troy, once told me that common sense was not really very common. If it were, then more people would have it.

I just recently read a wonderful article about the death of common sense which talks about the valuable common sense lessons we learned like when to come in out of the rain and don't spend more money than you have earned. Common Sense is reportedly dying because we don't accept those common sense values anymore. When I was a teenager I would leave the house without an umbrella when it was raining. My father would tell me that he has seen people get caught in the rain without an umbrella. But he has never seen anyone go out in the rain without one except me. Just recently a six year old boy was suspended from grade school because he bought a Boy Scout knife to class. The school has a zero tolerance policy when it comes to bringing weapons to school. I understand the school's position but common sense tells us to suspend a six year old child is not the answer to solving the problem of weapons at school.

One day while I was driving, Kai Lee, my grandson who was ten years old at the time, to school; he gave me an unusual response to something that I had said to him. He told me that what I had said didn't make common sense. I asked him was he saying that I didn't have common sense. He replied that I have common sense but I probably did not have it turned on. This is true for a lot of us. We have common sense but we don't use it as we should. For me, common sense begins with having a set of values and truths that guides my life. I look to Jesus Christ for guidance in making decisions that affect my life and the lives of others. There is a popular saying used by Christians that asks: "What would Jesus do." Jesus wants us to live our lives by following His commandments of loving God and loving our neighbor like ourselves. If we follow those commandments, we will make wise, good and common sense decisions.

My grandson was given a computer and he keeps it at my house so he can use it when he stays here. One day we were both in the computer room working on our computers when I decided to kid him about using his computer. I told him that he needed to ask permission from me when he wanted to use his computer. He is such a nice boy, and he just nodded his head in agreement. I then said that I didn't mind him using my (his) computer but he again needed to ask first. He looked at me and said that I had gone too far. He further stated that I had crossed the line. He said this was his computer not mine but he acknowledged that I could tell him when to use it. I respect him because he always sticks to his value system when dealing with me or others. This ability to do the right thing will protect him in the future from the many worldly temptations that he may face.

I see in my grandson, a future diplomat because he is always respectful but firm in responding back to me when he is right. My grandson not only has common sense, but a lot of other talents and gifts. The greatest gift he has is that he accepted Jesus Christ as his Lord and Savior. He knows that not only does Jesus love him but his family loves him also. This is common sense being turned on through The Holy Spirit. Common sense may seem to die in that it appears to change from generation to generation. What was unreasonable fifty years ago is reasonable today. And what is unreasonable today may have been reasonable fifty years ago. But the Holy Spirit is the same yesterday, today and tomorrow. As Christians, we always need to ask The Holy Spirit for guidance when making common sense decisions.

Your word is a lamp to my feet and a light to my path. I have sworn and confirmed that I will keep Your righteous judgments. I am afflicted very much; Revive me, O Lord, according to Your word. Accept, I pray, the freewill offerings of my mouth, O Lord, and teach me Your judgments. My life is continually in my hand, yet I do not forget Your law. The wicked have laid a snare for me, Yet I have not strayed from Your precepts. Your testimonies I have taken as a heritage forever, for they are the rejoicing of my heart. I have inclined my heart to perform Your statutes forever, to the very end. Psalm 119:105-112

ABUNDANT LIFE

I had begun the habit of spending more and more time in the bed. I suppose I had an excuse because I have had many health problems for some time. I was having trouble standing and walking for short periods of time. I should be grateful to still be alive because many people with my health problems have died as a result of them. I considered myself a Born Again Christian so why didn't I feel like getting up out of bed each morning and facing the world. I kept asking myself the same question until I realized that the Lord never promised me a life free of problems. But He did promise me an abundant life. I was going to church and reading my Bible on a regular basis but I still had these feelings of depression. It wasn't a lot of depression but there was some. The question was why was I depressed at all? I began to set aside a half hour in the morning to praise and worship the Lord. This seemed to make all of the difference in my attitude. Instead of lying in the bed and trying to sleep my life away, I had a new purpose for getting up and facing a new day.

The Lord spoke to me through The Holy Spirit and reaffirmed that He had promised me an abundant life. This is the life prayed for in the Lord's Prayer, **Matthew 6:9-14**. You start this prayer by acknowledging who God is by saying **"Our Father who are in heaven hallowed it be your name."** This is our way of praising God and telling Him that we know He is our creator. In our relationship with God, we must humble ourselves. **In John 3:30, John the Baptist says that Christ must increase and he must decrease.** This is so very true for us also. Christ must become first in our life. Whatever we accomplish in life, we should give the glory to God.

The next part of the Lord's Prayer is to pledge to follow His commandments when we pray **"Your kingdom come your will be done on earth as it is in heaven."** Then we pray: **"Give us this day our daily bread."** He has provided for us yesterday and our future is eternal life with Him. But while we are on this earth, He will take care of us one day at a time. We continue to pray **"Forgive us our trespasses as we forgive those who trespass against us."** This is so important that we be able to forgive people who we believe have done us wrong. Sometimes you hear people say I can forgive but I can't forget. Well the Lord promises to forget our sins and He asks that we do the same for those who have sinned against us. As for the idea that you can forgive but can't forget, I learned from my pastor, Rich Nathan that maybe you can't forget but you can choose not to remember. You can not have more than one thought in your head at the same time so think on those things that give glory to God. **The prayer ends with "Lead us not into temptation but deliver us from evil for yours is the kingdom and the power and the glory forever. Amen."** The Lord's Prayer tells us how to live the abundant life in just a few words. There is an age old question asked many times by many people and that question is" Why were we created and for what purpose. The Bible tells us that we were created by God in His image and that whatever we do; we are to do for the glory of Him.

If we are awaking everyday to live for Christ, then the focus on what we do is for His glory and not ours. This time that is given to us is invaluable and we should not waste it away on things that do not bring glory to Him. That doesn't mean that we can't enjoy the things that He has provided us on this earth but we should try to have a positive attitude and enjoy this life while we can. Spend your time wisely and always put the tasks that He has given you to do first. I can remember years ago before I had truly accepted Christ as my Lord and Savior, I was discussing the Bible with a friend of mine named Henry Simpson. I was saying that people are Christians just because they want an insurance policy against the finality of physical death. My friend told me that a good insurance policy also provides benefits while you are still alive. This is so true when you accept Jesus Christ as your Lord and Savior, He promises you salvation in the form of eternal life but He also promises you the salvation of an abundant life while you are still on this earth.

Then Jesus said to them again, "Most assuredly, I say to you, I am the door of the sheep. All who ever came before Me are thieves and robbers, but the sheep did not hear them. I am the door. If anyone enters by Me, he will be saved, and will go in and out and find pasture. The thief does not come except to steal, and to kill, and to destroy. I have come that they may have life, and that they may have it more abundantly." John 10:7-10

FRUIT OF THE SPIRIT

My wife, brother, sister and I are currently studying the Book of Galatians, which has been described as the Charter of Christian Liberty. The Apostle Paul says that Jesus' birth and death on the cross freed us from the penalty of the law of Abraham and Moses. This law given by God to the Jewish people was a standard to be used in guiding their behavior but because they are human, it was impossible for them to achieve compliance. The people were constantly sinning against God. So God sent His only begotten Son to earth to serve as a sacrifice in order to reconcile humans back to God. Faith in Christ was the bridge used to reconcile us with God and not our strict adherence to the law. The Bible tells us we are all sinners falling short of obeying the law. But through God's grace and mercy, we have a Savior in Jesus Christ who existed before the beginning of the world. He was sent by God to give us an abundant life while we are here on earth and to take us to Himself after our physical death. This process of accepting Christ as our Lord and Savior is called being **"Born Again."** In John 3:1-22, Jesus explains to Nicodemus about the new birth.

We are born physically through our mother's womb and eventually we will die a physical death. But being born again is a spiritual birth that places us eternally with Christ. This is Christ's promise of eternal life. When we go through this experience, Christ through The Holy Spirit makes us a new creature and gives us Christian characteristics called **"The Fruit of the Spirit."** But before the Apostle Paul talks about the Fruit of the Spirit in the fifth chapter of Galatians, he says that we Christians should walk in the Spirit so we won't fulfill the lusts of the flesh. Paul says that the Spirit and the flesh are contrary to each other and if you are led by the Spirit, you will not do the things of the flesh. He lists the characteristics of someone who has not accepted Christ in their heart as follows: adultery, fornication, uncleanness, lewdness, idolatry, sorcery, hatred, contentions, jealousies, outbursts of wrath, selfish ambitions, dissensions, heresies, envy, murder, drunkenness, and revelries. Paul says those practicing these characteristics will not inherit the Kingdom of God.

Paul then goes on to list the Fruit of the Spirit as follows; love, joy, peace, patience, kindness, goodness, faithfulness, gentleness and self-control. Paul further states we no longer need the law to guide and direct us. Our flesh with its passions and desires has been crucified with Christ and we now have the option of living and walking in the Spirit. In the seventh chapter of Matthew, Jesus warns us to watch out for false prophets. **Jesus says: "Beware of false prophets, who come to you in sheep's clothing, but inwardly they are ravenous wolves. You will know them by their fruits. Do men gather grapes from thornbushes or figs from thistles? Even so, every good tree bears good fruit, but a bad tree bears bad fruit. A good tree cannot bear bad fruit, nor can a bad tree bear good fruit. Every tree that does not bear good fruit is cut down and thrown into the fire. Therefore by their fruits you will know them." Matthew 7:15-20** The Fruit of the Spirit is described as the harvest or result of what we should see in someone in whom the Holy Spirit has been working. The evidence of the Fruit of the Spirit is a way of measuring the growth and positive change in a Christian. If we want to change, God would grant it if asked. The problem is that some of us do not want to change.

Love is the first fruit and is described in First Corinthians Chapter Thirteen as the greatest between love, faith and hope. This description of love is called *"Agape"* and is the highest form of love. This love is unconditional love and is distinguished from *"Storge"* or friendly love, *"Philia"* or family love and *"Eros"* or erotic love. **Joy** has been compared with happiness but joy is like an inner expression of happiness given by the Spirit and not an outer based human happiness depending on outer circumstances. Christian Joy is with us even in hard times. In the Book of James, the author says consider it all joy when you undergo trials and tribulations for you are being tested. I was diagnosed with prostate cancer in 1990 and have been living with this disease for over nineteen years. I never thought that I would consider getting cancer a joy but I now do because it has tested my faith in God. **Peace** is the quality that describes a person who is calm inside and outside even though his outer circumstances are in turmoil. **Longsuffering** as defined in The Webster Dictionary is bearing pain or trials calmly or without complaint. The life we are living is not a sprint but a marathon and we need patience to endure our problems so that we can obtain God's promise. **Kindness** is the act of being generous or warm hearted to someone or something. Mother Theresa was an excellent example of someone who was kind to others. **Goodness** is shown by moral and virtuous behavior and is closely linked to kindness. **Faithfulness** in Christ is complete loyalty to Him as our Lord and Savior. **Gentleness** is the quality of being meek and humble through the use of power and strength under control. **Self control** is self defined as having the ability to control your emotions and desires. Previously I would become upset at something someone would say about or do to me. But now, I know not to let it bother me. And initially when it sometimes does bother me, I have the Holy Spirit to remind me of what Jesus would have me do in this situation.

But the fruit of the Spirit is love, joy, peace, longsuffering, kindness, goodness, faithfulness, gentleness, self control. Against such there is no law. And those who are Christ's have crucified the flesh with its passions and desires. If we live in the Spirit, let us also walk in the Spirit. Let us not become conceited, provoking one another, envying one another. Galatians 5:22-26

ONE BODY

Have you ever thought how marvelous the human body is? All the different parts working together to allow us to function daily so that we can work, play, eat, sleep, wake and do many other tasks and duties that allow us to live our human lives as we know it. When I was hired as a disability claim examiner, I had to learn about how the human body functioned so I could make decisions on whether or not a person was disabled and unable to work any longer under the Social Security Disability law. We had physicians on staff who signed off on every case but it was important for the disability claims examiner to have a basic knowledge of how the body functioned; therefore I was introduced to the parts of the body including the circulatory, urinary, respiratory, nervous, immune, musculoskeletal, digestive, and endocrine systems. We had to review medical reports and along with the physician determine if the claimant had the physical ability to return to work. In my study and experience, I learned just how marvelous the human body is constructed. We have all these different parts working together in our body so we can function as a whole person.

We are amazed when we buy a car and the battery or tires last for five years or the engine last for over 100,000 miles. We are further amazed about how this car was built and all the parts seemed to work together. But it seems like every four or five years, we need to get a new car because the old one is wearing out. But the human body, although not indestructible, normally is good for over seventy years and in some cases has lasted for over one hundred and twenty years. Have you ever wondered what the human body is made of? Well when I was little, I was told that boys were made of scissors, snails and puppy dog tails and girls were made of sugar, spice and every thing nice. Guess what, I was fooled. In an article from Ezine Articles, James Lahey, reports that the human body is actually made up of fat, water, protein, carbohydrates, vitamins and minerals. Lahey talks about the 60-20-20 rule with 60 percent of your body being water, 20 percent fat, 20 percent protein and other nutrients. Men and women differ in that a woman's body will have more fat and the man's body will contain more protein and calcium.

Recently my wife was hospitalized for a heart related problem and had to go to her primary Physician, Terry Irwin M.D. for a follow up visit. Dr Irwin began to explain to us how the human heart works and we were both amazed at how the heart functioned in providing the life giving blood to the rest of the body. It is further amazing when you think about our brain, eyes, skin, arteries, veins, glands, bones and all the other many parts that make up our body. It is impossible for me to understand how someone could think that this all happened by chance. From an early age, we are taught that a creation can only come from a creator. God created us and grouped us into families. First we all descended from the first man and we all belong to the human family. Next we have our blood relationships where we are related to each other by physical birth. In my case, I am part of the Grant family on my father's side and the Shobe family on my mother's side. In some cases, we look like each other and carry the same or similar physical characteristics as another family member. As the singing group, Sister Sledge sang; **"We are family."**

I know that I love my family very much. I did not have any choice of whether I was going to be a member of the Grant and Shobe families. I was just born and there I was, a little boy named Marshall L. Grant Jr., son of Marshall L. Grant Sr. and Sara Jane Shobe. I was given a brother, Robert Douglas and sister, Alice Carole and I have been stuck with them all of my life and I love it. Although if you see them don't tell them I said this because I don't want them to think that I am a softie. In the twelfth chapter of the first Book of Corinthians, the Apostle Paul is talking about the body being one with many parts and he says that this is especially true for the body of Christ. Paul says that we were all baptized by one Spirit into one body and whether we are Jews or Greeks, slaves or free, we have been made to drink into one Spirit. As members of the human, family, we all need to love each other and work together for the. common good of us all.

For as we have many members in one body, but all members do not have the same function, so we, being many, are one body in Christ, and individually members of one another. Romans 12:4-5

Chapter Twelve:
MORE FAMILY STORIES

GRAPES AND BUCKEYES

THREE GUYS

DAMON

CELEBRATIONS

ADDIE'S KITCHEN

JULIE

MY NEPHEWS

DERRIANNA AND DIABETES

GRAPES AND BUCKEYES

My mother and I would listen to the Ohio State Buckeyes football games on the radio in the middle nineteen forties. We would listen to the game as we ate grapes. My mother was a big fan of Ohio State football and subsequently, she bought season tickets and attended the games with some of her friends. In fact, she was at the famous Snow Bowl at Ohio Stadium in 1950 when Michigan beat Ohio State by the score of nine to three. This game was played in very extreme weather conditions and no pass was completed or first down made by either team. I also went to some Ohio State games but didn't buy a ticket. One of my friends, Herbie Foster, taught me how to sneak in. Once we got into the stadium, we would hide in the lower level and when they started to play the national anthem, we would come out to find a seat. Today, we would probably be caught and arrested because of the tight security needed to prevent terrorism at large public gatherings.

But getting back to the middle nineteen forties, my mother and I spent a lot of Saturday afternoons listening to our Buckeyes. There was no television in those days just radio. In Poindexter Village where I lived, all the windows would be opened with the sound of radios playing. In fact on a hot summer night if Joe Louis was fighting, you could hear a stereo version of the announcer reporting the blow by blow account of the fight. Your imagination was so important prior to television coming on the scene. When you listened to shows like Lux Radio Theater, Gangbusters and The Fat Man your imagination had to fill in for what you couldn't see. Listening to football games was like that as well because you could not see the player running with or throwing the football. I don't remember who announced Ohio Sate football games on the radio in the nineteen forties and fifties. One of my favorite play by play announcers was Jimmy Crum who announced Ohio State basketball games during and after the time Ohio State won the national basketball championship in 1960. I can still hear him say,

"How about that sports fans, How about that." This became one of my father's favorite sayings as he would often say to me, "How about that Junebug, How about that."

Some of the great Ohio State football players that I remember were Fred "Curly" Morrison, Pandel Savic and Ray Hamilton. Fred Morison is alive and living in California and Pandel Savic is still with us living in Dublin, Ohio, a suburb of Columbus, Ohio. He has been a business associate of the great golfer Jack Nicklaus for many years. I don't know about Ray Hamilton. The last time I saw him was in 1968 at a friend's wedding. There was also Vic Janowicz, the Heisman Trophy Winner in 1950. There were other great Ohio State football players such as Les Horvath, the Heisman Trophy Winner in 1944 and the great Big Bill Willis, the legendary player of both Ohio State and the Cleveland Browns. Later on, we followed the exploits of the 1955 Heisman Trophy Winner, Howard "Hopalong" Cassidy, 1961 runner up to the Heisman Trophy Winner, Bob Ferguson and the 1974 and 1975 Heisman Trophy Winner, Archie Griffin. Since My mother's death in 1994, I have continued to follow Ohio State Football and have enjoyed the talents of Eddie George (1995) and Troy Smith (2006), both Heisman Trophy Winners.

In addition to Ohio State Football, My entire family and I loved to watch Ohio State Basketball on television during the time that Ohio State was competing for the NCAA National Championship. This was the time when Ohio State had such great players as Jerry Lucas, John Havlicek, and Mel Nowell and super subs like Dave Barker, who played high school basketball at Columbus St. Mary's High School. The Ohio State University went on to win the 1960 NCAA National Championship and were runner ups in 1961 and 1962. Ohio State Basketball continued to prosper under the guidance of Coach Fred Taylor for a number of years after winning the national championship that one time. Another famous player on that 1960 team but not a starter was Bobby Knight, who later became a great basketball coach at Indiana University and Texas Tech. Also on that Ohio State 1960 championship team were Larry Siegfried and Joe Roberts. Joe also played at Columbus East High School where Mel Nowell played basketball.

In addition to the Ohio State football games, my mother and I went to see Muhammad Ali win back the heavyweight championship from George Foreman in 1974. It is one of those memories of her that I will always treasure. She was quite a sports fan, especially concerning Ohio State. Today, when I am watching Ohio State Football, I sometimes think about her, with much love and joy about the times we shared listening to the Buckeyes and eating grapes.

Beloved, lets us love one another, for love is of God; and everyone who loves is born of God and knows God. He who does not love does not know God, for God is love. In this the love of God was manifested towards us, that God has sent His only begotten Son into the world, that we might live through Him. In this is love, not that we loved God, but that He loved us and sent His son to be the propitiation for our sins. Beloved, if God so loved us, we also ought to love one another. No one has seen God at any time. If we love one another, God abides in us, and His love has been perfected in us. 1 John 4:7-12

THREE GUYS

When I think of Kappa Alpha Psi Fraternity, My thoughts initially turn to three guys that have contributed so much to the fraternity. First there is Guy L. Grant, who was one of the ten original founders of the fraternity. Guy L. was just a twenty year old student at Indiana University when he along with nine other African American students founded Kappa Alpha Psi Fraternity in 1911. Guy was one of thirteen children born to Bob and Lucy Grant in New Albany, Indiana in 1891. At an early age, Guy L. had to take a leadership role in his family due to the death of an older brother and his father who were both named Robert.

According to the 1930 United States Census, an unmarried thirty eight year old Guy L. still lived at home with his mother, a sister and a few younger brothers. One of the brothers was my twenty two year old father to be, Marshall L. Grant Sr., who had just graduated from Law School. I believe that four of Guy L.'s brothers including my father became members of Kappa Alpha Psi Fraternity. Guy L. graduated from Indiana University Dental College and practiced dentistry in Indianapolis, Indiana for many years. He was the first Polemarch of Kappa Alpha Psi Alumni Chapter in Indianapolis, Indiana. He served for many years as the Grand Historian of the fraternity and was eventually given the title of Grand Historian Emeritus. Guy L. Grant died on November 11, 1973.

The second guy is Guy E. Russell who was born in 1912, one year after the founding of Kappa Alpha Psi Fraternity. Guy L.'s younger sister, Carrie, was Guy E.'s mother. She gave her son the same first name as her brother. Guy E., was affectionately known as Little Guy, and also became a member of Kappa Alpha Psi. He served his fraternity for many years until his death in 1996. He was the Polemarch of Alpha Chapter (Indiana University) in college and a member of the Grand Board of Directors in 1937. Little Guy was also Polemarch of the Indianapolis Alumni Chapter from 1945-1947. Little Guy was my first cousin but seemed more like my uncle since he was 25 years older than me. He surprised me one day by showing me my baby picture that he was carrying around in his wallet. He was a married man with three beautiful children and six grandchildren of his own. But he loved me enough to keep my picture in his wallet over the years.

The final Guy is my second cousin and the son of Little Guy This Guy was born in 1941 and is more like a first cousin since he is only 4 years younger than me. His name is Guy Evans Russell and like his father and great uncle, he is a lifetime member of Kappa Alpha Psi Fraternity. He served his fraternity as Vice Polemarch of Nu Chapter (Purdue University) in 1963 and continues to serve in the alumni chapter. A few years ago, he was presented with one of the first coins made in the likeness of Guy L. Grant. Although there are other Kappas in the family including myself, our family decided that he should be the one Kappa in the family entrusted with this honor. We are proud of and love all of our Kappa Guys and thankful for their service to their fraternity and family.

There are three other Guys in my life more important than My Kappa Guys. These Guys gave me life, continue to give me an abundant life and will ultimately give me an eternal life. Well you probably have guessed that I am talking about the Trinity of God, Jesus and the Holy Spirit. They are the three in one that we Christians believe in. God placed His only begotten Son on earth to serve as a sacrifice for our sins and reconcile us back to Him. After dying on the cross, Jesus rose from the dead and ascended to be with the Father. Jesus is preparing a place for us when He comes back to take us to be with Him but while we are here on this earth, He has given us a comforter, the Holy Spirit to lead us into all truth. They are three distinct persons but all three are together one God.

The word, "Trinity," is not in the Bible but God, Jesus and the Holy Spirit are used on occasion interchangeably in the Bible. In the first chapter of Ephesians, we see God functioning as a trinity of persons. In verse 4, God chooses who will be saved. The Son of Man redeems them in verse 7 and the Holy Spirit seals them in verse 13. I will always love my three Kappa Guys but they were created and given to me by my other three Guys; God, Jesus Christ and the Holy Spirit.

When all the people were baptized, it came to pass that Jesus also was baptized; and while He prayed, the heaven was opened. And the Holy Spirit descended in bodily form like a dove upon Him, and a voice came from heaven which said, "You are My beloved Son; in you I am well pleased." Luke 3:21-22

DAMON

My Uncle Doug and Aunt Hattie Belle adopted their baby son Damon in the early nineteen sixties. They had been childless for almost all of their married life which was longer than I had been on this earth. Both of them loved their son and doted on him very much. Before Damon and when we were little, they would care for us during part of the summer months. Now they could take all of that love and affection and give it to Damon. When my son died in 1978, my Uncle Doug and his son Damon came to the funeral. I noticed at the time that Aunt Hattie Belle didn't come with them. I briefly wondered why she didn't come but it was just a passing thought in my head. I probably thought that maybe she wasn't feeling well. But I never questioned her loyalty or love for me. I was going through one of the most horrible experiences that a father can go through so my thoughts turned away from why she was absent. There were plenty of other family members who were present along with countless friends, co-workers and church members. And I was kept busy keeping up with all of these people.

A few months passed following my son's death and the Lord was continuing to heal my sadness over losing him. I was still working for the Ohio Rehabilitation Services Commission and I had to attend a business meeting in Chicago, Illinois. I drove to Chicago and on the way back from Chicago; I stopped in Indianapolis, Indiana to visit with Aunt Hattie Belle. I knew that Uncle Doug was at work and Damon was in school, but this would give me a chance to talk with her. Some time into our conversation, she asked me how that son of mine was doing. The question caught me by surprise since I only had the one son and he had died. But before I had a chance to answer, she withdrew the question by turning her eyes away from me and mumbling softly "never mind". This seemed strange coming from her but again I let it pass. As I later found out, that at this time, Aunt Hattie Belle was in the early stages of Alzheimer's disease. Uncle Doug had not shared my aunt's illness with me but I can only imagine what he had to go through in seeing the love of his life become a different person.

Sometime after that visit with her, I learned that my sister and Uncle Doug had taken Aunt Hattie Belle to the Cleveland Clinic in Cleveland, Ohio to undergo a medical examination. What they received from the results of the evaluation was the worst possible news. Aunt Hattie Belle was diagnosed with Alzheimer's disease. Until this time, I had never heard of Alzheimer's disease and didn't know anybody who had it. The drive back to Indianapolis, Indiana from Cleveland, Ohio was a long trip and my sister told me that upon their return home to Indianapolis, my uncle went upstairs to his bedroom and began loudly crying and beating on the floor. He kept saying over and over "Oh Lord why can't it be me, why can't it be me." We always knew that Uncle Doug loved Aunt Hattie Belle very much and the way he received this news touched our hearts greatly. He had been a wonderful husband to her all of their married life. Even though they were childless for over twenty five years of marriage, she never had to work outside of the home.

However, when Aunt Hattie Belle heard Uncle Doug making all this noise crying, she asked my sister "What is the matter with Doug. Is he crazy?" Subsequently, Uncle Doug, become ill with cancer, and could not take care of her any longer without help and he arranged for her to live with her sister, my mother, in Columbus, Ohio. He would often drive to Columbus and spend time with her on the weekends as long as his health permitted. In 1978, my sister, Alice Carole, had a baby boy and when he was about five years of age, Aunt Hattie Belle began to get him confused with her son, Damon, who was now a grown man. She didn't recognize her son when he came to visit her but would always call my sister's son Damon. My sister's son was named Kyle and he would always let Aunt Hattie Belle know that he was not Damon. He would tell her over and over again that his name was Kyle and not Damon. But that wouldn't stop her from calling him Damon.

One day Kyle was about to get a spanking for something he had done. But before his mother could spank him, Aunt Hattie Belle stopped the spanking by saying that nobody was going to spank Damon. Unlike the past, when Kyle would tell Aunt Hattie Belle that he was not Damon, this time he remained silent. His mother told him over and over to tell Aunt Hattie Belle who he was. He looked up at Aunt Hattie Belle who was trying to protect him and then he looked at his mother with the switch. He thought about it for a few seconds and then he blurted out "my name is Damon." Aunt Hattie Belle passed away a few years later after Uncle Doug had died from cancer. And Kyle, now a grown man with a son of his own, never did received his much deserved spanking.

Correct your son and he will give you rest; Yes, he will give delight to your soul. Proverbs 29:17

CELEBRATIONS

As I watch the celebration of life services for Senator Ted Kennedy, My mind takes me back to the times in my life when I attended celebration services for my loved ones. The first occasion occurred in 1950 when my cousin, who was nineteen years older than me died. He was a thirty two year old physician named Dr. Walter R. Shobe and we were all very proud of his achievements. Then in a time frame of five months, I lost my grandmother and two uncles These deaths in 1951 began with the heart attack suffered by Uncle Lawrence in March, who was stricken while watching a boxing match on television. Than in June 1951, my grandmother, Lucy Grant, died at age eighty three. She would have been eighty four on August 13, 1951. This was a big loss for our family because she was the matriarch and mother of thirteen children. After my grandmother's death, my uncle Dave came to visit with my father in Columbus, Ohio. He stayed with us for a few weeks and then returned to Indianapolis, Indiana, his home.

Shortly after Uncle Dave's return home, he was found dead on a public bus of a heart attack in August 1951. He had been running to catch the bus and collapsed after boarding it. I had watched my father at all three funerals or celebrations as I prefer to call them. I only saw him cry at the one for Uncle Dave. I guess he tried to stay as brave for us as long as he could. My Uncle Lawrence, Uncle Dave and my grandmother all lived together along with my Uncle Charlie and Aunt Bernice. My Aunt Stella then died in 1964 and Uncle Everett, my mother's brother, passed away a year later in 1965. Uncle Charlie, a life long bachelor, finally married in 1951 after his mother's death and stayed married for almost thirty seven years until his wife, Julia, died in March 1988. Aunt Bernice died in 1984 and Uncle Charlie was the last of Lucy Grant's children to pass away and he died in June of 1992 at the age of eighty eight ... Another death that was hard for me to take was the death of my brother's first wife Claudia in 1959. She was only seventeen when she died giving birth to my brother's first son Robert Douglas Jr. Her heart stopped beating during delivery and she went into a coma. She died the next morning with only my brother being present at her side. She never got to see her beautiful son, but she did dream about him before he was born.

In her dream, she saw him in show business which actually happened. Robert Jr. performed in Broadway shows, movies and television shows under his middle name Douglas. He graduated from The Ohio State University and received his masters from Temple University. He is currently an artist and teacher living with his wife, Eileen Smith Grant and working in New York City. My brother, Doug, remarried in 1963 and along with his lovely wife, Addie, had four more sons together, Tony, Tim, David and Chris Grant. My father suffered a stroke in 1973 and lay in a coma for three weeks before he passed away. His older brother, Guy L. Grant, one of ten founders of Kappa Alpha Psi Fraternity, had passed away three weeks earlier. Our immediate family was unable to go to Uncle Guy's funeral because of my father's illness and this was a double blow for our family in 1973. It goes without saying, that I loved my father very much and was very much saddened by the passing of my Uncle Guy. Since 1973, I have also lost Uncle Orville, Aunt Carrie and Uncle Wilbur on my father's side and Uncle Wood and Aunt Hattie Belle on my mother's side. Also Uncle Doug died in 1982, a few years before his wife, Aunt Hattie Belle.

In 2000, my beloved cousin Bernard Shobe passed away. I remember we both attended Uncle Wood's funeral and Bernard was tearfully saying, "We're next." I knew what he meant because by that time, I had only one uncle left alive. I have attended many life celebrations for my family and friends since being a thirteen year old child in 1951. But the toughest celebration I had to attend was for my son, Marshall L. Grant lll. He died a few months shy of his eighth birthday in 1978 of unknown causes. Just five years earlier, I had attended the celebration in the same church for my father, Marshall L. Grant Sr. Since that time, the pastor, Phale D. Hale who performed both of those celebrations, has also passed away. My mother, Sara Grant, passed away in 1994 at age eighty seven. Words cannot express how much my brother, Doug, sister Alice and I loved her. She was the glue that held our family together. I have had other deaths in my family that are just as painful to mention, including some of my cousins, but these come to the forefront of my mind. In reading 1 Corinthians, the Fifteenth Chapter, verses 50 through 58, the Apostle Paul writes about our final victory in which the followers of Christ will have their death swallowed up by victory.

"O death, where is your sting? O Hades, where is your victory? The sting of death is sin, and the strength of sin is the law. But thanks be to God, who gives us the victory through, our Lord Jesus Christ. 1 Corinthians 15:55-57

ADDIE'S KITCHEN

Addie Grant is known for hospitality by all of those who come to visit her and my brother Doug. She is always cooking something delicious and if not, she will go in the kitchen and whip up a tasty meal in a jiffy. One of her dishes is especially a favorite of my sister's son, Kyle. This dish is a tuna and noodles casserole. Kyle would ask for it when he came home on his breaks from Heidelberg College. When Addie has dinner for the family, she always has a smorgasbord of food prepared for your enjoyment. There are usually plenty of desserts including pies and cakes. Both she and my brother have plenty of food in the house. In fact, one of her younger sons, David, would sometimes come to his mother's house and do some quick shopping.

I always enjoyed going to their house because I was going to get something to eat that my wife wouldn't buy for me because of my bad eating habits. Addie buys a lot of young people food because she has six grandchildren and has watched all of them and still is watching two today while her son, David and his wife, Carolyn work. She also watches my sister's grandson Grant Gibson and she does it for free as she does for her own grandchildren. She doesn't have to do this but she does it out of love and responsibility for her nephew Kyle Gibson, Grant's father. Grant is getting a wonderful opportunity to interact with Addie's grandchildren, Julia Addie and Jon David. Yes little Julie is named for both of her grandmothers, Julia Huber and Addie Grant. Every time I go to her house, Addie is always doing something unless she is not feeling well.

She is cooking, cleaning or chasing after the kids. She doesn't do much chasing because she is training them to come to her when she calls them. She also makes them pick up after themselves and say thank you when someone gives them something. She is a firm believer in providing discipline to children under her care and supervision. It must be working because all of her sons have grown up to get college degrees with four of them receiving their Master Degrees. They all have good jobs and wonderful families and stay in contact with their parents as often as possible. In fact, I see the second oldest son, Anthony, who lives in Chicago, here in Columbus more than I see the two youngest sons who live here. He makes frequent visits to see his parents and the rest of his family. I should add that he is the only unmarried son and has more time to stay in contact with the rest of his family. I have a wonderful relationship with all of my nephews.

Doug and Addie celebrated their forty sixth wedding anniversary in April 2009. It seems like only yesterday that I went to Addie's house to be the best man at her and his wedding in April of 1963. This was about seventh months before the assassination of our beloved President John F. Kennedy and over a year before I finished college. After their marriage, they moved into the upper half of our family duplex home located at 1507-1509 East Long Street, Columbus, Ohio. Not only did Addie cook meals for my brother, she also cooked meals for my father and me. In 1973, Doug and Addie built a beautiful big ranch home near Westerville, Ohio, a suburb of Columbus, Ohio. She still reminds me about that cake she baked that I almost ate all of it before it had cooled. My wife has a complaint about me like that because she had taken a lot of time to bake a lemon meringue pie and I ate most of it before it had cooled. My wife has not baked a lemon meringue pie since. Addie did not do me the way my wife did. She has continued to cook and bake even though she knows that I will eat up all of her food. In fact, after feeding you, she will send you away with some food that you can eat later. Today, because of my health, I am restricted to a special diet that my wife prepares and I eat it at home. Now when I go over to visit Addie and my brother, I can't eat what she has prepared. I miss that part of my visit. I am hoping for success in losing weight so that I can once again eat the food prepared by Addie in **Addie's Kitchen.**

"For I was hungry and you gave Me food; I was thirsty and you gave Me drink; I was a stranger and you took Me in; I was naked and you clothed Me; I was sick and you visited Me; I was in prison and you came to Me." **Then the righteous will answer him, saying, "Lord, when did we see You hungry and feed You, or thirsty and give You drink? When did we see You a stranger and take You in,**

or naked and clothe You? Or when did we see You sick, or in prison, and come to You? And the King will answer and say to them, *"assuredly, I say to you, inasmuch as you did it to one of the least of these My brethren, you did it to Me."* Matthew 25:35-40

JULIE

I have just finished listening to a song about me by Julia Addie Grant. Little Julie just turned two years old this October of 2009 but she is already an accomplished singer in my view. She has been talking and singing for sometime now and surprisingly, she sings in key. I am hesitant to call her an accomplished singer just as many were hesitant to say that President Obama deserved the Nobel Peace Prize. But like Obama I am awarding her this honor based on the promise that she has shown. She is eager to sing for you and has learned a few songs taught to her by her grandparents, Doug and Addie. One of her favorites is "This Little Light of Mine' and another is the "Star Spangled Banner." I told her grandfather, my brother, that she will probably be ready to sing the Star Spangled Banner at the Super Bowl when she is five years old. At first, I was just joking but now this seems like it could be a possibility.

She is also able to relate to you by locking her eyes onto your eyes. She loves to have you read to her and you can see her in the other room coming toward you with a book out stretched in her hand and her eyes looking straight in to your eyes. You know that she is bringing this book for you to read to her. Not only is she smart but she seems to have good common sense. Her cousin, Grant Gibson, plays with her a few days of the week. Grant is one month younger than Julie and he has a hearty appetite. Not only does he eat his food but he grabs Julie's food. Little Julie would pick up her goodies in one hand but to protect against Grant eating all of her food, she now uses both hands. This reminds me of when my wife and I were first married. My wife would eat one kernel of popcorn at a time while I would take fistfuls of popcorn. My wife had to adjust her thinking and she started to take fistfuls of popcorn in order to keep up with me.

I am a lover of music and especially the piano and singing. My favorite female singer is Dinah Washington. She died many years ago at the age of thirty nine but I still listen to her music today. Other female singers that I like listening to are Billie Holiday, Ella Fitzgerald and Mariah Carey. My favorite male singer is Frank Sinatra with Nat King Cole coming in a close second. Other male singers that I enjoy are Louis Armstrong, Lou Rawls, Tony Bennett and Brook Benton. There are of course many other singers that I like. I can't read the future but I think that Julie has the ability to join that list of great singers. My only hope is that she will grow up and become whatever she wants and fulfill her dreams in accordance with the glory of God.

Perhaps Grant can someday accompany her on the piano. He seems to have a talent for the piano because every time he comes over to my house, he wants to play it. And he doesn't just bang on it but he picks out a melody using both the treble and bass keys. Both Julie and Grant are being raised together and hopefully one day they will be very close to each other. I would love to be around to see Julie and Grant grow up and see what they become but the Lord has already given me a glimpse. Julie's five year older brother Jon David is also smart and knows the names of some of the Presidents of the United States and most of the books of the Bible. He serves as a big brother to both Julie and Grant.

God seems to have given Julie the talent of singing and with proper nourishment from her loved ones, God will turn that talent into a gift to be used for his glory. I am very proud of her and what she has accomplished at the tender young age of two. However, this is just the beginning and it will take her loving family and the village of teachers, counselors, ministers, physicians and others to help her grow and develop along the way. Hillary Clinton was correct when she said that it takes a village to raise a child. That was so true for us when we lived and grew up in Poindexter Village and later on Long Street. Julie's grandparents, Doug and Addie, are daily providing their grandchildren with Bible scriptures so they can implant them in their hearts.

Your word I have hidden in my heart, that I might not sin against You. Blessed are You, O Lord! Teach me Your statutes. With my lips I have declared all the judgments of Your mouth. I have rejoiced in the way of Your testimonies, as much as in all riches. I will meditate on Your precepts, and contemplate Your ways. I will delight myself in Your statutes; I will not forget Your word. Psalm 119:11-16

My Nephews

Robert Douglas Grant Jr. who was born on May 10, 1959 is my oldest nephew and he lives with his wife Eileen in New York, New York. I have previously written about him and his remarkable achievements at such a young and tender age. Now I would like to focus on my remaining five nephews, four are sons of my brother, Doug and his wife, Addie. The youngest of the remaining five nephews is my sister Alice's son. All of these remaining five nephews are members of Kappa Alpha Psi Fraternity. I have spoken of Kappa Alpha Psi in past writings and this is an international fraternity which my uncle Guy L. Grant was one of the ten original founders. There are many male members of the Grant family who are members of this fraternity including me. I am proud of my nephews for following in my footsteps. My second oldest nephew, Anthony Romero Grant is a graduate of Howard University and has a Masters in Business Administration from Indiana University. He is self employed as a financial expert and also gives good financial advice to his family members. He helps us all to prepare our taxes and provides computer advice and service when he comes home to visit his parents and family and we appreciate him for this very much. Tony is a very giving person and is involved in many charities in the Chicago area. He is also very close to all of his nieces and nephews and serves as a wonderful uncle to them.

My third oldest nephew is named Timothy Avery Grant and he is an executive with Abbot Laboratories and works in the San Francisco area. His job takes him all over the world. Tim is a graduate of my Alma Mater, Ohio University in Athens, Ohio and has received his Master's Degree from Franklin University. He is married to his wife, of seventeen years, Marti and together they have two children Marissa Nicole and Nicholas Avery. Despite his success in the business world, Tim's secret desire is to be a chef and maybe after he retires, he will pursue that ambition. My fourth oldest nephew, David Todd Grant is a graduate of the Ohio State University in Columbus, Ohio. He was a champion wrestler in high school and in addition to owning a State Farm Insurance Agency; David is also the wrestling coach for Westerville North High School in Westerville, Ohio. In fact, He has guided three of his wrestlers to state wrestling championships. He and his wife Carolyn have two children, Jon David and Julia Addie and I have previously written about Julie and Jon David.

The fifth oldest nephew is Christopher Tyrone Grant and he is also a graduate of Ohio University in Athens, Ohio. Chris is married to his wife, Marcia and together they have two sons, Joshua Ryan and Jacob Tyler. Chris also works for State Farm Insurance Company and has received his Master's Degree from Ohio Dominican University. Chris and Marcia took my wife and me to the Kappa Reunion on May 30, 2009 and this reunion was the catalyst for writing these stories. I will always be grateful to Chris and Marcia for taking me to the reunion. My sixth oldest nephew is Kyle Grant Gibson, who is my sister Alice's son. His father is Calvin Gibson who has appeared in many television shows and commercials. Kyle is a graduate of Heidelberg College and has received his Master's Degree from Ashland University. He is currently a vice principal in the Columbus, Ohio Public School System. Kyle is interested in pursuing his Doctorate Degree in Education and I believe he will achieve that degree someday. Kyle is the father of a wonderful little boy named Grant Avery Gibson who looks just like Kyle. Little Grant is also the apple of my sister Alice's eye.

I love all of my nephews and they have helped me in ways that my beloved deceased son, Little Marshall would have if he were alive today. They all have my best interests at heart just as I have their best interests at heart. They have also been very kind and thoughtful to their Aunt Delores and she loves them very much also. What I most appreciate about them is that they have a wonderful relationship with and love for each other. My brother's five sons treat my sister's son Kyle just like a brother even though he is their cousin. They have mentored to him and provided positive role models for him to use by their examples. The oldest son, Robert Jr. is nineteen years older than Kyle and has helped to care for him when he was a little boy. In fact, all the boys served as role models for the younger ones and this was because of Doug and Addie's parenting skills. Doug and Addie both valued hard work and getting a good education. This has paid off because all of the boys have received their college degrees and have good jobs.

My advice to my nephews and others is to put their faith, hope and trust in Jesus Christ and let Him guide and direct them. They will never regret it and Jesus will give them an abundant life until He takes them home to be with Him.

But without faith it is impossible to please Him, for he who comes to God must believe that He is, and that He is a rewarder of those who diligently seek Him. Hebrews 11:6

DERRIANNA AND DIABETES

My wife and I have a little ten year old great granddaughter who is just adorable. I suppose everyone thinks that their little great granddaughter is adorable. But this time it is really true. She is also smart and talented. I remember when she was just a toddler; I offered her a graham cracker. I broke a whole one in half and extended the half to her. She passed by the half that I had extended and then secured the half that I had held back. Once she got the held back half, she took the extended half. My wife has been trying to spend more time with her and help in guiding and shaping her development. She was able to give her ballet lessons this spring as an introduction to the arts. She seemed to like the lessons and hopefully she will continue with them in the future. My wife enjoys looking for clothes, games and toys for Derrianna. I think my wife just likes to shop period. But shopping for her kids and grandkids is always a pleasure for her. Just recently, my wife took Derrianna to a Jonas Brothers concert. They took pictures and bought souvenirs at the concert. Derrianna was so excited about going to see them as any normal pre teen or teenage girl would be.

I am beginning to see her grow up right before my eyes. My wife also bought a keyboard that Derrianna enjoys playing when she comes over to visit us. Every time that she comes to visit us, she always comes to find me and gives me a hug and kiss. And she always gives me a hug and kiss when she leaves to go back home. My wife smiles and says that she never gives her a hug and kiss when coming or going. One day, when she came to visit us, she saw a syringe that I had left out on the table. I have diabetes and need to take insulin on a daily basis. She looked at the syringe and asked me "what was that for?" I told her that I had diabetes and I used the syringe to give myself insulin. I explained that this was medicine that I needed to take to keep my blood sugars down. I don't know whether she fully grasped what I was saying or not. But she seemed to be satisfied with my answer. Other questions that she has asked include how old I am and are my wife and I married? She then asked how long have we been married.? I don't know why she is asking the married question. Maybe it is because her parents are not married or because so many couples today are not married.

I am concerned about Derrianna and my other great grandchildren not being raised with Christian values. Today with the moral decline in our country and the world, it is getting more difficult to raise our children with Christian values. There is so much outside influence on our children that it is hard for even Christian parents to compete with the outside world when trying to pass down our values to our children. When I think about my children, grand children and great grandchildren, I realized now that I may not have provided the leadership that I should have in the past and I have deep regrets about this. But this is not the time to look back and find blame but to look ahead and provide the Christian leadership needed to give my great grand children the tools necessary to be successful in this world and the hope of salvation in the world to come. I am calling on my children, grandchildren, my wife and myself to do the things necessary to provide faith, hope and love for all of our family members. Some of the things we can do as parents are to make sure we set the example, and then see that our children are reading the Bible and other Christian materials and books. The most important decision we can make is to accept Jesus Christ as our Lord and Savior and follow his commandments. We need to take our children to church and then along with them practice what Christ teaches us.

One day Derrianna came to visit us and brought along her new friend. As usual, she came in the house looking for me to give a big hug and kiss. I was in my bedroom and on my dresser was a used syringe. This time, however, she had brought her friend up to the bedroom with her. After she hugged and kissed me, she noticed the syringe on my dresser. She then asked me again what the syringe was for. I repeated that it was for use in treatment for my diabetes. This seemed to satisfied her and she told her friend, "Its alright, you can give him a hug". "He just has diabetes and you can't catch it". Her friend then felt free to give me a hug. Both my wife and I see a lot of potential in Derrianna and we are and will be constantly praying for her future Christian development. She is a beautiful child and one day she will grow up to be a very beautiful woman. I want her to fully understand our love for her and better yet,

God's love for her. Anyone who reads this message please keep us, her and all little children in your prayers. **Glory Be To God.**

I rejoiced greatly that I have found some of your children walking in truth, as we received commandment from the Father. And now I plead with you, lady, not as though I wrote a new commandment to you, but that which we have had from the beginning: that we love one another. This is love, that we walk according to His commandments. This is the commandment, that as you have heard from the beginning, you should walk in it. 2 John 1:4-6

Chapter Thirteen:
SPECIAL STORIES

THANKSGIVING

CHRISTMAS

EASTER

GOD AND GUNS

LOVE AND MARRIAGE

HEART OF HEARTS

GUILTY

ALPHA AND OMEGA

EPILOGUE

THANKSGIVING

In just another three days, I will be celebrating my seventy second Thanksgivings Day although I don't remember some of the first ones. And I indeed have a lot to be thankful for. My health is being managed very well and my wife's health is looking good despite the scare that we had two weeks ago when she had to be rushed to the hospital because of a rapid heart beat. We still don't know why this occurred but with proper medical treatment, her heart beat returned to normal almost immediately. She has just seen the doctor and he gave her a good prognosis. Thanksgiving Day has always been one of my favorite holidays especially because of the many different and delicious kinds of food and desserts. Unfortunately, I have always eaten more than I should have except for one Thanksgiving that I remember. And that was the Thanksgiving, when my father was in the hospital in November 1973 dying from the effects of a stroke he had incurred a few weeks earlier. I didn't have much of an appetite but I tried to eat anyway. The meal tasted terrible and I just could not eat it.

Wikipedia, the online encyclopedia, describes Thanksgiving Day as a harvest festival to give thanks for the harvest and to express gratitude in general. This holiday may have religious origins but is now identified mostly as a secular holiday. It is celebrated primarily in the United States and Canada. According to the history that we learned in school, the first Thanksgiving took place at the Plymouth Colony located at what today is Plymouth, Massachusetts. Other interpretations of this event mark it as the beginning of genocide against the natives found here by the Pilgrims after they had departed from the Mayflower Ship that had brought them across the Atlantic Ocean to this new land. I am not going to discuss the merits of these other interpretations but I believe Plymouth Colony was the site of the first Thanksgiving. If you are in Canada, Thanksgiving Day is celebrated on the second Monday in October and in the United States, it is held on the fourth Thursday in November.

The first modern Thanksgiving can be traced back to 1863, When President Abraham Lincoln, proclaimed a holiday to be thankful and celebrated in November of each year. Before that time in 1777, all of the thirteen colonies joined in a thanksgiving celebration to take note of a victory of the British at Saratoga but it was only celebrated once. President George Washington proclaimed a national day of thanksgiving but it did not have wide support. Sarah Josepha Hale, a magazine editor, over a forty year period, championed the cause for a national thanksgiving holiday and this led to President Lincoln's action in giving us a day to be thankful. After being changed a couple of times, the date for Thanksgiving Day was set in 1941, declared to be the fourth Thursday in November and at this time Congress made it a legal holiday. Even though I always look forward to Thanksgiving Day, I am troubled by it not being celebrated as a day to give thanks to God. But when I think about it, this day of Thanksgiving is a legal holiday and in this country, we have separation of church and state.

Therefore it is not surprising that the Thanksgiving Day proclamation does not tell us who to give thanks to. We have freedom of religion and we can choose who to worship and give thanks or not to worship and not give thanks at all. If you are a follower of Jesus Christ, then you are instructed in Ephesians 5:20 to give thanks for everything to God the Father in the name of our Lord, Jesus Christ. In Romans 14:6, the Bible tells us we should give thanks to Him whether it is a special day or not or whether we eat or not. Thanking God is not something that you can have Congress make a law for us to follow. God has given us the power to choose to follow Jesus Christ or not. Because of what happened on the cross over two thousand years ago, I am free of the law. By loving Christ and putting all of my hope and faith in him, I don't need a legal holiday to tell me that I should be thankful to God. I am thankful every morning when I wake up in my right mind and before I go to bed at night.

Thanksgiving Day is a special day set aside once a year so that all Americans, including us Christians can take the time to give thanks to God and to continue to build our loving relationships with each other including family and friends. May God continue to bless us and the

United States of America. In Jesus' precious name, I pray these blessings. Amen

Oh, give thanks to the Lord! Call upon his name; make known His deeds among the peoples! Sing to him, sing psalms to Him; Talk of all His wondrous works! Glory in His holy name; Let the hearts of those rejoice who seek the Lord! Seek the Lord and His strength; Seek His face evermore! Psalm 105:1-4

CHRISTMAS

M y earliest memories of Christmas began when I was a child living
in Poindexter Village. I always thought that the Christmas lights
in the apartment of Dorothy Wright directly facing us were so beautiful.
These lights were multi colored and big unlike the little lights people
display today. I can still see them in my mind telling me that Christmas
is near. My mother always said that she could tell I knew Christmas was
approaching because I would sing my favorite Christmas song; "Santa
Claus is coming to Town." For those of you who don't know it or may
not remember; it starts out with the words; "Oh you better watch out,
you better not cry, you better not pout, I'm telling you why; Santa
Claus is coming to town." This song was written in 1934 by J. Fred
Coots and Haven Gillespie and was first sung on Eddie Cantor's radio
show in November 1934. This song is still popular today and is used to
remind children that Santa knows if they have been good or bad. I can
remember going to bed with great anticipation of waking up to find
many presents for me under the Christmas tree.

This tradition has been carried on with my own immediate family.
My wife and I have received a lot of pleasure from seeing our children
react to receiving their presents on Christmas morning. I believe that
I received more joy in giving to my children than receiving gifts from
my parents as a child. That old Christian saying; "It is more blessed to
give than to receive." is still as true as ever. One Christmas when I was a
young child, my father gave me a train set among other presents but he
also bought my mother a ring. For some reason, I became jealous of him
giving her the ring and I cried because I did not get one. I have asked
myself, in the past, why was I jealous? My only answer is as a human
being, I was born with this big defect called a sinful nature. One of the
many characteristics of a sinful nature is jealously. This subject of gift
giving and receiving brings me to why we celebrate Christmas? When I
was working for the State of Ohio, during one Christmas season, one of

our secretaries put a big sign on the front of her desk that said; "Happy Birthday Jesus."

Upon seeing it, management ordered her to take it down. There were other signs on desks celebrating Christmas but they said things like; "Have a Merry Christmas and a Happy New Year.' These signs were deemed to be appropriate. When this occurred, I wondered why a sign saying happy birthday Jesus was considered inappropriate since I thought this is why Christmas is celebrated. At that time, I was not a born again Christian, so the issue quickly went away. But in later years, I began to question why we as a nation and individuals celebrate Christmas. Some of the information I found out was astonishing. If we were to think about it, many of our religious practices are based on intellect, experiences and tradition which are a part of our understanding and in many cases acceptable. But the ultimate authority of understanding what God wants us to do should be based on the Holy Scriptures. And the major way to find that out is to read and study the scriptures for ourselves.

Not only is Christmas celebrated by Christians but also by non Christians. The origin of Christmas lies in its pagan roots and not in the Holy Bible. Today's practice of celebrating Christmas with Santa Claus, reindeers, Christmas trees, mistletoe and gift giving did not originate in the Holy Bible but have pre Christian or secular themes and origins. I went to Christmas Eve services yesterday at my church, Vineyard Columbus, and again heard a wonderful sermon by my pastor; Rich Nathan. Pastor Nathan talked about what the world would be like if Jesus had never been born. He used the example of the movie; It's A Wonderful Life, starring Jimmy Stewart and Donna Reed. Jimmy Stewart playing the part of George Bailey who wishes that he had never been born. In this Movie, his guardian angel grants his wish and George then sees how many people were affected negatively because he was never born. What happened in this movie is nothing compared to what would have happened if Christ had never been born. Think of how bad it is today and imagine what it would be like without Christ's influence in this world.

When Christ came into this dark world, He brought a bright light indeed, Himself. Before He came, the world was a very different place. People were indiscriminately slaughtered and children were sacrificed to various gods. The hospitals that we go to when we are sick came about through Christianity. This is so true in my hometown of Columbus, Ohio as mostly all the hospitals were founded by the church. The lovingly way we treat each other during Christmas and sometimes throughout the year comes from Christ and the light that he brought into the world. **He is the light of the world.**

"And this is the condemnation, that the light has come into the world, and men loved darkness rather than light, because their deeds were evil. For everyone practicing evil hates the light and does not come to the light, lest his deeds should be exposed. But he who does the truth comes to the light, that his deeds may be clearly seen, that they have been done in God." John 3:19-21

EASTER

Easter of course is always a special time of the year. I remember when I was a child we would always get new clothes at Easter. My mother would dress us in our new outfits and take us to church. The Easter Bunny was a big hit at our house during Easter. He would bring us a basket filled with Easter eggs, jelly beans, candies and usually a chocolate Easter Bunny. My mother would cook us a special meal usually beginning with a ham and other goodies. Easter was also a sign that summer was not far away and we would soon be out of school. At Franklin Park, there was usually an Easter egg hunt for the children in the area. This is a tradition that was done at the White House in Washington D.C and still continues until this day. There are many memorable Easters but the one that I remember the most was in March 1978 which was a month after my son died. I was attending church with my wife and infant grandson, Derrick, and the pastor began to talk about Christ rising from the dead to be with the Father. I started to cry thinking about my son and I used my grandson to cover my face so no one would see my tears. That message of Christ's resurrection gave me hope that I would some day be reunited with my son again. My tears were not only of sadness but also joy.

My memories of Easter are of the passion plays put on to depict the crucifixion and resurrection of my Lord and Savior Jesus Christ. In some cultures, People volunteer to portray Christ even to the point of having spikes pierce their hands and their body being nailed to a cross. As realistic as this is, it can't begin to compare to the actual crucifixion of Jesus Christ. I also remember Easter from a legendary movie titled "Easter Parade" staring Fred Astaire, Judy Garland, Peter Lawford and Ann Miller. This movie was made in 1948 when I was just eleven years old and still in elementary school. The movie tells the story of a dancing team that breaks up on Easter because the female member, Ann Miller, wants to be a solo act. The male partner, Fred Astaire, wants to prove to his ex partner that he can replace her and make a star of the next dancer he meets which turns out to be Judy Garland. To make a long story short, Fred is successful and he and Judy Garland celebrate their success by walking in the Easter Parade a year from his breakup with his first partner. Until I became a Christian, this was probably the way I thought about Easter.

Just like Christmas, Easter has its pagan roots. In a report by History. Com, Easter is a Christian festival that contains many pre Christian traditions. According to St. Bede, an eighteenth century historian, Easter's origin goes back to the Teutonic mythology. The name Easter was originally derived from the word Eostre. Eostre was an ancient Greek goddess of spring and she returned to earth after a long cold winter bringing with her the warmth and light of spring. Scholars believe that the Christian Church changed this spring festival to a celebration of Christ's resurrection. There is also a connection between the Jewish Passover and the Easter celebration in that it was during Passover 30 A.D. that Jesus was crucified. Passover is the time designated to celebrate the Israelites release from bondage and slavery after three hundred years. In different versions of the Holy Bible you will find the terms "Easter and Passover" being used interchangeably. According to History.Com; "The early Christians, many of whom were of Jewish origin, were brought up in the Hebrew tradition and regarded Easter as a new feature of the Passover tradition festival; a commemoration of the advent of the messiah as foretold by the prophets."

For we Christians, Easter is a great day of hope that because of Christ's death and resurrection, our sinful nature died with him and we now are free from the responsibility of having to sin. We also will be with Christ again one day because He promised to prepare a place and someday come to take us to where He is. When I was little, I didn't know the true significance of the meaning of Easter. I had to accept Jesus Christ as my Lord and Savior to understand what He truly did for me and the many others who depend on, trust in, rely on and cling to Him for their salvation. I can face the future with all of its uncertainties knowing that I need not fear what will happen to me because that was taken care of over two thousand years ago on a cross at Calvary. Easter is also a time that brings many people to church who have not attended since the last Easter. If you are a regular church member it is advisable that you come early to church on Easter Sunday so that you can get a seat because it is usually crowded on this day. Some churches have sunrise services on this special day. In any event, this is an opportunity for the Gospel to reach those who may not be receiving it on a regular basis. I love the celebration and the hope that Easter brings to all of us who have accepted that wonderful gift of salvation bought and paid for with the priceless body and precious blood of Jesus Christ.

But I do not want you to be ignorant, brethren, concerning those who have fallen asleep, lest you sorrow as others who have no hope. For if we believe that Jesus died and rose again, even so God will bring with Him those who sleep in Jesus. 1 Thessalonians 4:13-14

GOD AND GUNS

I have just finished listening to a National Rifle Association robot call that encourages citizens like me to protest against the United Nations attempt to ban guns throughout the world. The NRA wanted me to listen to their taped information from the president of the NRA and then talk to a live person about this issue. I don't usually take part in these kinds of telephone surveys but I thought that it was my duty to give my comments. Once the live interviewer came on the phone, I began to tell him about my support for the second amendment which gives all Americans the right to bear arms. But then I added that there are too many guns on the streets and in the hands of people who are abusing this right to bear arms. I told the NRA interviewer that the NRA ought to find a way to help keep guns out of the hands of people who abused them. He agreed with me but as I continue to make my point, he hung up on me. I guess he wanted my opinion but only if it coincided with his. But what he probably really wanted was a donation of money.

The second amendment of the constitution reads as follows: "A well regulated militia, being necessary to the security of a free state, the right of the people to keep and bear arms, shall not be infringed. What this means has been discussed and disputed since the amendment was written. I won't pretend to be an expert on the constitution and try to interpret this amendment. I do know that I believe in the right to have a gun for protection and recreational target shooting. I don't believe that guns should be accessible to everyone who wants one. These two opinions seem to be in conflict and they probably are. This is where the problem is. How do we as a people continue to give our citizens the right to bear arms and at the same time keep guns out of the hands of irresponsible people? That was the question that I was asking of the NRA interviewer when he hung up on me.

As I told the NRA interviewer, I do believe in our constitutional right to keep and to bear arms but with every privilege and right there is a duty and obligation that goes along with it. Too many people are being killed and maimed by the intentional and negligent use of firearms. The old saying is that" Guns don't kill, people do." As a responsible society, we must find a way to balance the right to have a gun with the right to be safe from the irresponsible and indiscriminate use of guns. But the NRA interviewer didn't want to listen to another side of the argument about keeping and bearing arms. He just wanted to push his point of view, so he just hung up the phone on me.

As a young man, I served my country as a United States Marine. I was taught how to use firearms and became good in how to use them. I spent time on the firing range shooting a 45 semi-automatic pistol used by military policemen, which was my assignment during my last six months of duty. I also qualified as an expert rifleman in the use of the M1 rifle during my time in the Marines. I am no stranger to having and using guns or weapons as we called them in the Marines. Years later as a civilian, a friend of mine reintroduced me to guns and I would periodically go to the firing range and fire his weapons. Eventually my friend bought me a revolver and later I traded it in for a 44 Smith and Wesson semi-automatic pistol. I kept this pistol until my grandson was born and started living in my house. I removed the pistol from my house because I didn't want to take the chance that he could ever find it and accidentally shoot himself.

As a Christian, I believe the answer to this very difficult problem is an individual response to what Christ would have us do about the keeping and bearing of arms. Some people that have guns carry them wherever they go inside or outside their house or when they go to bed, or to the bathroom. They are constantly thinking about their physical survival. Others carry guns in order to be able to physically abuse other people. Maybe the answer lies in having gun owners be trained, licensed and insured when owning and operating a gun just as we do for automobile owners. If we followed the commandments of Jesus Christ, we would have no need of guns for our defense from or our revenge towards others. Jesus taught us that perfect love for Him casts out fear (1 John 4:18) and that we should return hatred and violence with love for our enemies.

"You have heard that it was said, "You shall Love your neighbor and hate your enemy." But I say to you, love your enemies, bless those who curse you, do good to those who hate you, and pray for those who spitefully use you and persecute you, that you may be sons of your Father in heaven; for He makes His sun rise on the evil and on the good, and sends rain on the just and on the unjust. For if you love those who love you, what reward have you? Do not even the tax collectors do the same? And if you greet your brethren only, what do you do more than others? Do not even the tax collectors do so? Therefore you shall be perfect, just as your Father in heaven is perfect." **Matthew 5:43-48**

LOVE AND MARRIAGE

Previously I have mentioned how my little ten year old great granddaughter asked my wife and me if we were married. And if so, how long have we been married. We were able to tell her that we have been married for over forty two years. Some children today don't come into contact with a lot of married people. There isn't the commitment to marriage as there was when I was a little boy. We lived in Poindexter Village, a public housing apartment complex and mostly everyone I knew living together as man and woman were married. Today, you find households with only the mother and her children. Sometimes the father is living with them but he is not married to the mother and far too many times he is not working. There are instances where both the mothers and fathers have children with multiple partners. I know of situations in the past where a woman became pregnant and the father married her not because he wanted to but rather because he wanted his baby to be born in wedlock. That was back in the days when marriage was still a widely respected institution. I was watching the Judge Hatchett Show one day and an alleged father being sued for paternity said the following: "Mama's baby, Daddy's maybe." This underscores the changed social pattern and the way it seems concerning paternity issues today.

In 2002, I attended my nephew, David's, wedding and at the reception, the master of ceremonies asked the guests to sing a song using the word love in the lyrics. I remember my cousin Norma's family from Philadelphia, Pennsylvania singing the renowned Frank Sinatra hit titled "Love and Marriage." The lyrics are as follow: "Love and marriage, Love and marriage go together like a horse and carriage." That is the way most people would think about marriage back in my childhood days. If you fell in love with a member of the opposite sex, you wanted to marry them and live happily ever after. But today and for many years, we haven't needed the use of a horse and carriage. Today we ride in what was initially called a horseless carriage. The car was one of the great

337

inventions of the late nineteenth and early twentieth centuries. Not only did the automobile eliminate the horse as a means of transportation but it provided a means for privacy that allowed men and women to become intimate in their relationships faster than in past times.

The Apostle Paul in talking about marriage said the following: **"But I say to the unmarried and to the widows: It is good for them if they remain even as I am; but if they cannot exercise self-control, let them marry. For it is better to marry than to burn with passion."1 Corinthians 7:8-9** The Bible spends a lot of time on marriage and the issues surrounding it. Beginning in the first book of the Bible, God creates man (Genesis 2:7) and then gives him a companion, Eve (Genesis 2:21-25). In the Old Testament God lets man have more than one wife but this leads to many problems such as jealousy, having favorites and being unfair to some of the wives. But in the nineteenth chapter of Matthew, Jesus says that there should be one man with one wife. The Bible addresses the sexual practices of Adultery; **(Leviticus 20:10; Deuteronomy 22:22; Hebrews 13:4)**, Incest; **(Leviticus 18)**, Homosexuality; **(Leviticus 18:22; 20:13; Romans 1:24-28**, Rape; **(Deuteronomy 22:23-29)**, Fornication; **(Exodus 22:16-17)**, Prostitution; **(Deuteronomy 22:16-17)**, and Bestiality; **(Leviticus 20:15-16)**.

The Bible speaks loudly on the side of marriage between two people of the opposite sex, who are faithful to each other, in the following passages: **Drink water from your cistern, and running water from your own well. Should your fountains be dispersed abroad, streams of water in the streets? Let them be only your own, and not for strangers with you. Let your fountain be blessed, and rejoice with the wife of your youth. As a loving deer and a graceful doe, let her breasts satisfy you at all times; and always be enraptured with her love. For why should you, my son, be enraptured by an immoral woman, and be embraced in the arms of a seductress? Proverbs 5:15-20**

The big issue today is not just whether people of the opposite sex should get married but whether people of the same sex can marry each other. Some people say yes and others say no. There have been a few states that have allowed marriage between same sex couples because of judicial decisions saying it is legal. Sometimes those judicial decisions have been over turned by the people voting on the issue. I don't know what the answer should be under our constitution; that is an issue for the courts to decide. In the United States of America we have the freedom to choose what religion we want or not to choose any religion at all. So our laws cannot be based on the religious values of some, a few or many of our citizens. But as for me, I will choose the Lord Jesus Christ and the values that he has given to those of us who have accepted Him as our Lord and Savior. I believe in Christian marriage between persons of the opposite sex with Jesus Christ as the Head of the family.

Then the rib which the Lord God had taken from man He made into a woman, and He brought her to the man. And Adam said: "This is now bone of my bones and flesh of my flesh; she shall be called Woman, because she was taken out of Man." Therefore a man shall leave his father and mother and be joined to his wife, and they shall become one flesh. Genesis 2:22-24

HEART OF HEARTS

We are blessed in this world if we are able to develop a close relationship with other people. I consider it a blessing that I have experienced a number of close friendships growing up, in school, in the Marine Corps and at work. I am a member of a great college fraternity which continues to provide me with friends from all over the world. My closest friends however are members of my immediate family. When I was little I didn't necessarily pal around with my brother and sister because of our age difference. We each had our own friends but since, we have been grown; we have gradually grown closer to each other. We obviously have a lot in common but we also truly have a love for each other and want to be in each other's company as much as possible. My wife made a comment about our relationship, which I considered to be a compliment. She said; "You three are thicker than thieves." Well we do care and look out for each other. We socialize, exercise and study the Bible together. We also spend holidays and sometimes vacations together.

There is however one person closer to me than anyone and this is my wife, Delores. I met her over 43 years ago and we have been married over 42 years. We have been through a lot together, both good and bad times. But we have handled both the good and bad the same by relying on the Lord Jesus Christ for help and courage. When our son, who was almost eight years old, died, my wife was a pillar of strength for myself and others. I knew the tremendous love that she had for our son and all of our other children but this was a time when a lot of people would be watching to see how she would react to this terrible tragedy. She had to show that her faith produces action and become a witness for Jesus Christ. Many of our friends mentioned how she had been a witness for Christ through her behavior. Those of us who profess to be Christians should understand that our best witness is our behavior. One of my favorite expressions attributed to St. Francis of Assisi is; "Preach the word constantly and when necessary use words." As Christians, we think that we have to verbally tell other people about Jesus but people primarily learn about him through our actions. I remember one time when I was joking with my wife about man being the head of the wife and I had found a scripture which I believed made my point. This was when I was using scripture to prove a point and not to grow in Christ.

I had found this scripture in the book of Ephesians that stated that the husband was the head of the wife. I thought that I had proved my point. But she told me to keep on reading further. I continued to read and much to my surprise I read that the husband was the head of the wife as Christ was the head of the church which included me if I was a follower of Christ. The husband being head of his wife is in effect only if he submits to Christ as the head of him. These scriptures read as follows: **"Wives, submit to your own husbands, as to the Lord. For the husband is the head of the wife, as also Christ is the head of the church; and He is the savior of the body. Therefore, just as the church is subject to Christ, so let the wives be to their husbands in everything. Husbands, love your wives, just as Christ also loved the church and gave himself for her." Ephesians 5:22-25** The issue expressed in Ephesians is not about husbands controlling wives but about husbands loving wives as they love their own bodies. In 1st Corinthians, Chapter Eleven, the Apostle Paul says the following: **"But I want you to know that the head of every man is Christ, the head of the woman is man, and the head of Christ is God."1 Corinthians 11:3**

When I think about my wife and what she has meant to me over the years; I consider her to be my heart of hearts. She is my closest friend in this world and that is how it should be between a husband and wife. She has given me care, comfort, romance and spiritual advice and I love her just as much as I did when we were both young. In fact, I probably love her more since I am older and hopefully wiser. But I must confess that there is some one who I love more and is closer to me and that is my Lord and Savior, Jesus Christ. You see, He is the one who gave her to me on a temporary basis. She won't belong to me always but Christ will be with me eternally. But while my wife and I are both on this earth I will enjoy her companionship and love and give thanks to God for giving her to me. As I am writing this, tomorrow is Valentines Day and to you Delores, I give you all my love in the name of Jesus Christ.

"But from the beginning of the creation, God made them male and female. For this reason a man shall leave his father and mother and be joined to his wife, and the two shall become one flesh; so then they are no longer two, but one flesh. Therefore what God has joined together, let not man separate." **Mark 10:6-9**

GUILTY

During the early days following the death of Christ, Many Christians were put on trial and convicted for being a Christian. Many times their conviction meant that they had to forfeit their life. I wonder what would happen if I were accused of being a Christian in a country where being a follower of Christ was a crime punishable by death. Would there be enough evidence to convict me? Would I want to be found innocent of the charge of being a Christian? Would I need a lawyer to defend me? Because I believe that I am a Christian, I don't see any value in hiring a lawyer for a hopeless case. However, I think that there is one lawyer, Mr. Deville Satan who would be eager to defend me. Mr. Satan would tell me that just because I believe there is a Jesus Christ and think that I am a Christian doesn't mean that I am a follower of Him. Furthermore just because I attend church doesn't make me a Christian anymore than standing in a forest makes me a tree. I know that I drove the church bus to pick up senior citizens. But picking up senior citizens for church doesn't mean that I am a Christian.

Mr. Satan thinks he would probably have no problem in defending me against the charges of being a Christian. However, he advises me not to get on the witness stand because I could be asked about being seen worshipping and praising Jesus Christ. But as of now, this evidence is only hearsay and Mr. Satan thinks that I can't be convicted on such flimsy circumstantial evidence. According to Mr. Satan, being seen worshipping Jesus will surely convict me of being a Christian and he further states that I should avoid humbling myself, praising and submitting to Jesus Christ as my Lord and Savior. I should also avoid prayer at all costs because this is one of the behaviors that can be used against me when they are trying to convict me of being a Christian. And I should never be caught reading the Holy Bible and applying its principles. I should try not to mention that faith, hope and love are an important part of my thinking.

I need especially to emphasize that my love for God and others is conditional based on what they do for me. Never show in public the Fruit of The Spirit such as Love, Joy, Peace, Gentleness, Goodness, Kindness, Faith, Meekness and Patience. If I follow the advice of my lawyer, Mr. Satan, I should have no problem in convincing a court that I am not a follower of Christ. **But I can't save my physical life at the expense of denying Christ as my Lord and Savior.** I can't say that I don't look to the Lord Jesus Christ for my salvation past, present and future. I can't say that Jesus Christ is not the beginning and end of my life. I can't say that Christ didn't die on the cross to have my sins forgiven and reconcile me to God. I can't say any of these things. What I can say is that I am guilty of clinging to, depending on, trusting in and relying on Jesus Christ as my Lord and Savior and I am guilty of believing that He died and rose up to be with the Father and will come back for me one day. Despite Mr. Satan's defense, **I am guilty as charged of being a follower of Jesus Christ.**

I am blessed to live in a country where I have the right to worship my Lord and Savior, Jesus Christ, without fear of being killed or ridiculed for it. This country's values are based on freedom of religion and that means the right not to believe in God if I so desire. Faith in a Higher Power is not something you can legislate or dictate. My conversion did not come about because of something someone made me do. It came about because God chose me and sent His Holy Spirit to minister to me. I would pray that if I lived in a country that outlawed Christianity, I would have the courage to confess Christ as my Lord and Savior. But if I don't follow his commandments in this free country, I am in fact denying Him. So those of us who profess to be Christians should remember every day that we are awake, we have another opportunity to tell the world who Jesus is and what He is doing in our life by our actions.

For I know that this will turn out for my deliverance through your prayer and the supply of the Spirit of Jesus Christ, according to my earnest expectation and hope that in nothing I shall be ashamed, but with all boldness, as always, so now also Christ will be magnified in my body, whether by life or by death. For to me,

to live is Christ, and to die is gain. But if I live on in the flesh, this will mean fruit from my labor: yet what I shall choose I cannot tell. For I am hard pressed between the two, having a desire to depart and be with Christ, which is far better. Nevertheless to remain in the flesh is more needful for you. Philippians 1:19-24

ALPHA AND OMEGA

Many years ago when I first pledged to my fraternity, Kappa Alpha Psi, I had to learn the Greek Alphabet. I still remember most of the letters although I had to research the internet to list them in order. In case you are interested they are as follows: Alpha, Beta, Gamma, Delta, Epsilon, Zeta, Eta, Theta, Iota, Kappa, Lambda, Mu, Nu, Xi, Omicron, Pi, Rho, Sigma, Tau, Upsilon, Phi, Chi, Psi, and Omega. The letter Delta is important to me because it is the name of my fraternity's chapter on the Wilberforce University campus in the State of Ohio. This was where I was first inducted into Kappa Alpha Psi Fraternity in 1960. Wilberforce University is the nation's oldest private African American university and was named in honor of the great 18th century abolitionist, William Wilberforce. My fraternity's chapter at my alma mater, Ohio University, is named Epsilon Lambda and this chapter was created in 1966, two years after my graduation.

Other Greek Letters that have a special significance for me are the letters Nu, Pi and Phi. When put in the order we Kappas used them, they are Phi Nu Pi and have a very special significance for members of our fraternity. I wish that I could tell you the meaning of Phi Nu Pi but you will have to cross the burning sands into Kappa Land to learn this. My brother Doug would like to know what Phi Nu Pi means but neither his four Kappa sons nor I will tell him. Kappa Alpha Psi Fraternity was founded in 1911 on the Indiana University Campus by the following men: Elder W. Diggs, Byron K. Armstrong, Ezra D. Alexander, Henry T. Asher, Marcus P. Blakemore, Paul W. Caine, George W. Edmonds, Guy L. Grant, Edward G. Irvin and John M. Lee.

Every fraternity can list some well known members and Kappa Alpha Psi has many such members. For example there is Ralph Abernathy, civil rights leader, Tavis Smiley, talk show host; Johnny Cochran Jr., outstanding lawyer; Bill Russell and Oscar Robertson; basketball greats; Arthur Ashe, tennis great and General Daniel Chappie James Jr. first black four star general in the United States military. Before accepting Jesus Christ as my Lord and Savior, my favorite Greek word was Kappa. This of course, is the name of my fraternity, Kappa Alpha Psi, and my uncle, Guy L. Grant, was one of the ten founders. In addition to my uncle and me there are other male members of my family that also belong to this fraternity.

However now when I think of the Greek alphabet, I have begun to focus also on Alpha and Omega. These other two letters belong to Alpha Phi Alpha and Omega Psi Phi fraternities. Martin Luther King Jr. is an Alpha Man and Jessie Jackson is an Omega Man. These three fraternities were founded within five years of each other beginning in 1906 and all its members are primarily African-Americans. They are friendly toward each other and at the same time compete for new members. But I am finding myself thinking more about Alpha and Omega than about Kappa. Why is this so? I am not an Alpha Man nor an Omega Man. **I am a Kappa Man.**

It would seem strange that I would spend so much time thinking about Alpha and Omega when I am Kappa through and through. But it is true, this focus on Alpha and Omega gives me great joy, even much greater joy than I could ever get from just thinking only about Kappa. I have joined my fraternity, Kappa Alpha Psi, for life but I have given my life to Alpha and Omega for life and eternity. You may be wondering what is it about Alpha and Omega that makes it so special in my life that it would make Kappa number three when it comes to these Greek letters.

When I think of Alpha and Omega, I think about the lyrics in the song "He is Yahweh" which describes my Lord and Savior as follows: "The Creator God, The Great I am, The Lord of All, Rose of Sharon, The Righteous One and the Three-in-One." Further according to the lyrics of this song "He is the one who makes me happy and gives me peace. He brings me comfort and turns the bitter into sweet. He stirs up my passion and is rising up in me. He fills my hunger with everything I need."

So I am not only a Kappa Man but I am also an Alpha and Omega Man. Alpha is the first letter of the Greek alphabet and Omega is the last letter. And Jesus Christ is **The Alpha and Omega**, the first and last; the beginning and end in my life. I worship Him in spirit and truth and look to Him for my help and my salvation.

"I am the Alpha and the Omega, the Beginning and the End, the First and the Last." **Revelation 22:13**

EPILOGUE

Writing about my life experiences started out with a few stories about my fraternity on the Ohio University Campus during the late 1950's and early 1960's and gradually grew to include all facets of my life experiences. It is amazing to me that I was able to remember all the information that I used in the stories. I can remember wishing that I had kept a diary when I was younger so perhaps I could write a book; but the things I wrote about have been dormant in my head for many years. Once I started writing about my life, I continued to receive inspiration from God to keep going and now I have written over one hundred thousand words. This afforded me the opportunity to read and study scripture that I may not have read if not for writing this book. This process has been a serious and inspired learning experience for me. Hopefully, I have grown in Christian wisdom since I began writing. I told my wife that I thought that God was allowing me to write a book but He was probably using this opportunity to teach me His Word.

My brother Doug, who has edited everything I have written, said that he believes he has grown spiritually since I began writing because he had to look up and study every Bible verse contained in my work. Not only does he review these verses but he reads what proceeds or follows and the Word becomes implanted in his heart. He, my sister, my wife and I have just finished studying the Book of Galatians and we are now reading the Book of John. We, like my wife, are beginning to develop a habit of studying God's Word and are benefiting greatly as a result. My sister recently told me that she had an opportunity to provide some words of comfort to a friend who had just lost her grandfather. In the past, she would not have been able to do this. But since she has given herself to God and is now consistently studying His Word, God has equipped her to minister to others in need. When my son died many years ago, I had a friend, Ronald Harris, who gave me words of comfort from God. I have never forgotten what he said to me and even though

Ronald has passed away, I still think of him often. God is wonderful to us and will equip us to serve Him if we asked in faith.

As I am completing this epilogue, my sister in law, Addie Grant, is recuperating from surgery and I am thankful that she is doing much better. It is shown everyday over and over that God is so good to us. My mother in law, Katherine Snoddy is ninety one years old and she is in reasonably good health. I told her that I want her to be at my eightieth birthday party which is over seven years away. Besides I need her to stay in good health in case she has to take care of me. She knows that I am not joking since when we are riding together, she always gets out of the back seat first so she can help me out of the car. However recently, she has been house bound because of swelling in her feet. She is being treated for this condition but so far the swelling continues. She has developed a fan club at our church and after services her church friends ask my wife how she is doing and when will she be able to return to church. We hope and pray that she will get better and be able to walk again. We are very optimistic because her mother lived to be one hundred and one years old. My mother in law is still a sweet and beautiful woman as beauty always stands out at any age.

One of our childhood friends, Donald Spurlock, has recently died. Donald lived next door to us on Long Street and I still remember him along with his parents, Richard and Ruth and his brother Richard Jr. They have all passed now. I can still see Donald sitting on the back porch with his English Springer Spaniel, Corky, feeding him some food. When we first moved to that neighborhood, we would go next door to the Spurlock's house to watch television. Eventually my father bought us a television set. All the houses that were on my block between Taylor Avenue and Parkwood have been torn down to provide land for the Columbus East High School expansion. The school has built additional classrooms, a beautiful gymnasium and a parking lot on the land. Although the house is gone, I still have my precious memories that no one can take away from me. And the church, St. Philip Lutheran that was built across the street shortly after we moved there is still standing and this is where my brother, Doug, attends with his wife Addie.

There has been a time lapse since what I wrote above and what I am writing now. My beautiful mother in law, Katherine J. Snoddy, passed away a few months ago on September 3, 2010, at the age of ninety one. She would have been ninety two on December 28, 2010. Our family misses her very much but is comforted in the fact that she was a believer in the hope that Christ gives to those who have accepted Him as their Lord and Savior. But the Lord has blessed our family with a new member, Kylen Michael Gibson, who was born on November 30, 2010 in Columbus, Ohio. He is my nephew Kyle Gibson's son and the little brother of Grant Avery Gibson.

Then Job arose, tore his robe, and shave his head; and he fell to the ground and worshipped. And he said: "Naked I came from my mother's womb, and naked shall I return there. The Lord gave, and the Lord has taken away; Blessed be the name of the Lord." Job 1:20-21

INDEX